FLIP FLOP
Fantasy

Christina Laflamme

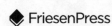

FriesenPress

Suite 300 - 990 Fort St
Victoria, BC, V8V 3K2
Canada

www.friesenpress.com

ISBN
978-1-5255-1216-2 (Hardcover)
978-1-5255-1217-9 (Paperback)
978-1-5255-1218-6 (eBook)

1. BIOGRAPHY & AUTOBIOGRAPHY, ADVENTURERS & EXPLORERS

Distributed to the trade by The Ingram Book Company

My Wheel is in the dark, -
I cannot see a spoke,
Yet know its dripping feet
Go round and round.

My foot is on the tide -
An unfrequented road,
Yet have all roads
A "clearing" at the end.

Some have resigned the loom,
Some in the busy tomb
Find quaint employ,
Some with new stately feet
Pass Royal through the gate,
Flinging the problem back at you and me.

- Emily Dickinson

For Abby, Mathieu, Colby, and Maya,
my nieces and nephews.

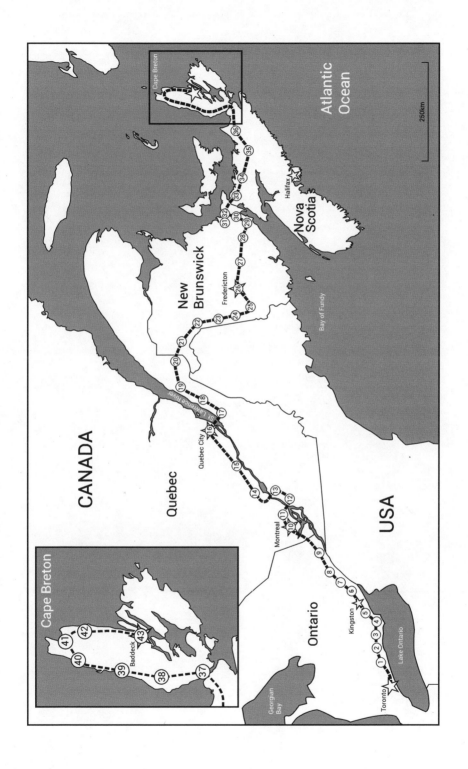

LAND ACKNOWLEDGMENT

I would like to begin by acknowledging the First Nations whose traditional, and often unceded, territories I passed through on my journey:

(Toronto, ON) – Originally Tkaronto by the Haudenosaunee, meaning "where there are trees standing in the water is the traditional territory of the Haudenosaunee, the Huron-Wendat, and the territory of the Mississaugas of the New Credit First Nation. The territory was the subject of the *Dish With One Spoon* Wampum Belt Covenant, an agreement between the Iroquois Confederacy and the Ojibwe and allied nations to peaceably share and care for the resources around the Great Lakes. This territory is also covered by the Upper Canada Treaties.

(Kingston, ON) – Traditional territory of the Anishinaabeg and Haudenosaunee Peoples.

(Montreal, QC) – Traditional territory of the Kanien'keha:ka (Mohawk), a place which has long served as a site of meeting and exchange amongst nations.

(Québec, QC) – the traditional territory unceded territory of the Abenaki and Wabenaki Confederacy and the Wolastoqiyik (Maliseet).

(NB, NS) – This territory is covered by the "Treaties of Peace and Friendship" which Wolastoqiyik (Maliseet)and Mi'kmaq peoples first signed with the British Crown in 1725. The treaties did not deal with surrender of lands and resources but in fact recognized Mi'kmaq and Wolastoqiyik (Maliseet) title and established the rules for what was to be an ongoing relationship between nations.

Thank you – Meegwetch – Niá:wen – Welaliog – Merci for your hospitality and safe passage!

SOURCE: Canadian Association of University Teachers (CAUT) Guide to Acknowledging Traditional Territory
https://www.caut.ca/docs/default-source/professional-advice/list---territorial-acknowledgement-by-province.pdf?sfvrsn=12

Table of Contents

"Despite everything, I believe that people are really good at heart."
- Anne Frank

PROLOGUE

I was forty-one years old when I began my solo two thousand six hundred kilometer bicycle ride, beginning in Toronto and culminating at the end of The Cabot Trail on Canada's east coast. I am not a long-distance cyclist. I am a marathon runner. When I started running marathons I read one book by a female marathon runner and then I began. I have run fifty-two marathons to date. When the idea to do this long-distance bike ride came to me, I similarly wanted to read one book by a female who had done this or something similar on her own. I couldn't find that book. So I decided I would write it. I had no experience with long-distance bicycle rides, and I have no experience with writing books.

I knew that embarking on a trip like this, alone as a woman, would bring about some unique challenges and vulnerabilities. If I couldn't learn how another woman had dealt with those things, then I could at least share how I did with other women who might be, like I was, quite trepidatiously considering some sort of similarly intimidating foray.

Less than ten days after I finished my bike ride, I heard about the book *Wild* by Cheryl Strayed. Soon thereafter, I also found *Girl in the Woods* by Aspen Matis. When I looked for a female solo-adventure book before my trip, I only looked at Mountain Equipment Coop's book selection. This explains why I didn't stumble upon these books, and I'm sure many others like them that exist, since these memoirs are not sold there. They should be. In the end, it's a blessing. If I'd found these books before my ride, I might never have written this one.

The main purpose of my book is simply to relay how I, as a woman alone, pulled off this ride; everything from what I packed in my panniers to how I dealt with the many challenges I encountered along the way: physical, environmental, geographical, spiritual, and mental—even for a quasi-loner like me, riding solo for six, eight, ten hours a day, and then spending most every evening by myself, too, is a lot of time to spend alone.

A secondary purpose of this book was to share the good stories of the good people I knew I would meet along the way. The media would have us believe that we live in a big, bad, scary world where no one can be trusted. Every time a damaged or defective soul does something bad or awful we all hear about it and read about it and talk about it; it's front-page news. We are taught to fear.

I am not downplaying the horror of the muggings, the attacks, and the murders; all the awful things that do, sadly, horribly, happen. It breaks my heart and even discourages me at moments. But. These damaged and defective souls have taken up an unfair amount of space in our consciousness. These transgressions actually make up a minor part of the total sum of daily human interactions. We have a skewed perception of humanity, of each other, as a result. I don't wish to discount the negative that happens in our world, but I do want to give some balance, share some of the positive, tell some of the other stories; the good stories.

I have been an Airbnb and Couchsurfing host (and guest) for over five years, since early 2012. I live in a tiny, bachelor apartment. When I have guests, we sleep in the same small room in separate beds. In the beginning, friends and family were a bit aghast. "You let *men* stay with you?" "Do you lock up your valuables?" "Aren't you afraid they might be some nutbar?" Yes, I have had many single men stay with me. No, I do not lock up my valuables. And, no, I think most everyone is just like you and me: nice and good at heart. I eventually came up with a standard retort for all raised eyebrows: "If you want to see the shitty side of humans, go watch the news or read the papers. I get to see the beautiful side of humans over and over again." It was through years of these wonderful interactions with so many different strangers and always having lovely experiences in their company that I knew I would be okay on my ride.

And when I say, "I knew I would be okay," I mean to say that I was pretty sure. Of course I was scared. Damaged and defective souls (as I always refer to them, simply calling them evil does not seek to understand) do exist. But I wasn't prepared to just lie down and die and let life pass me by because there is danger out there. Instead, I prepared, I vowed to stay aware, to be smart, to listen to and trust my instincts, and to go.

There is a saying: "Prepare for the worst and hope for the best." I'm not a fan of this saying. It is simply not good enough. My spin on it is this: "Prepare for the worst but *expect* the best." Because as Melody and Janet, a pair of female cyclists I met along my ride through Ivy Lea, Ontario put it: "There has to be more of us than them or we all wouldn't still be here." Exactly.

And so, despite messages from the media and society that it is unsafe for me to do something like this alone because I am a woman, and despite my own sleepless nights preceding the ride when I was filled with self-doubt, anxiety, and fear, I literally had no choice but to go. The adventure called me resolutely.

This book is not only intended for women. Our shared humanity and the impact we have on each other's lives are not exclusive to one gender. That impact can happen in the briefest of moments and can be either profoundly positive or deeply negative. The better understanding we have of each other; men of women, women of men, men of men, and women of women, the happier and safer we will all together be.

What I did not foresee when I set out that quiet morning on July fifth, 2016, from my home in Toronto, was the journey of self-discovery and self-affirmation that unfurled as poignantly and plainly as the path beneath my wheels. Thus, thirdly, this book is an account of that emotional expedition too.

I hope these pages serve a practical purpose to all fellow adventurers but particularly to lone females. I also hope they serve as a testament to the goodness of people and restore a bit of our faith in each other. And, ultimately, in ourselves.

I knew in my heart that women are strong and capable and that people are good. And this summer I basically bet my life on it. I rode two thousand six hundred kilometers all the way to the east coast alone, and there I found what I didn't even know I was looking for: my own self-acceptance.

A SHORT HISTORY
OF BICYCLES

I received my first two-wheel bicycle from my Aunt Denyse as a First Communion present in grade two. It was pink and white and had a long, cushy, white banana seat. The chain guard was white and polka-dotted with strawberries and read: "Strawberry Delight." My goodness, I loved that bike.

I remember my dad taking me to The Old Road, a short stretch of abandoned street near our apartment building on Nonquon Road in Oshawa, to learn how to ride without training wheels. I learned quickly. What a feeling. I felt powerful, fast, and free.

Strawberry Delight: my gateway drug.

When she couldn't come with us for whatever reason, (I suspect she just needed a break), my mother used to send my older sister Carolyn and me to church on Sundays by ourselves. We did not want to go but she forced us, being the good, God-fearing woman she is. The church, Saint Gregory's, was just over three kilometres away from where we lived, a very long walk for a seven-year-old and a nine-year-old. Sometimes we walked, sometimes she put us on the bus. But after I got my bicycle, Carolyn and I asked if we could ride our bikes. My mother said no, it was too dangerous because I was still just learning to ride a two-wheeler.

It was pretty easy to get around the obstacle of no permission. We lived on the second floor of our apartment building and the bike room was on the main floor. We accepted our mother's decision, left for church, went straight to the bike room, got out our bikes (watching our balcony carefully all the while), and off we went like good little Catholic children to church.

Church was terribly boring, of course. Like the lack of permission from our mother, we were also able to easily remedy this unfavourable situation. We sat in the back pew, acted up, and laughed our little heads off the whole time. It was fun.

The thrill of sneaking our bikes out, the goofing off during mass; we were on a high as we rode our bikes home. That is, until a lady backing her car out of her driveway one Sunday knocked me right off my contraband bicycle.

The lady jumped out of her car. "Omigod, omigod! I didn't see you! Are you okay?" she shrieked.

I told her I was fine.

"Give me your phone number. I want to call your mother and make sure you're all right."

I gave her our number.

As we rode away, Carolyn so gently and lovingly explained to me the bigger problem that was now looming. "You're so stupid! That lady is going to tell Mom we were on our bikes!"

Fuck.

Carolyn and I came home and sat on the couch in the two-bedroom apartment where we three lived (my parents are divorced), waiting with dread and foreboding for that damn phone to ring. Eventually, it did. It was her, the lady who had bumped into me on my bicycle with her car. We could tell by my mother's shrill "What?" and barely restrained "I see." There was no way the detail about us being on bicycles could be carelessly omitted from the lady's version of events. Was there? Well, a kid can hope. My mother freaked on us when she got off the phone. We were grounded from our bicycles.

We served our time, and eventually of course, she finally let us ride our bikes to church. She went over ad nauseam about being very, very careful and riding on the sidewalk and stopping before every driveway and obeying traffic lights and…on and on… We agreed to it all.

Those rides to church on our bicycles were intoxicating. Saint Gregory's seemed so far, and the journey there felt like a real adventure. And of course we did not come straight home as our mother had instructed. How would she know how long it takes two little kids to ride three kilometres on bicycles? We loved riding our bicycles, Carolyn and I.

Before long it was time for a big-girl bike for me. My mom took me to Canadian Tire. It was the summer before grade four. It was a red Supercycle and to me it looked absolutely huge. But the salesman assured us that it was the right size for me. I was allowed to choose what colour tape the handlebars would be wrapped with. I chose white.

We rode the shit out of our bikes, that summer; Carolyn, me, and Selena and April, twins who also lived in our building. We were a little posse, riding our bikes on The Old Road, through the creek, in the graveyard.

One afternoon we were zooming through the paved schoolyard area behind Queen Elizabeth Public School. We were all riding as fast as we could. I was last in the line of our little armada, being the youngest and still a bit awkward on my new, big bike. One, two, three. They all zoomed ahead and disappeared to the right of the portable and around to the front of the school. I pedaled with all my might toward the portable, ready to make the same turn and catch up. Then the chain fell off my bicycle.

It all happened in a millisecond. Unable to brake, I smashed into the long side of the portable, scraping my palms and knees on its gravel perimeter. I howled, I wailed. I waited to be found and rescued, the centre of attention with my bloody hands and knees. I bawled, on and on; loud and dramatic. I waited and waited. *Well, for fuck's sake. How long is it going to take for them to notice that I am missing?*

My Oscar-winning, albeit sincere, show of tears had been in vain. I was all cried out. I got up, walked my bike back onto the pavement, and dusted myself off. Then one, two, three…Carolyn, Selena, and April turned up.

"Where the hell were you?" Carolyn yelled.

"My chain fell off and I fell," I said weakly.

Then I saw my sister register my bloody palms and knees and my now calm face. "Wow, you're taking this really well," she said, impressed.

Approval from my big sister. I felt myself grow in height. Two inches.

"Yeah, I'm okay." I said bravely. *She shall never know the puddle I just cried.* I realized I'd just earned some respect. I felt like the shit.

I went through high school and university without a bike. This is probably for the best. I probably would have ridden it to my drunken death.

After university, in 1998, I worked at a Greek restaurant called Christina's on Danforth Avenue. When customers asked if it was named after me, I lied matter-of-factly: "Of course."

At the beginning of August in Toronto there is a celebration of all things Greek called "Taste of the Danforth." My goodness, what mayhem. We sold every last chicken, lamb, and pork kebab in the house. In that one weekend I made a cool thousand dollars. That was huge money for me at that time. I did two things. The first is funny. I got a perm. Who the hell gets a perm in the late nineties? I just wanted to wash and go, and leave it a big curly mess. My new crazy hairdo was not only practical, it was fun.

The other thing I bought was a bicycle: a red Peugeot. I named it "Freedom." Everyone knew my bicycle by her name. I rode that thing everywhere; to and from work, to friends' places, early morning, late night. I think my favourite time to ride was after finishing the night shift at The Black Bull in downtown Toronto. I would ride home at 3:30 in the morning as the city slept, as late-night partyers straggled home, and the streets were practically void of cars. I could just fly. I rode my bicycle always. If my friends and I were going to a club, I would get all decked out in my crazy rave wear with my crazy rave shoes, hop on my bicycle, and meet them there. I called it "Heels on Wheels." People would ask me, "Omigod, how do you ride with those shoes?"

I would always tell them, "Left, right, left, right."

In 2008, I bought my first car. I was thirty-four years old. I lived downtown, and I bought it to get to and from my new career as a French teacher in Thornhill. I loved my little car; a red Toyota Yaris. I called it my "toy yo-yo." I started driving to all kinds of fun places; exploring. I drove all over Ontario, to Montreal, and to New York City twice.

And then I just kept driving my car. I remember one day my sister Angela gave me a surprise visit at The Black Bull where I was still waitressing on evenings and weekends for extra money. I told her, "I'm almost done. If you want to wait, I can drive you home."

She came to a dead stop. She looked shocked, I dare say, alarmed. "You mean you didn't ride your bicycle here? Why didn't you ride your bicycle here?" she asked, looking stern, serious, and perplexed. She wanted an answer.

I felt my cheeks burn. Yeah. I would never normally pass up an opportunity to ride my bicycle.

In July of 2011, I set off on yet another spontaneous weekend car trip to visit my friend Doug in Pittsburgh. I saw my precious red Peugeot locked up in front of my thirty-story building as I drove away. There she sat, old, rusty and faithful, my precious Freedom. Well, some jerk stole her that weekend. I never saw her again. I was pretty upset. I loved that bike. My fate was now sealed. And this is how a passionate cyclist becomes a mindless motorist without even realizing it.

I shudder.

Finally, one glorious day, after an unfortunate-cum-fortunate series of events—another story entirely involving shady car salesmen, outrageous and corrupt insurance hikes, crazy parking and speeding tickets, the whole mess of it—in April of 2013, I sold my damn car. I felt like the smartest person in the world. Now, each morning, instead of spending forty-five minutes driving and raging and effectively wasting time, I spend an hour reading. Instead of spending another forty-five minutes (or more) driving home each evening, I spend another hour reading. I read thirteen novels in the first two months of commuting using public transit. Instead of spending a thousand dollars each month on car payments, insurance, parking, gas, and tickets, I now spend $240 a month on a GTA pass (public transit pass) and with the rest I buy or do whatever the hell I want. (Mostly I waste it. Ugh.)

And guess what was among the very first things I bought with my new-found extra disposable income? The stars re-align, Zen restores, and the head screws itself back on. Yes, a bicycle. I chose an inexpensive 7-speed Raleigh Detour 2.5.

I honestly don't think that riding my bicycle halfway across the country would have even occurred to me if I still owned a car. Since all I own for transportation is a bicycle, that's what I thought to use to make the trek. And since my impulsive brain does not seem to know the difference between "idea" and "decision made," my fate was sealed.

Cabot Trail, baby, here I come.

HOW I PREPARED

I did a handful of weekend biking and camping trips to prepare. First, I rode from my apartment in Toronto to meet my cousin Danny and his girlfriend Krissie, in Hamilton, Ontario. Eighty kilometres long, the trek took me just over four hours. This was my very first long-distance ride. Ever. Although my bicycle was pannier-free, it gave me some gauge of my speed; about 20km/hr. I stayed overnight at their place and took the GO Train (the commuter train) back the next day.

For my next training ride, I rode from my apartment to my dad and Helen's house in Whitby, Ontario. I had panniers this time with some overnight stuff. And wine for Helen and me and beer for my dad. I stayed overnight at their place and I rode home the next morning. One hundred four kilometres total.

Next, I rode from my apartment to my Aunt Amy's house in London, Ontario and back; a four hundred kilometre trek. I broke it up over four days; one hundred twenty kilometres to Paris on the Friday night (after my day of teaching and in a light rain, I might add), eighty kilometres to London on Saturday, and then the reverse back over Sunday and holiday Monday. It was a success. I stayed at a motel in Paris and with my aunt in London. Camping was not part of the mix yet.

Next, my friend Craig and I rode our bicycles from Toronto Island to Niagara Falls and back; a trek of about three hundred kilometres over a few days. We gorilla camped (also known as stealth camping or wild camping; it is basically setting up camp in a non-designated camping area, and is somewhat akin to trespassing) along the way. This was a completely new and absolutely exciting concept for me. I loved it, but with regards to preparing myself to do the same for my big bike ride, it was of limited use. After all, I wasn't alone. Would I love it as much if it were just me? What about starting those fires in the pouring rain? I'd left that fun task to Craig. What would I do when I was alone?

There was one time during that ride to The Falls, however, when I *was* alone. Craig and I had set up our tent among some trees beside the water and on a fairly steep angle due to lack of much choice for our proper concealment. It was at the Bronte Harbour Yacht Club. There was a jazz festival going on in town. Lots of foot traffic. He left me in the tent to go back into town to get water.

He wasn't gone long before I became overcome with fear. The rustling of the trees. A twig breaking. *Do I hear voices?* I wasn't afraid of animals here, right beside a bustling town. Also, I had dog spray on hand. What I feared was a human; drunken kids who might harass me, or some strange man who might rob or attack me. I tried to remind myself that the odds are astronomically stacked against that happening. The number of good and harmless people far outnumber the damaged and defective. And the odds of one of those rare, damaged, or defective humans being in just the same place I am are also enormously unlikely. However. It is still possible. And thus, there I was, afraid.

In the end, of course, no boogieman in a hockey mask ended up appearing. Craig returned and all was fine. I felt safe again. But this summer there would be no knight in shining armour to give me a potentially false sense of security. There would just be me. Me and my belief in the goodness of humans.

Gulp.

Next, I rode from my apartment to Bronte Creek Provincial Park in Oakville where I camped overnight by myself. A friend came to visit for a couple of hours and helped me tie up my hammock tent for the first time. My hammock tent is a completely enclosed, zip-shut tent that is suspended between two trees like a hammock. It's a thing of genius; unfathomably comfortable and completely dry and clean as it never has to touch the ground, not even to set it up.

The knot-tying to securely keep my tent suspended looked simple enough until I actually tried it myself. In the end, I let my friend hang my hammock tent for me, watching closely and learning, for "next time." I rode home the next day; a total ride of one hundred and twenty kilometres and my first time camping alone.

My last trial run was from my apartment to the place that would also be my destination on day one of my big ride: seventy-four kilometres east to Darlington Provincial Park. This time no friend came to visit or help. The task of tying up my hammock tent was all on me. It took me hours. I should have waited to open the wine, perhaps? After watching YouTube videos on my iPhone, trying my own "logical and creative" approaches, and finally, sending texts to my friend who'd helped me last time, including photos of each step of my knot-making process, I finally got it.

My father drove from Whitby to come have coffee with me in the morning. While he was there, the lady from the lot across from mine came over to chat. She was camping there with her husband and two children. They had offered me firewood the night before as well as extra hamburgers and hotdogs they had. I had wanted to partake in their kindness but I was there to test that I had properly prepared and could make do on my own. I felt forced to decline both offers. Now she came over, asking about my hammock tent.

The three of us struck up a conversation. I told her what I was up to, preparing for a major bicycle ride from Toronto to the East Coast and The Cabot Trail.

She said, "I kept telling my husband last night: 'She's so brave!'"

"Oh, well, we'll see. I haven't done it yet." I replied.

"Oh, she'll do it. I have no doubts," my dad said.

I think my family thinks I can do anything. I wonder if they have any clue how scared I am right now.

"Inaction breeds doubt and fear. Action breeds confidence and courage. If you want to conquer fear, do not sit home and think about it. Go out and get busy."
-Dale Carnegie

EXCERPTS OF ANXIETY

JUNE 8

I'm scared to death.

Christina.

Remember. Fear is a wonderful feeling. Fear means that we are on the brink of learning new things and that our spirit will grow, whether through success or through failure.

Ugh.

The start date is less than a month away. I feel both ready and not ready whatsoever. I have the same attitude that I remember having during my first ultra-marathon. I had run fifty kilometres the first day; Saturday, July thirty-first. I was to return the second day on Sunday, August first, to run forty-two kilometres. An ultra-marathon and a regular marathon back to back. They call this particular piece of madness "Conquer the Canuck." It was 2004. I was rigid, stiff, and sore the Saturday night, after having run the gruelling fifty kilometres that day, my first ultra-marathon. I knew that day two was not going to be possible.

But.

I was there. I'd rented the car and the motel room. I woke the next morning and this is when I had that same feeling I'm having now. I was just in a state of fear, of disbelief that I was perhaps actually going to go through with this? I thus became, providentially, very short-sighted. *Well, I'll just show up at the* start line. Then, at the start line, I thought, *Well, I'll just start and see what happens.* And then, after the first loop, I thought, *Well, I'll try one more.* And so on. Eventually I categorically shocked myself. I finished that disgusting race.

I know I'm capable, that people are good, and that all things are possible. *Tout est possible.* I know, I know. But the truth is: I'm petrified. I don't really know what I've signed up for. I'm a marathon runner, not a cyclist. I'm not even an experienced camper. I just keep telling myself that I am simply going on a little bike ride each day. "The journey of a thousand miles begins with one step," isn't that right Lao Tzu? Hello?

Echoes. Crickets. Sigh.

If I think about the plan as a whole, I feel overwhelmed. I lose sleep. I drown in anxiety. I don't know what will happen. But I guess I'll just "show up at the start line." I'll just set out and see.

JUNE 11

Money. Not once in my life have I been able to sit down and hash out a specific and detailed budget. In looking at the big, round numbers and in doing some rudimentary division, I should be just fine.

Anyway, what else should I do with a whole summer off by myself? I might as well do something utterly exceptional, right?

This may feel scary and even strange, but anything else feels just plain wrong.

JUNE 20

I just spent another unexpected five hundred dollars at Mountain Equipment Co-op. Good grief.

When camping this past weekend with my family, I was stunned to see how tiny each my dad's and my sister Angela's sleeping bags were. I was in shock since my sleeping bag takes up nearly one whole of my two side panniers. I was there to buy a new one like theirs. I also bought a retractable handsaw with a 7-inch blade. *Sexy.* I had borrowed my sister Carolyn's axe over the weekend and quickly learned how dangerous and impractical it was for cutting branches from fallen tree limbs. The limbs are small and thin, you need to hold them with one hand and wielding an axe with only the other is inefficient and slippery. A saw is definitely the perfect tool for this task.

I also bought shorts for riding, a 775mL pot to match the 500mL one I already have (probably not necessary but this way I can cook beans for breakfast and make coffee at the same time...dreamy) and a few other clothing items I may or may not return. (P.S. I returned nothing.)

When I told the lady helping me with all my sleeping bag questions what I was planning, she broke out into the hugest smile. She lit up and told me she had just returned from a cycling/camping trip herself. It empowered me to see how happy she was about her experience and for me on the brink of mine. I meant to ask her if she'd done the trip alone or with a group but I got side-tracked with the super-fun practice of stuffing my soon-to-be-purchased, amazing new sleeping bag into this little miracle thing called a stuff sack.

That's still the most unknown variable: not camping, not the amount of cycling, but me doing this as a woman by myself. I wish I knew more and felt more confident, or knew a woman who had done this, even through a book. I wish I knew why I wanted to do this, desperately, yet wholly unconfidently. Well, even if it is stupid or risky, and even if not many women do something like this alone, it looks like I am going ahead and doing it. So excited, so scared.

JUNE 28

Another night of fitful, unrestful sleep. It's anxiety. It's so many things. It's just...the trip.

At this point I am just stewing and over-thinking and drumming up worries simply because I have the time.

One week until the great departure.

JUNE 30

The last day of school was today. I decided to get one last pedicure before the big bike ride. Fittingly, I chose China Glaze's "Flip Flop Fantasy;" a pretty, bright orangey-pink. I love it. And how appropriate. I wore flip-flops for all of my practice cycling/camping weekend trips and never had any issue so I am just going to go with those as my footwear for now. "If it isn't broken, don't fix it," as the saying goes.

When I'm not bursting with anticipation and excitement my nerves seem to be absolutely shot. Five days. The wait is killing me.

JULY 3

I just bought a ukulele for my trip.

There are less than forty-eight hours to go. I just want to fill my head and body and soul with learning and growth and exploration and wonder and delicious, wholesome, natural foods from local farms I pass and the sounds and smells of nature as opposed to the same old, silly, stagnant city pacifiers I continually turn to (spending, spending, spending) like an automated, idiotic robot.

I just want to go already...

Ontario

*"Anyway, what else should I do with a whole summer off by myself?
I might as well do something utterly exceptional, right?"*

JULY 5TH – DAY 1

I awake minutes before my alarm, just shy of five in the morning. It is finally the fifth of July. As I gain consciousness and become aware of the new day, I realize with bewilderment: This. Is. It.

I eat some Triscuits with peanut butter and jam and have a double espresso with milk. My mind is racing, my heart is pounding. I am, beyond words, excited. But I am calm. I am going through the motions of my morning routines in a state of shock; the beginning of my adventure is finally now. This day has been twenty months in the dreaming.

My tiny bachelor apartment is perfectly quiet and still. The city is silent and asleep somewhere below my tenth-floor balcony. My panniers are already packed and mounted onto my bicycle. I am ready.

Or so I hope.

I do a final visual inspection of my beloved little flat to make sure it is in pristine condition for my Airbnb guests who will arrive later in the day. Then I leave the key on the dining room table, awkwardly squeeze and steer my widely-loaded steed out the front door, and leave the door unlocked.

In the quiet void of dawn, excitedly but unceremoniously, I begin.

I am immersed in the glorious silence of this early-Tuesday Toronto morning, but inside me a volcano is erupting, a heart is bursting, my eyes are wide, and I am being pulled, drawn, and dragged absolutely toward a mysterious goal, a fate I know next-to-nothing about. I'm excited, and I'm scared.

My bike is heavy. Last night, my friend Tony popped by to say goodbye to me and wish me luck. I asked him to pick my bike up, with all its loaded panniers, and estimate how much he thinks it weighs. He said fifty or sixty pounds. I think it weighs more; maybe seventy or eighty. Either way, it's far from light. But I invite the hard work, the weight training for my thirsty, able muscles. I likewise invite the exercise of riding sixty to eighty kilometres a day, every day. I love, I need to keep busy and to keep fit. This crazy bike ride to the end of the Cabot Trail will more than fulfill both of those personal requirements.

I have not scheduled any rest days. I don't know if that is feasible, to ride every day for hours and hours, day in and day out, without taking a day off. Time will tell.

My planning of the route was brief, simple, and incomplete. I don't like to over-research or over-plan things, whether it be an evening out or a vacation to another continent. I much prefer to discover than to expect. I want to be open to what comes my way. And so I did what I always do; as little scheduling and detailing as possible. I basically divided the total number of kilometres I will need to travel (at least two thousand four hundred twenty-five) by the number of days I have available to ride (at most fifty-five). I did this by searching up a cycling itinerary on Google Maps from my address in Toronto to Baddeck, Nova Scotia, then adding three hundred kilometres, which is the length of the Cabot Trail itself. In the little online inquiry I did regarding The Cabot Trail, Baddeck is the town that is mentioned as a common starting point. This gave me a minimum daily requirement of only forty-four kilometres, but I intend to do sixty or eighty, to fill the days, and to leave myself lots of cushion time, just in case. In case of what, I dare not think.

I booked online my first few days of campsites. I was wary to book any further ahead than that. Who knows what will happen? I will take things as they come and decide and plan things as I go along. What other choice do I really have? *I have no idea what the hell I'm doing.*

I begin pedaling.

I follow the directions on the Google Maps itinerary on my iPhone, mounted using an armband phone carrier wrapped around the stem at the handlebars. I pedal east on Davisville, south to the Kay Gardner Beltline Trail, through Mount Pleasant Cemetery, and then east on Moore as the red-hot sun rises in a cloudless sky. Toronto sleeps still. I have always loved being out in the streets at this time of day; usually it's for a morning run. I have never risen this early in the morning for a bicycle ride.

I follow along with the growing traffic until joining up with the Pan Am Trail in Scarborough. It is beautiful and scenic and follows right along Lake Ontario. I pass little makeshift Inuksuk monuments built along the shore. Everywhere I look there are wild wood lilies, just like the ones I had tattooed on my arm only months before this trip. I interpret their abundant presence to be blazes left for me by Mother nature herself, assuring me I am on the right path. The trail is perfectly manicured and flat. I smile as the sun hits my face and the wind cools my already-glistening skin.

Petticoat Creek in Pickering is picturesque and lovely with its little suspension bridges and lush, green trees. Frenchman's Bay Yacht Club is also incredibly quaint and pretty. I stop there to use the washroom and fill my water bottle. These beautiful neighbourhoods are next door to Toronto, only minutes away, yet I knew nothing of them. Already the thrill of discovery is upon me.

Everyone I pass says good morning and smiles. It is uplifting. It's like my favourite saying from the Talmud: We do not see things as they are, we see things as *we* are. Everyone is happy and friendly because I am exactly where I'm supposed to be, following my crazy heart, my wild spirit is unleashed and breathing.

I pass a gourmet hotdog stand and savour the gorgeous smells of delicious pork and beef fat. Sigh. I am under a self-imposed ban on pork and beef for the duration of this trip. During my trial cycling/camping weekend trips, I ate dozens upon dozens of hotdogs. I love them. They are delicious and the perfect camping food. That's just why I had to ban them, for fear of eating one million of them during this extended excursion. I miss them already.

Exactly seventy-four kilometres and six-and-a-half hours after leaving this morning I arrive at Darlington Provincial Park. I'm thrilled. My first accomplishment.

After only one day of riding, though, I am already worried about the long days of sun exposure on my face. My forehead and eyes are covered fine. It is my cheeks, nose and neck that I am worried about. My arms are covered by my white, long-sleeved Lululemon t-shirt. My legs are exposed but I am not worried about them. They can get as black as coal and they will still not have caught up to how much sun exposure our faces and upper bodies get in a lifetime.

Although I have more than enough raw nuts and protein bars on me and have no need to buy anything from the campground store, I go there and curiously look around anyway. The prices for food are marked up about three hundred percent from the regular grocery store prices. I buy a can of beans for my breakfast tomorrow morning but make a mental note to avoid shopping at campground stores whenever possible.

The first mission upon arriving to my campsite is always the same: set up the hammock tent. Rain or a loss of sobriety could happen at any moment, after all. Always make sure that shelter is taken care of first.

I change into a bikini and a cheap, tangerine Joe Cotton dress that I refer to as simply, my camping dress (I brought two, the other is navy) and cycle over to the beach. I sit there for a bit, just watching the water. I am in a state of calm, complete bliss. Then I cycle to the shower, then back to my site. I feed the birds with some leftover bread from a sandwich I ate earlier from Tim Horton's. It's probably not wise leaving breadcrumbs out, they might attract other more pesky animals, but I can't help it. I want the birds to come visit. They are completely freaking out over their newfound meal, chirping away to each other. It's funny. I almost feel like I can understand what they're saying to each other, and it includes some "Fuck, yeahs." when translated into human. They come and go, pecking and stealing away their dinner, crumb by crumb. At one point, one bird flies down, picks up one of the breadcrumbs, throws it back down, picks up a different one, throws *it* back down, then finally decides on a third before flying off with it. Funny little guy.

It's now seven-thirty in the evening. The sun won't set until nine, but nevertheless I think I shall start my fire now. I am dead tired after my long ride in the sweltering thirty-one degree heat.

When the sun goes down, so shall I.

"Nothing compares to the simple pleasure of riding a bicycle."
-President John F. Kennedy

JULY 6TH – DAY 2

In the morning I heat water over the fire in the smaller of my two pots and make my sacred morning coffee. It is this: one packet of Nescafé Sweet and Creamy instant coffee with one packet of Starbucks Blond Roast instant coffee. It is the perfect blend of strong, tasty, and simple.

As I sit savouring the moment, the smells of nature and the caffeine, a woman from the neighbouring campsite approaches. She comes bearing two logs of wood, offering them to me. Her name is Cathy and she is a teacher, too, but with the Brant Huron Superior School Board. She reminds me of the woman from the family who had camped across from me at this very park during my last practice bike/camp trip. Now at this same park, as I embark on the journey I had told the previous woman about, here is another kind soul, also extending warmth and offering help to me.

I was feeling disappointed in myself for having set out from Darlington a full three hours later than planned. Rushing and deadlines, even self-imposed and for logical reasons like avoiding the hottest sun of the early afternoons, just don't seem to be part of the DNA of this ride, I am already learning. But now, just a few minutes on my way to my next destination, the disappointment subsides and I cannot wipe the smile from my face. I am cruising along a typical country road. On my left are beautiful farmhouses and lush green crops that go on for acres and acres. On my right, a CN train zooms by. I love that sound; the train whistling and the rhythmic rattling of the tracks. Today the sun is hot but not cruel. I couldn't be happier.

There is something ironic about the name Darlington Nuclear Waterfront Trail, isn't there?

I pass through the Darlington Hydro Upper and Lower Soccer Fields (they are just fields, no soccer pitches) in Clarington. Somewhere around here, deep in the breadth of the Ontario Power Generation grounds, I have a major Google Maps failure. It has taken me along dusty, gravelly roads to a locked fence gate that simply has a stop sign affixed to it. Behind it is some sort of industrial factory site. But according to Google Maps, this is where I am supposed to be and where I am supposed to continue through. Day two and I am already lost and having GPS issues. I have no back-up paper maps. Self-doubt about the whole trip hits me like a tsunami.

It is twenty-seven degrees. The thought of backtracking along these roads in this heat does not sound fun at all. But, what choice do I have? I turn my bicycle around and start pedaling.

Instead of straight backtracking the way I came, I decide to go east and along the fence of the plant. I use the compass app on my iPhone to guide me. I go up a short but steep hill. I make it all the way up. Woot! Woot! At the top, two men in a truck happen by. They slow and roll their window down and ask what the heck I am doing there. I tell them I am lost and now I am trying to find my way back to any major street. They tell me I am headed in the wrong direction and that the only thing I would find this way was myself in a lake. Okay. I turn myself around and begin the straight backtrack out the way I came.

There are many, many uphill gravel roads around here. Lucky me. I am still trapped within this Ontario Power Generation road maze when I come to a fork in the road that does not look familiar from my way in. On Google Maps, the cross road I am at only goes to the left. In actuality, this road prolongs in both directions. Was it only recently extended, perhaps? I remain stopped here while I try to figure out how to get out of this industrial, dusty, nightmarish labyrinth.

Thankfully, a truck happens to pass by. The friendly and helpful man inside gives me directions. He says that just to the right there will be a turnabout that will bring me to the South Service Road. Perfect. Very soon, I arrive at the turnabout. Hallelujah.

Short-lived hallelujah.

The turnabout leads to Energy Drive East, Energy Drive West, and Holt Road. No mention of a service road. I stay put at the side of the road and wait. Not long later, yet another truck happens by. The two nice boys inside inform me that Energy Drive East *is* the South Service Road. Right. I guess Ontario Power Generation felt the need to remove the universally-recognizable and helpful name of "service road" and replace it with a stupid name associated with their stupid company. Fantastic.

While I'm moaning and complaining, I might as well mention that the Waterfront Trail, along today's stretch, goes back and forth between lakeside trail, which is sometimes gravel, and service road. If I were to do this route again, I would act like a car on Google Maps for this first part of today's route.

I am now on Lake Road in Bowmanville. A VIA Rail train zooms past and gets me to thinking. There is just something about trains, something romantic and nostalgic. When I was a kid, we had a book at home called *All Aboard!* It was a book about two kids who take the train to travel across the country, from one coast to the other. I loved this book. And ever since I have had a penchant for train rides and a dream of doing a similar cross-Canada train trip. When I left on this bicycle journey only yesterday, the plan was to fly home from Sydney or Halifax at the end. But I already know in my heart that that is not the right fit nor the essence of what I am doing. Too fast, too high tech. It has hit me like a ton of bricks, it just feels right, and the decision is already made: I will take the train home.

I am out of water when I happen to be passing a company called Atlantic Lifts Limited, in Bowmanville, just at the same moment when a food truck is pulling up and sounding its horn. I pull in and buy an egg salad sandwich on whole-wheat, a tuna fish salad sandwich on whole-wheat and two bottles of water for $11. What timing. I chat with a couple of the employees who have come out to buy their lunch. When they see me and my loaded-up bicycle, they ask questions. I have fun telling them that I rode from Toronto. They gasp. I smile. I get quite a kick out of this little scenario, shocking people with the story of my little adventure. Their excited reactions help put vigour in my stride. Then I tell them where I am headed: the Cabot Trail on the east coast. They can't believe it.

The truth of the matter is: neither can I.

Soon after this little pit stop, I pass the Samuel Wilmot nature Area, just outside of Bowmanville. There, I come upon a little path into the woods. I can see a viewing platform a short way down the path into the trees on my right. I am curious. I dismount my bike and prop it against a tree.

As I approach, I see that the platform is closed. A sign says: "Please stay out." Like it was an invitation, I hop the barrier. I have never before seen a viewing deck that looks out onto nothing but a massive field of tall, swaying reeds, waving and languishing in the wind. It is incredible. I wasn't expecting this poignant cache of natural beauty. A veritable sea of green grass, high as small trees, dancing, populace and buoyant, yet deafeningly silent. I feel like a welcome trespasser so long as I likewise stay hush. And I do.

After the nature area, the intermittent trail peters out and then the "Waterfront Trail" becomes a never-ending stretch of road called Lakeshore Road where there is not a stitch of shade, not a soul to be found, and not a single sound, save for the electric buzz in the air from the overhanging power lines that you almost don't notice until you do, and then you marvel at how quietly thunderous it is.

I stop at a grocery store just before arriving to my destination: a little sailboat, "Old Flat Top," that I have rented for the night through Airbnb. Blessed be grocery stores and their arctic, blasting air-conditioning. It is hot, hot, hot out. I also stop for a bottle of wine at the LCBO (the Liquor Control Board of Ontario, or, simply, the liquor store). It's just "bicycle minutes" away from the marina where my sailboat home-for-the-evening is. Perfect. I ride over and settle into my charming naval digs. I lock my bike up on the dock and transport my heavy panniers onto the boat. I open the wine, settle down with my new ukulele, and practice three songs: "You Are My Sunshine," "Amazing Grace," and "Happy Birthday." It was my older sister Carolyn's birthday on the fourth. I learned it for her.

I have the coolest pink guitar at home and it has sat atop my bookshelf for over eight years now. I have always joked that not one but both my legs would have to be broken for me to be able to sit long enough to practice and to build those callouses on my fingertips like my dad told me I'd have to suffer through to make any real progress. It's just too big and too time-consuming for go-go-go me. And too painful. But the ukulele is perfect. "Guitar for dummies," I call it.

Or, guitar for extreme Type-A chicks with ADD.

Soon I head out to The Jailhouse Pub, minutes away, for some dinner. I have a tasty Greek salad and a glass of red. I meet two lovely women about my age and we three start up a lovely little conversation. I love chatting randomly with strangers. Even at home in my thirty-story building I love to initiate and engage in small talk with people in the elevators. Often I think people almost look relieved that I have broken the ice. I hate when I hear people say that Toronto is unfriendly. Not true. Perhaps people are just shy, nervous, preoccupied. Anyway, what did that wise guy Mahatma say? "Be the change..." If you think someone or somewhere is unfriendly, *be friendly*. I can attest to the fact that it works.

Suddenly a crew of sailors walk in, white uniforms and all. They are in their early twenties, I would say. They start flirting with the two women I was speaking with and the women are absolutely eating up the attention. Not one of the sailors pays *me* any mind. Of course not, I suppose. I have spent the day sweating and cycling under a hot sun. My hair is kinked with sweat and salt and coiffed into a lovely helmet head. My face is streaked with runny mascara and dirt. And it's just as well. I want no part of the unfolding debauchery. Boys and partying are furthest from my mind. Wine and ukulele on a gently rocking sailboat overlooking the water is more what I am in the mood for. It's my cue to leave.

I go out to my bicycle, which I had humorously parked at the end of a long string of gorgeous motorcycles. A couple of the owners of the motorbikes are there and we strike up a conversation. I tell them about my journey and they are incredulous and supportive. Their names are Phil and Jerry. We all add each other on Facebook and they tell me they will definitely be following my journey. My crazy little bike ride is a great conversation piece; a key to open doors to new, wonderful people. I knew it would be.

Today I rode sixty kilometres in thirty-degree heat. It's early in the ride, but, so far, so great.

*"You know, 'Why? Why?' A very American, finger-snapping question.
I do something magnificent and mysterious, this thing, and I got a practical
'Why?' And the beauty of it is, I didn't have any why."*
-Philippe Petit, Man on Wire.

JULY 7ᵀᴴ – DAY 3

In the morning I awake, make coffee, sit on the deck, and watch the sunrise. It is cloudy, but I see the sun for a few brief minutes before she tucks back away, behind the clouds, where she belongs, in my opinion, for the long, hot, daytime ride ahead of me. There is no one around, just me and the seagulls. It is peaceful, serene, and still.

Ideally, I should set out on my bicycle at dawn to clock in as many kilometres as possible in the cooler mornings, avoiding the hottest sun that shines mid-afternoon. But this won't always be possible and it is best that I find ways to deal with the sun rather than trying to avoid it. Yesterday I bought a pink bandanna at the Dollar Store to wear around my face as I ride. I won't win any fashion awards or get endorsed by the cool kids, but it will be smart and my skin will thank me.

I ride over to The Buttermilk Café on King Street West. I order three sunnyside up eggs, home fries, with buttered in-house-made rye toast. It is divine. And a watermelon wedge. This place is great and my waitress, Heather, is smiley and friendly.

I ride back to the marina. In total I have four panniers for this ride. Two big side panniers attached to my back rack. One contains my tent, sleeping bag, and a bicycle repair kit. The other contains my clothes. Then I have a smaller pannier that sits atop my rack. It contains all my toiletries. Finally, I have a small pannier mounted to my handlebars for food. All are detached and in the boat. I reattach my toiletries pannier on my bike, and ride to the marina washrooms to shower. I am combing my wet hair at the communal sinks when an older lady enters. She says hello and asks me if I am boating here.

"No, I'm cycling, actually."

I then tell her a bit about what I am doing. She becomes downright animated.

"Can I give a donation?" she asks, excitedly.

So sweet, so funny. But I am just doing this for the heck of it. In truth, I don't even know why I am doing this, just that I needed to—this adventure called me by name. "No, but thank you." I tell her.

"Can I get a picture with you?" she asks.

I laugh and agree.

We walk outside together. She introduces me to her husband and her two friends. They are all boating there. She and her husband are from Toronto, both retired from working for the Attorney General. We take the picture and say our goodbyes. She wishes me well but, in the same breath, tells me I won't need it. I love this woman. Her name is Anne. I love that she is exuberant and supportive and not pessimistic and doubtful. The fact that I am a woman doing this on my own is clearly not a worry with this friendly, fiery lady. Twenty months ago, when I began telling people what I was thinking of doing, I got some raised eyebrows. "By yourself?" they asked, sceptically.

Is that crazy? Reckless? Dangerous? Stupid? It is if you believe that the world is a bad place full of ill-intentioned people. I don't happen to share that view, and clearly, neither does Anne. Bless her.

I set out for my day's ride at twenty to ten. The forecast calls for a high of thirty-two with some cloud. I don my pink bandanna. I look like a pirate, like the bad guy in an old black and white cops and robbers film. I look ridiculous. I don't care at all.

Today I mess up my route. I am too busy being so goddamned happy and tra-la-la-ing along that I miss the turn for Old Danforth Road. Google Maps reconfigures my directions and tells me I should turn left onto Shelter Valley Road. However, I look at the map and that seems like an unnecessary divergence when County Road Two continues straight toward my destination. I continue straight. I quickly realize why Google Maps has not recommended this route. There is no paved shoulder and the gravel shoulder is quite treacherous for a bicycle. I am forced to share the narrow road with passing motorists. I pray no one is texting and driving here.

A short while later, I stumble upon the pretty little Township of Wicklow where I pass beautiful Wicklow Beach. The water is beckoning me to come say hello with my hot feet to its cool shore. I stop, and so does a black van, just a little ways down the road. It just sits there. I watch it, waiting, but no one emerges from it. I carefully set my heavy bike onto its kickstand. When I finally have it balanced and secure (it's not easy), I walk down to the beach. Two gentlemen get out of the van and do the same. I see them looking over at me.

I take off my flip-flops and walk my hot, dusty feet in the cool, shallow water of the beach. It feels unspeakably refreshing. I think about resting here an hour, going for a swim. But I decide against it. I am too keen on locking in kilometres and exploring. I have not traveled far enough or long enough yet to feel secure taking "time off."

Plus those guys are watching me.

I take a good look at the two men. I pause and I think. I try to forget about external messages of fear from the media, the blanket advice of "don't talk to strangers," paranoid images from horror movies. Instead, I try to read them, give this situation some thought and evaluation. My gut tells me that they are harmless. I assume that they must live here and that my pirate get-up and loaded-up bicycle and I must stick out like a sore thumb. I return to my bike and they return to the van. Of course I have some of those wild thoughts; thoughts that these two strangers might want to harm me. But it is way more likely that they are just nice people. It's what my instinct is telling me. They look curious, not menacing.

"Hello." I call out.

I ride over, closer to the van, inside where they are once again seated. The three of us strike up a conversation. I tell them about my journey and what I am planning. They are impressed and full of smiles. Both men are warm and encouraging. I am happy to have met them.

We say our goodbyes and I begin pedaling down the road. They wave as they pass me. I wave back. Then I see them stop and turn the van around. I laugh. I wonder what is up now. They slow as they pass me. The driver blurts out: "But where do you sleep?" and "How do you know where to go?" and "How did you know what to pack?" And on and on. He has overcome his shyness and now has a million questions and they are rapid-fire pouring out of him. It's pretty cute.

The young man doing all the talking is named Ramneet. He tells me he has a farm here and if I need any help or accommodations I am welcome at his place. He also tells me he has a restaurant in Little India in Toronto and I am invited to visit it. I sure will. I love Indian food. It's my favourite type of cuisine. Another kind, beautiful stranger. We add each other on Facebook, he wishes me good luck, and I give my standard reply.

"Thanks. I'll need it."

The van disappears down the road and I continue on in the opposite direction, smiling.

Although yesterday there wasn't a speck of shade to be found anywhere, today there is a lot. Lush trees with a lot of beautiful, welcoming coolness to protect me as I ride. It is ironic and perhaps unnecessary, then, that I am in what I have already come to call "full pirate gear" today: that fashionable pink bandanna wrapped around my face, tucked under my sunglasses, over my ears, and tied at the back. It covers my entire face and neck. It is perfect protection from the sun.

The route is charming and pretty today. There are many big, beautiful country homes, sprinkled with Muskoka chairs on rolling lawns.

I'm out of water. I decide I will ask the next homeowner I see if I can fill my bottle. The next human I see turns out to be in the next township, called Lakeport. The smiley gentleman on his front lawn gladly obliges. I wish him a good day, and he me.

Next I stop at Vito's Restaurant and Pizzeria in Colborne. Here I meet a friendly, chatty couple: Dick, 80, and Jane, 73. "I'm sure you've seen our books," they joke. They clearly get a kick out of the irony of their famous names.

I sit down and they begin to chat with me. It is like they have been expecting me. We get right into the thick of conversation. I learn that Dick has non-Hodgkin's lymphoma cancer and four stints in his heart. Jane chirps in that she's been trying to knock him off for years. We all laugh. They tell me about Chauga, a healing tea made from dying yellow birch trees. The trees try to heal themselves and in so doing they grow little burrows on their bark. The tea is made from these burrows. Dick and Jane are actually from Toronto. They tell me about their three children. They tell me about the music band they are in. I like their page on Facebook. We talk about the recent shootings of the innocent black men in Baton Rouge, Louisiana and in Falcon Heights, Minnesota. Together, we feel sadness, dismay, horror, and shock. In our short conversation, we have shared about life, personal and the world at large, the good and the bad. I feel as though I am dropping in on old friends. Who said I was doing this bike ride alone, anyway? I finish my salad, we say our goodbyes, and off I go again.

Along these country roads I have seen countless Canadian flags waving proudly from quaint, country homes. I love our flag, its simplicity, and that there is something from nature on it. I love that it is original and not flashy. It's just really *nice*.

Just like Canadians, eh?

In the early afternoon I arrive at Presqu'Ile Provincial Park. It is massive and gorgeous. The trees must be fifty feet tall. My particular site, lot number 211, is stunning. The floor is a soft, cushy ground made of pretty, fallen, amber pine needles, fine mulch, and a blend of new and old leaves. I am in awe of the grandeur of the trees, the beauty of the woods, and all the fresh grassy, smoky, oaky smells.

The trees are so numerous on my lot that I actually have the luxury of needing to decide which two to hang my hammock tent from instead of being thankful there are two that are manageable for hanging at all. The trees need to be far enough apart but not too far in order to hang it properly. I pick a spot. Also, here the fire pit is embedded into the ground; a small detail, perhaps, but a cool perk.

I happen to be across from the two park host sites. These are campers that volunteer to be of help to any campers who might need it. A woman from the ambassador campsite adjacent to mine has come over to speak with me. Her name is Sherri. She and her husband, Marc, were noticing that I am on a bicycle. She has come to ask questions and to offer any help I might need. I love that my bicycle draws people toward me. I am happy to talk about my adventure and to meet these new, friendly people.

After Sherri leaves, I take care of duty number one: setting up the hammock tent. Then I go for a short bike ride to the park store, mostly for something to do. I buy a bag of potato chips and a litre of milk. So much for my plan of eating all natural foods and fresh produce from the stands I pass as I ride. In actuality what I pass are corner stores and gas stations and Tim Horton's. Oh, well. It was a delicious dream while it lasted.

When I return, I find that some kind stranger has left me a pile of kindling beside my firewood. How sweet. Earlier, when I arrived, a little boy from one of the host sites had eagerly asked me if I needed any help. I had said I didn't and thanked him. My guess is this wood comes from him. I will have to keep an eye out for him to say thank you.

The Internet connection is spotty at best here at Presqu'Ile. I feel much more alone without it. I must check Facebook one million times a day, up from only half a million times per day when I am at home.

The mosquitoes are eating me alive. Oh, man. What can I do but douse myself with insect repellent over and over, despite that I hate putting alcohol-based chemicals onto my already beat-up skin from the sun. Well, I may be ageing myself on the outside but my soul is drinking from the fountain of youth.

So far I have been lucky. All three nights I have slept near enough to the water that I hear the waves crash on the shore the whole night long. How the sound of the water soothes the soul.

Today I travelled forty-two kilometres under intensely sunny skies and a high of thirty degrees. Tomorrow should be interesting. The forecast calls for clouds all morning with a forty percent chance of lightning and rain in the early afternoon. During the two practice weekend cycle trips that included camping, I didn't encounter any rain. It is the one situation I have absolutely no experience with and my gear has never been tested against. I will be sure to leave early tomorrow. I have a sixty-two kilometre ride planned.

In the middle of the night as I lie asleep in my hammock tent, I wake and hear the raccoons having their way with my small food pannier. Although I had looked for a branch to suspend it from, there were none low enough to be reached. Still, in the middle of the late, dark night, I get up and look again. Nope. Still no low branches. None have mysteriously sprouted while I slept. I take the rope that I usually use to suspend my food from trees and wrap it around and around the pannier. There will be no getting into it now, she says.

Silly city girl.

In the morning, I find two furry little guys rocking out beside the picnic table, partying it up with the nuts and raisins from my food pannier. They look drunk with feast and victory. I am actually impressed with their work. They had gnawed and bitten their way around the rope and through the durable and thick nylon and plastic casing of the pannier. I shoo them away and begin cleaning up the mess. Despite the many nuts and raisins on the ground and already eaten by my little friends, there are still quite a few left in the pannier. I decide to throw them all into the forest beside my site. Heck, they earned it.

Really, it is a blessing in disguise. I had way over-packed and quite frankly that much of my homemade trail mix was heavy. Plus, I enjoy stopping for food, even if it is truck-stop and coffee shop sandwiches. It breaks up the day and grants me the opportunity to meet and talk with people.

As I am packing up my camp, the chipmunks discover the goldmine I have just left for all the wildlife there among the trees. They are going bonkers, making that high-speed ticker-tape sound I have already come to recognize from them. It goes on and on. They are shrilly chipping and rapidly trilling to each other the news of their great find. I laugh. It is cool to see them scamper off with their fat, stuffed cheeks.

Bye, little guys. I'm off, again.

"When I ride in the mornings, my shadow is ten feet tall
because The Sun knows that is exactly how I feel."

JULY 8TH – DAY 4

And on the fourth day, it rained.

Just minutes after I set out, Murphy's Law, down comes the rain. Okay, here goes nothing. Also, I have no Internet connection, thus no Google Maps for the first thirteen kilometres. I am only able to figure out my way because the friendly and helpful man who owns the little store just outside the front entrance of Presqu'Ile Provincial Park came to chat with me as I sat on the picnic table in front of his shop, fiddling with my phone. He's from Toronto, too. He lives and works there eight months, then comes and lives out here and works his little shop for four months. Sounds like a pretty nice life. He let me use his Galaxy phone, which, unlike my iPhone, was getting full reception, to figure out the first little bit of my journey.

The rain is steady and unapologetic, telling me it is time to separate the eager little girls from the real women. Hard rain. About ten minutes of that, then thunder, too. I am both invigorated and scared, part girl, part woman. But what do you do? Stopping is the same as going; wet and sopping. I keep going. At least it is warm out. Pedaling keeps you warm, too. A voice in my head taunts me: *Welcome to the reality of your little flip-flop fantasy, my dear.*

After about thirteen kilometres, I finally spot a little restaurant on the side of the road called The Mason Jar; warm food, a place to dry up a bit, and Wi-Fi. There is perfect Internet connection, which I enjoy using over a hot, hearty breakfast of three sunnyside up eggs, home fries and rye toast with butter.

Here I do my daily administration: I upload all my previous day's pictures to Facebook for storage. I create a new photo album each day and confine the privacy settings to just me. I don't have enough space on my phone to let them accumulate there. I take a lot of photos. Also, this way they are safe and secure should something happen to my phone. I do my daily post, too, on Facebook. I relay just the basic facts of my progress with a few photos. These daily posts let my family and friends know I am okay. They also act as a vehicle for me to feel their love and support as they post encouraging messages and like my photos. All the feedback I get from these posts helps me immensely and prevents me from feeling isolated and alone. Finally, I email my daily notes and observations, mostly written through voice text, to a dedicated email account I set up expressly for this purpose. By doing this daily administration, should anything happen to me or my phone, only one day's photos and notes would be lost.

My phone, in life in general, but exponentially more so on this trip, is my life. On this trip it is my telephone, GPS, camera, note-taker, itinerary, connection to home. I try not to think about how dependent I am on it. It stresses me right the hell out.

The rye bread here is just dripping with butter. Well done, The Mason Jar. I add raspberry jam and voilà: a slice of heaven. I eat my breakfast, then tuck the leftovers into my 750mL cooking pot. In it already are my leftover veggie dogs and beans from this morning. This is a great system. It clips shut and doesn't leak. It's perfect. I take my napkin and start cleaning the black soot from the outer bottom of the pot off before putting it back in my pannier. I see a man watching me curiously as I clean the pot and pack up my food. I'd love to know what he's thinking.

The restaurant is a charming and simple little diner where the service is warm and friendly and where the old boys, fifty-ish, call the old men, seventy-ish, "young fellas" and where everyone knows everybody else. I love places like this. I value being privy to these snapshots of a kind of living other than mine in the big city.

I am worried that I will again not have Internet connection once I leave The Mason Jar so I take screen shots of each stretch of the route that remains between here and Sandbanks Provincial Park, my next destination. The rain is slowing. Off I go.

I inhale deeply the wonderfully rustic smells of the country, manure and grass and dirt, brought alive and swimming in air by the wet of the rain; things you never smell in downtown Toronto. These are the verdant scents that awaken long-sleeping memories from my childhood. I remember a road trip to Quebec, to the farm of the brother-in-law of my Great-Uncle René, in the outskirts of Acton Vale. It was my dad, his second wife Lisa, my sister Carolyn, and me. I remember the foal and the chickens and Tante Elise's craftwork of the little potpourri bonnets she made in her trailer home. Fond flashbacks flood my brain, my heart, in an instant. The nostalgic aroma of the farm.

Suddenly, as I am riding along Bedgley Road, a massive, ferocious-looking, leashless dog comes bounding out of one house's backyard, menacing and barking, coming straight at me. "No no no!" I say in a highly alarmed but surprisingly controlled voice. I pull over immediately and grab for my dog spray. The dog is tearing straight toward me, and fast. I fumble with the side zipper of my toiletries pannier, which is, quite inconveniently, atop my back rack. Milliseconds feel like minutes.

Then, just as suddenly, the dog stops at the end of the driveway. I suppose it feels satisfied that it has done its duty of ensuring I am not coming to trespass, that it has sufficiently scared the fucking shit out of me. As soon as I realize I am going to be okay, I break into a full sweat; forehead, chest, back. Cautiously, still no dog spray in hand, I get back onto my bicycle and contrive to gingerly ride away. A few minutes later, a safe distance away from the big, bad house dog, I pull over and move my dog spray from the unreachable side pouch of my toiletries pannier in the back to the reachable side pouch of my handlebar food pannier. Smarter.

The city girl is learning.

The rain has now stopped but the clouds are thankfully still full and present. Yesterday was all about colours: acres of green corn stalks with emerald leaves, blue lake, fields of blonde wheat, cobalt sky, and orangey-red wild lilies. Today is all about the animals: fastidious raccoons, excited chipmunks, majestic horses, lazy cows, cock-a-doodle-doing roosters, and super scary dogs. I sure am getting my country on. It's wonderful. I call out hellos to them all (except the dog).

And then, bless, a winery. Prince Edward County, I learn, is second only to Niagara for number of wineries. This one is the Karlo Estates Winery. It is a big, beautiful, red barn with freshly-painted white mouldings around the windows, walls of handsomely worn slats of wood, and a silo at the back. Inside, everything is made of wood: the loft, the floors, the bar, the shelves, the barrels. I take a deep breath. It smells wonderful. Antiques ornament the lumber planks; a rocking chair, a piano, an old cash register, a buffet, a hand-held cow bell, and an old telephone. It is positively charming. I do two wine tastings and buy a bottle of the Triumvirate.

Soon Google Maps brings me to a nine-kilometre stretch along the Millennium Trail. The first half is hard-packed dirt and easy to ride. The last half is made of chunky gravel with many large, rough boulders. It is difficult, slow, and stressful to ride. With a heavy load like mine, it is quite precarious. I know exactly how to make this a bit less painful. I pull over and uncork my bottle of Triumvirate. I sip a bit from my stainless steel, stem-less wine glass. I have a cigarette, too. I carry on. The path, magically, seems friendlier and more fun.

A bit further along, still on the Millennium Trail, on a lovely little bridge, I pull over again. I pull out the 750mL pot from my food pannier and eat all my leftovers. When I finish, I wash the pot and my spoon with the tiniest bit of water from my one-litre water bottle and a baby wipe. Baby wipes are essential in life in general but especially when camping. Convenient uses of baby wipes for camping include: ass-wiping, nose-blowing, refreshing the hot, dirty face (surprisingly they always feel cool), dish-washing, picnic table cleaning (they are durable), and more.

The road after The Millennium Trail is also not ideal with no paved shoulder and only a narrow, gravel one. I am forced to ride on the road and share it with motorists. Drivers coast wide around. Bless them.

I stop at "The Local Store" about eight kilometres before my destination, hoping to find food as I am all out. It turns out to be more of a local arts and crafts store. It's charming, but not what I need. I do meet a friendly lady named Mary-Ann, though. She asks where I rode in from. We have a great conversation and she tells me where I can find a proper grocery store. I set off again.

She honks as she passes me in her car. A bit farther on, I come to a house where a lady is standing on the front lawn, waving excitedly at me. It's Mary-Ann—this is her house. She beckons me over and offers me dinner, which I decline because I am exhausted and I just want to get to my site. She gives me a county map, which may definitely prove useful in light of the loss of Internet connection I experienced this morning. Mary-Ann is a sweet lady, eager to help.

And then, because the day had not already been long and challenging enough with the rain and without Internet and due to the gravelly path of the Millennium Trail, with only three kilometres to go, I get a flat tire. I pull over to the side of the road and attempt to pump the back tire. It takes. We'll see how long it holds. I hope I can at least make it to the park. What a day. Thank goodness I have wine.

Sandbanks Provincial Park is beautiful. It is winding and hilly, not flat like so many others. My site, lot 313, is the most private I have had so far this trip and throughout all my practice trips. However, there is a fire ban. I can't cook the rice I just bought at a little deli just outside the park. I snack on the local cheese curds I also bought there. I guess that's dinner.

Once my hammock tent is up, I sit down at my picnic table, in a zombie state. I'm exhausted. It's not just the riding. It's the adrenaline flowing all day, the rain, the searching for somewhere dry, the observing, the soaking in of it all…it is a constant attack on the senses. At the end of these days, my brain is tired. I sit and I sit, then I sit some more. The park store is open for another hour. And even though I have not had a proper dinner, I just don't know if I can make it. I'm that wiped. And grumpy. And perhaps a bit tipsy from the Triumvirate.

My buddies, the mosquitoes, begin to arrive. I spray and I spray; I cover myself with bug repellant. My forearm is aching from so much spraying from the damn pump bottle. I make a mental note to buy aerosol spray for my next bottle.

Dusk settles in slowly, almost imperceptibly, like dust on a mantle. I continue to just sit there, like a bump on a log, unable to move. I sit and watch the light slowly slip away, like an entire orchestra of rays, taking sneaky little steps back, back, back, behind a curtain of trees and a horizon I cannot see. Yep. I'm tipsy. I'm not going to the park store. I'm sitting here and playing my ukulele instead. It is dark, darker, pitch black, absolutely void of light like is only possible out in nature during a fire ban. It's perfect. This is living.

With no fire to tend to, instead I play. I sip, I smoke, I write, I play. All this as the wind blows gently, and the trees create a quiet, momentous choir of white noise. I am transported by the peace, the beauty, nature, the thrill of this adventure I am on. I can't help but wonder: what led me here? Where did the idea to do this crazy bike ride come from, anyway? Why was I so dead set on doing it even though I had never done anything like this before? Does it even matter? I am thankful. Boundlessly thankful. How will I ever relay to anyone this incredible feeling inside me?

Up to and including today, I had planned and booked my accommodations online before leaving. The first four days. From here on in, it's "come what may." I do not find this worrisome or stressful. In fact, I find it exciting. It's a little adventure within an adventure. Tomorrow, so long as I travel about fifty kilometres, I can end wherever I want. Will I gorilla camp? Have my first motel stay? Perhaps I will Couchsurf; I sent out a couple of requests. But truthfully, I prefer to camp. I would rather sleep beneath the stars and amid the smells of leaves and trees and pine needles and clean, crisp air. And my hammock tent? It is like sleeping in the palm of Mother Nature's own hand. It is a cocoon, a womb, a soft, fluffy cloud.

Today I travelled sixty-two kilometres in twenty-eight degree temperatures with my first taste of rain. At two in the morning, it returns. Light raindrops on the fly of my hammock wake me. What soft, soothing rhythm. I am blessed. I am soon lulled back to a perfect sleep.

"I've either lost my mind or finally got it right."

JULY 9ᵀᴴ – DAY 5

The fire ban means cold coffee. The instant coffee packets do not dissolve easily in cold water but eventually they do. I sit at my picnic table, in my little outdoor living room. I light a cigarette. I sip the cold coffee. Then, like ice slowly being melted from a windshield, an unusual visual begins to illuminate slowly, subtly, all around me. I look up and all around.

It is snowing pine needles!

What a sight. There is nothing to say or anyone to say it to. Beholden, I sit there and watch the mass of tiny light green spines come tumbling, twirling down, thick in the air, a soft swarm. What a wonder.

I pack up my camp, and then take a look at my bike. The air that took yesterday has all escaped and the flat has returned. I decide I had better let someone who knows what they're doing change the tube and watch closely. I feel that if I attempt it at my current stage of expertise, or lack thereof, I am likely to fuck it up even further. It can hold air temporarily; hopefully long enough for it to get me to someone who can help. As I pass I scan the campsites for one with bicycles but don't find one.

I leave my campground and despite the worry of fixing my flat tire, I cannot help but go to the crisp, cool water of Lake Ontario. I step my flip-flopped feet into the wonderfully wet and soothing shore. What a beautiful beach of super soft, velvety, ultra-fine sand. I can't see the dunes and would love to. But I need to tend to this tire and take advantage of this motivation to get riding. Sandbanks, you and I have unfinished business, my friends.

I stop at the park office and ask if anyone knows how to change a flat. I am in luck. The lady walks me over to the park workshop where "the guy" who knows how to change a flat is. He and his two coworkers help me, and they do it with big, friendly smiles. Upon my request, the main guy shows me what he is doing as he does it. He also tells me how he, too, did the Cabot Trail by bicycle when he was younger. He tells me how he flew down one of the mountains, no brakes, full speed, about ninety kilometres an hour. He was going so fast that he blew out both tires.

"From the heat?" I ask.

He confirms my guess. Good to know. I will remember this for when I get there. My bicycle is all fixed and I am off once again.

Wait a second.

He said *mountain*.

He said *one of the mountains*.

Oh, man.

Even though it is getting late, I am starved and need to eat. I eat at the Park restaurant. I have four sunnyside up eggs, rye toast with butter and jam, hash browns with green peppers, onions, and mushrooms, 500 mL of milk and a large coffee.

Today I finally change into my other outfit for riding. I only brought two. After four days of riding in the same clothes, the shirt from my first outfit is getting downright grimy, I could barely pull it onto my arms this morning. I feel like Queen of the Universe in my clean clothes.

Today the clouds are a masterpiece. There are mountains in the sky. What is the best art gallery there ever was and ever will be, showcasing daily the most stunning chefs-d'oeuvre in the world? The sky, of course.

Two nights in a row with a non-electric campsite is one night too many. My single charge for my phone is out, so is my ten-charge, and I'm at ten percent on my phone. Luckily I am on one long stretch of one road only. There is no need to stay logged onto Google Maps. It is just forty-three kilometres along Highway 33, no turns whatsoever. I will be fine. I am thankful for the break on my data usage, too. I can only imagine what my phone bill will be like. (P.S. Thankfully, I incurred no extra charges.)

After three hours of riding, I stop on the side of the road to eat my leftover toast from breakfast this morning with one of the two mini cans of Bush's maple beans that the park office gave me, which were left over from a promotion. Yuck. Maple beans. But I eat it all.

Not long after, I happen upon another winery: Bergeron Winery. I do three tastings. I buy a bottle of the Gamay, which is the type of wine I most often drink when I am in Paris, France, where I usually spend my summers off. It is a purchase based as much on nostalgia as it is on taste. While I am there I charge my array of electronics. Charging these things takes time, though. I haven't brought any of them back to life much at all when the ants in my pants are restless and I am on the road once again.

But not for long. Another winery. Thirty-Three Vines Winery. Although I am already stocked for this evening, I decide to stop. It is right here in my path and therefore part of the journey and who am I to meddle with such a lovely fate? I chat with Beth who sits in the old, refurbished locomotive car where the tastings and sales take place. I do three tastings. I buy the Blueberry Baco Noir. I am now very well-equipped for tonight. I pray I don't drink both bottles.

Indeed I am well-equipped with wine but I am completely out of food. *Priorities, woman.* Finally I come to The Old Conway General Store. I am hoping for some sort of sandwich but there are none. I am forced to settle for some jalapeño cheddar potato chips. At the counter, Wayne explains to me that he just opened this store about a week ago and he is not yet set up for debit or credit purchases. I am crushed. I have no cash. My devastation and hunger must be obvious. He tells me the chips are on the house.

This reminds me of another time, many years ago. I had been out trail riding all morning in the hot, hot sun on my Surly Instigator, up and down Toronto's Don Trails. My Surly has a super-jacked mega front shock, perfect for riding through the nature trails, over boulders and raised tree roots. My ride ended at Riverdale Park. I was hungry as a bear and parched as paper. I rode over to my favourite café in the whole city: The Rooster on Broadview Avenue. I grabbed an M-bar and a carton of milk. I waited in line. I got to the front, only to see a sign: "Cash only." Then, like now in front of kind-hearted Wayne, I was crushed. The guy behind the counter at The Rooster simply said, "If I let you have it, will you come back later and pay?"

I was incredulous. I did come back and pay later, but not before getting a tattoo on the back of my neck of two words that make up my personal religion: "Love. Karma."

I had wanted this tattoo for a while and this simple act of trust and kindness from The Rooster told me this was the day to do it. The guy behind the counter showed some faith in a stranger and I thought that was beautiful. I've never forgotten it and I continually strive to pay it forward. And now here is Wayne, committing the same beautiful act of kindness.

I now have everything I need to party: the sun on my face, the joy in my heart from riding my bicycle, salty snacks, cigarettes, wine, and my ukulele. I stop along the side of the road, I hop the guard-rail and I climb down the big boulders, out of view from the road. I sing, I eat, I sip, I smoke, I play. Life is wonderful.

After a lazy fifty kilometres of riding, I arrive at Finkle's Shore Park, which borders the northeastern tip of Lake Ontario. I have a few more chips, a few more sips, and another cigarette. It is spacious and beautiful here. A young couple is doing some stand-up paddle boarding. The trees here are large and looming, giving lots of protective shade. I sit in the gazebo. I still don't know where I will stay this evening. I am halfway between where I started this morning and where I need to get to tomorrow. I will start keeping an eye out for motels or Bed & Breakfasts or even a spot to gorilla camp. I am in no rush.

Or am I?

Suddenly there is a massive, ominous, dark cloud on the horizon and the wind picks up swiftly. It looks and smells like rain. I know what's next, and soon. Now I *am* in a rush. I stop at a family restaurant in the town, Bath, I find myself in. There is a lady entering at the same time. I ask her if she knows of a Bed & Breakfast nearby.

She looks at my loaded bicycle, then at me. In one breath, this is what she says to me: "Yes, there is one down the road, and there is one just over on such-and-such street, or you can just stay at my place. We just set up the tent in our backyard yesterday; it's ready to go. You can sleep there and you can shower in the morning."

Just like that. She writes her name, Mary, her address and her phone number on a piece of paper and goes on her way as if we had just had a casual conversation about the weather. I am stunned. I carefully fold the precious piece of paper and put it into my food pannier.

I decide not to eat at the family restaurant because it is full and busy. Instead I backtrack maybe fifty meters and go to The Loyalist Pub. Locking up my bicycle outside (all bags stay with the bike), I am thrilled to hear live music from inside. I order the black bean burrito with salad and, my favourite, French dressing. And a glass of wine. And then a second. And this is how I meet another lovely lady, also named Mary.

Mary is the friendly, fast, and efficient lone waitress at the pub. We strike up a conversation and continue to chat warmly while she works. I tell her what I am up to with my little bike ride. She thinks it's fantastic. She is supportive and kind. With each new supportive woman I meet I feel less and less like a freak. It's hard not to sometimes feel that way back home where I know no one who is doing the same thing as I am, a crazy summer-long bike ride, nor anything remotely similar, and when nearly all my friends and colleagues are married with children. But now that I am out here and doing my thing, in my element, I am finding alliance and affirmation through the outpouring of support, from both old friends and new.

I charge my phone and extra batteries as I chat with Mary and listen to the man play his guitar and sing his original songs. Finally, it is time to go. Mary and I add each other on Facebook. I am off again.

I set off toward the Bed & Breakfast that Mary had told me about. As I near it, I see a pathway that leads to a small parkette on the water, Lake Ontario. I go there instead, still contemplating gorilla camping. Ironically, there is a tent pitched and a kayak banked on the shore. I venture near the tent and sure enough there is a person inside, fast sleep. I call out a hello. I want to ask if he is gorilla camping and pick his brain about the topic if he is. But there is no movement from inside the tent. I look around to see if there is somewhere I can pitch my hammock tent. There isn't. All the trees are closely clustered and are full of long, dense branches. I think again about Mary's offer. Already on this trip I have declined many kind offers of food and help, feeling that I should not accept if I don't need it. But there is the other part of me that absolutely wants to partake in these beautiful acts of kindness and generosity. I stand aside my bicycle in the parkette and deliberate.

Finally, I decide on Mary's house. I am drawn to her caring nature, and I want this lovely story to tell. And, most importantly, I need to get over this notion that I should not accept kindness, warmth, and caring because I have enough money, because "I don't need it." I do need it. It is not just an offer of free accommodations, it is love. And we all need love.

I knock timidly on the door. A man opens it, takes one look at me, and says: "You must be the lady Mary was speaking about."

I assume I definitely am. He opens the door wide and invites me inside.

Mary, her husband, and her great-grandson, JJ, are all home. They are a lovely family; down-to-Earth and welcoming. Their house is beautiful and they have lots of fun, expensive toys in the driveway. JJ is the cutest. The tent in the backyard is immaculately clean, spacious, and comfortable on their soft, lush lawn. By nine at night I am all settled in and ready for sleep. Mary offers to make me coffee or tea but I politely decline. Inside the tent in the fast-fading light, I have my wine and my ukulele ready to go.

It's like that dark, threatening cloud from earlier guided me to stop here in Bath, then held out until I was safely sheltered here in this tent in Mary's backyard, for only now does the rain begin to rhythmically drum down, hypnotizing me into a sound, deep sleep. I pedaled fifty-four kilometres today in twenty-four degree heat and mostly sunny skies. Thank you, rain, for guiding me, for holding out, and for now chanting to me, surrounding me like arms, cooing me into this much-needed slumber…

*"Someone telling me I can't do something is the second best fuel toward accomplishing goals. Just watch me. But the very best fuel is someone telling me I **can**."*

JULY 10TH – DAY 6

In the morning, I shower while everyone still sleeps. Mary has left me a towel to use. I write a thank you note. I make sure the tent is in as pristine condition as when I arrived. I leave quietly, just after seven in the morning.

Not far from Mary's house is a Mac's Milk. I buy two chicken Caesar wraps, four cheese sticks, a banana, an apple, two protein bars, and a coffee. I use the washroom and set out at eight o'clock sharp. It is cloudy and cool with an occasional break of sun. There is even a light sun shower. It is a warm, refreshing little treat. Not little, actually. It is a wonderful treat. There are no small gifts, especially from nature.

Today there are strong headwinds. Rain threatens all day but never arrives.

I stop at the Tim Horton's in Kingston.

A gentleman is entering at the same time as me. "You're pretty brave riding in those flip-flops. I have scars on my legs from riding a bike like that as a kid." he says to me.

I smile. I don't expect anyone to understand, much less endorse, my choice of footwear. Every army has its uniform, after all. In the cycling world, there are jerseys, padded shorts, footwear, lots of gear, and clothing all specific and recognizable to this subculture. I have none of it. I find the jerseys to be loud and ugly. I would feel like a fraud wearing them anyway. I don't need the padded shorts—I have built-in padding, you might say. And in all of my trial cycle trips, I wore flip-flops because that was what I found in my closet and they worked just fine, as it turned out. I'm open to other footwear but the need simply hasn't presented itself. I will continue to wear them until they no longer work. Sounds logical to me, even if others don't get it. There's nothing wrong with wanting or having all that fancy and flashy gear, of course. I'm just saying that it's not for me and there's more than one way to cook an egg, after all.

One of the many great things about this ride is that everybody says hello: runners, walkers, cyclists, and people sitting on their front lawns. Truckers wave, motorcyclists wave. Everyone takes one look and understands what I am up to. I'm wearing not only my heart on my sleeve but my whole life, too. Some may say I am vulnerable on this ride, I say exposed, advertising, shouting out this awesome thing I am up to. And people are responding. It's invigorating.

When I am at home in Toronto, every time a speeding fire truck or ambulance passes with its sirens going, I make the sign of the cross. I don't believe in God anymore, but maybe the person or people that these emergency vehicles are rushing to do. I do it for them. I do like and miss the rituals, songs, and community associated with my old religion, Catholicism. I continue to do this simple sign of support, long after I have given up any ties with it. As I ride along each day, I am seeing a lot of dead animals. With each lifeless creature I see, I become less and less immune, the desensitization of fast, city life unravels a bit more. I don't become more accustomed to seeing these deceased little beings of nature, instead I grow more and more sensitive and upset. Somewhere along the way, I have begun making the sign of the cross for every innocent dead animal that I pass. There are many. Poor little guys.

"Good job!" a female cyclist calls to me as she passes me along the last stretch of my route on Highway 2 before I arrive at my destination of Gananoque.

"Thanks! You, too!" I call back.

I arrive at exactly one in the afternoon to the quaint network of cabins on Howe Island Ferry Road in Gananoque. The cabins sit on the bank of the St. Lawrence River, and one of them is occupied by my little sister, Angela, while she works in theatre here for the summer. Her cabin is charmingly small and terribly cute. My sister gives great hugs. It is wonderful to see her.

We walk along the grounds, we go down to the water, we eat cheese, and I drink wine. I nap in my hammock tent while she goes for a run and does our laundry. She is a good little sister to her travelling, tired, and slightly intoxicated older sister.

The other cabins are occupied by other members of the theatre company. Angela and I walk to one of the other cabins where everyone is congregated, playing cards. After the game, many of us walk down to the water and smoke cigarettes. It is beautiful; the setting sun, the colours on the lake and in the clouds, slate grey and purplish-blue sky streaked with powder pink and orange and fiery red. I finish a second bottle of wine. Oops. Riding tomorrow should be fun.

My sister invites me to sleep on the couch in her little living room, but I choose to sleep in my hammock tent outside instead. It is just too comfortable, I can't resist.

Today I rode fifty-seven kilometres in a misty rain against strong winds. And had two bottles of wine.

I sleep like a dead log in the deep, dark woods.

"Two of the best tools I have for completing these crazy feats are naïveté and ignorance. And then, once I'm in the thick of it, pride comes swooping in as a close third."

JULY 11ᵀᴴ – DAY 7

I wake just after five. It has rained hard through the night, which did wake me temporarily and I loved it. I adore the soothing march of raindrop feet on my tent fly and being suspended right there amidst the parade, the outpour, all the while keeping completely dry as I slightly swing as if in a cradle.

I packed a Bivy sack (essentially a very expensive, army-style, sleeping bag-sized tent) and a ground mat (for warmth from the ground, which is cold even in the summer) for this trip but have not used either during any of my trial runs nor any of the nights camping thus far. I did not even use the ground mat during the one night I slept on the ground in Mary's backyard. It is early in the trip but I think I may leave these two items behind here with my sister. I'm nervous to make such a drastic decision this soon into my ride. Marc and Sherri, from Presqu'Ile Provincial Park, had told me about a hiker they met once. He only had a hammock tent. He told them that on the very rare occasion when he cannot find trees on which to hang it, he simply lays it out on the ground. I may follow his lead.

Thanks to Angela, I am again in fresh riding gear. What a treat. My destination today is Brockville. I don't have my accommodations booked, but I have my eye on the St. Lawrence Park. It is waterside and if it does not offer camping, I will gorilla camp. I am excited to do this.

After much contemplation, I decide that indeed I will leave my Bivy sack and ground mat with my sister, along with my binoculars and my compact but difficult-to-use can opener that I bought years ago in Paris. I reassure myself that my sleeping bag is brand-new, down filled, and good to as low as 0°. Sure, I may get chilled if I have to sleep on the ground but it is summer and I will survive. Famous last words?

My sister prepares a bag of green and white snow peas for me to take on my ride. Any opportunity to eat raw vegetables is welcome.

Thank-you and good-bye, Angela-la. I love you!

I pass through the little town of Gananoque. How pretty it is. Angela told me that there would be many Dollar Stores and even a Canadian Tire on my way through. However, before I reach any of those, I come across Donovan's Hardware. I much prefer to shop at independently-owned businesses. I stop in. What a wondrous shop. Inside there are shelves upon shelves of all sorts of interesting stuff: regular hardware store wares, old wood stoves, antique dishes, vintage clothes, used books, hats, dolls, toys... I can't resist taking photos. It is like stepping back in time and finding yourself in a messy, over-flowing shop of obscurities.

I need two more tent pegs for the fly of my hammock tent. The owner sells me some dirty, old, rusty metal pegs for twenty-five cents apiece. He said these would be better than tent pegs, which can bend and snap. (He is right.) There is a framed newspaper article near the cash register explaining the store's one hundred forty-two-year history. I am fascinated. Charlie Donovan himself, over ninety years old, is serving me. I am honoured. I also buy a normal can opener.

Yesterday the clouds were full, far-reaching, and fluffy. Today the sky is blue and the clouds are thin and spread out like a long, stretched, and tearing knot of cotton candy. It's beautiful.

I am passing through the lovely little town of Ivy Lea when I meet two cyclists named Melody and Janet. They are friendly and asking questions about my trip. I tell them where I am headed and that I have no accommodations booked and that I am considering gorilla camping. They both seem to think this is a perfectly fine idea and even suggest that once I reach Brockville I go down to the marina, that I might find a good place to pitch my tent there. I add Melody and Janet on Facebook and I am off again.

It is a beautiful day. The path is paved but shadeless. As I am riding, I notice a large, black fly perched on the back of my right hand. It is sitting on the white fabric of my thumb-holed sleeve. It looks massive. I shoo it away with my left hand. When it doesn't move I, irrationally, completely freak out. I shriek as I swat and flail and simultaneously forget to continue steering my bicycle. I fall off it.

Shame, shame, city girl.

My knee is bleeding but I am okay. I can't help but laugh at myself. A fly. A damn fly. I get up, dust myself off, and carry on. But not for long.

Another damn flat back tire. What the hell is going on? Is my load simply too heavy? Two flats in seven days? That is not a sustainable ratio. There are still seventeen kilometres until Brockville. Oh, man. It is hard work, riding a bicycle on a flat tire, especially with all this weight. And, in all likelihood, I am fucking up the wheel frame by doing so. I give it a pump, also hard work with just my little hand pump and in the hot, hot sun. The air takes. It is another slow leak, like last time. For this detail and small grace, I am thankful. I pull over every two kilometres to painstakingly pump the tire back up.

With only one kilometre left until St. Lawrence Park, where I am hoping to eke out some sort of accommodations for the night, I see Mark's Union Tire & Alignment. The word "tire" leaps out at me like a bullfrog and gives me hope. My arms are sore and weak, like rubber, from all the tire pumping. And all the stops are making the day's route take forever. To top it all off, it is damn hot out.

I approach and ask the gentleman behind the desk if anyone there might be able to help me change my tire. He replies no, this is a car tire shop, but that he will put my bike in his truck and drive me over to the bike repair shop about five kilometres away. This man, this complete stranger, is already out of his chair, looking for his keys, ready to take me to the bike shop.

"It's okay. It is a slow leak. I can make it there. But thank you." I stutter graciously. Of course I would love to accept this generous offer, but my pride is telling me that taking a ride, even when I have a flat, would be "cheating." I want to ride every inch of the way from Toronto to the end of the Cabot Trail. I simply cannot accept a ride under this challenging and laborious but not dire circumstance. I'm tougher than that.

Ride, stop, pump, ride, stop, pump. I finally arrive at Cranks Bicycle Shoppe on King Street West in Brockville. While super-friendly Scott fixes my bicycle, I go over to The Union Jack Pub and have their veggie burger and fries and, quite uncharacteristically, a pint of beer, Coors Light. The veggie burger is divine. The patty is a Portobello mushroom head and is topped with feta, onion, and green peppers. It is, hands down, the best veggie burger I have ever had.

The waitresses are friendly and during our chat they offer me a place to stay if I don't find accommodations. I was told this might happen when I arrive out east; these open doors, these kind souls. But I am still in Ontario and it is already, beautifully, happening. I thank the girls and tell them I will keep their offer in mind. Truthfully, I feel incredibly drawn to explore the gorilla-camping possibility. It is comforting to know I now have a contingency plan.

I go back to Cranks. I tell Scott about my little bike ride and how I am looking for somewhere to stay that night. He tells me to go to St. Lawrence Park, that there is indeed camping there. Perfect. As I am paying, I ask him about the Cranks water bottles. I ask if they are five hundred millilitres.

"Well, there is enough room for almost a full bottle of wine. You'd have to have a good swig first, though."

My mind is blown. It's like Scott read my thoughts. That is exactly why I was eyeing the bottle: for leftover wine and for day drinking as I ride. I laugh incredulously.

"I'll take one." I tell him.

"It's on the house," he replies.

The water bottle is instantly sacred to me.

It is at St. Lawrence Park that I learn about the St. Lawrence Park's program for cyclists. Basically, a cheaper rate is given to self-supported cyclists such as myself at the string of parks located along the St. Lawrence River. Furthermore, smiley Steve at the front desk explains to me that they would never turn away a self-supported cyclist; they would always find room. How wonderful. I appreciate this sensitivity as "self-supported cyclists," new vernacular for me, are not as mobile to find alternative accommodations in the face of no vacancy, are more vulnerable to the elements, and are generally more tired at day's end than their motorist counterparts. The regular rate for a night of camping ranges from $29 to $40.25 but for me and my loaded-up bicycle it is only $10.50. Sweet.

I tell Steve that the only catch is that I need trees for my hammock tent. Steve walks with me over to the area reserved for cyclists.

"Right there are two trees that will work," I tell him and point over to the left.

He doesn't seem convinced. He tells me it's too close to the walkway, that there might be foot traffic that would bother me. "You know what? We're not busy. I'll give you a private site for the same price."

He takes me up a stone pathway leading to the top of a hill to a completely private site where I can see the lake to the east, thanks to my higher altitude. The shower and washroom are just steps to the south. The site is lush green, completely surrounded by tall, beautiful trees; countless possibilities for my hammock tent. To top it all off, the fire pit has a grill.

Steve and I walk back to the office to fill out the paperwork.

"Actually, that's the site where the incident happened," he tells me on our way.

The *incident*? That sounds intriguing.

"What incident?" I ask, quite curious.

He tells me that last year there was a huge dispute between a father and his son's girlfriend about, I kid you not, whether the Earth is flat or not. The son's girlfriend insisted that the Earth is flat while the father, of course, argued that it is round. I listen incredulously. The argument became so heated that the father began throwing all of their belongings into the fire, including their propane tank. There was a huge explosion and an ensuing out-of-control fire. The fire department came, the media came. The story made all the newspapers. Even Bill Maher mentioned the incident on his night-time talk show. I am cracking up. What a story. I couldn't make this stuff up if I tried. I love that my particular little campsite is basically famous.

I set up my hammock tent, collect some firewood, saw it into burnable pieces, take a shower, and then go and sit at the end of a park dock while the sun sinks below the trees behind me. It has been a long, trying, wonderful day. I rode fifty-six kilometres in twenty-eight degree heat, was attacked by a common fly, and rode with a flat. And look at me now, on this dock, feet in water, sitting here among such beauty, nature and the St. Lawrence River in all her majesty, and with a huge sense of accomplishment, freedom, and a pride that just would not be felt had I not come here the way I came, on a bicycle, riding all day long, hot and sweaty, bloody-kneed, enduring, and surmounting the challenges and the unglamorous hiccups. I think: How am I so fortunate to end up here like this? I thought I was some sort of weirdo, but maybe I'm actually some kind of genius. I smile. I feel like the smartest, most fortunate, richest, most appreciative, happiest girl in the world.

"I feel lost, I feel high, I feel alone, I feel free."

JULY 12ᵀᴴ – DAY 8

I set out for my day's ride at nine-thirty. My mind is adrift and I pedal as if on automatic pilot. I pull over to take a photo of a little, blue church.

A woman driving by in her minivan rolls her window down. "Are you from here?" she asks.

"No," I reply.

"Oh, let me tell you something about the church then."

She pulls over and we have a lovely chat. She tells me a bit about the history of the church; that it is a historic site built in 1809 and was rebuilt in 1845. Barbara Heck, founder of Methodism in North America, is buried here. I am impressed at how knowledgeable she is. I tell her about the excursion I am on and my goal of getting to and riding The Cabot Trail.

Her name is Gloria and she lives on Myers Point just across from the church. "A little cottage on the river, nothing fancy." she tells me. "We live there year-round."

"Sounds heavenly." I respond.

"You're welcome anytime." she says.

At Gloria's encouragement, I go right up and into the church. Here is where I meet Dave. I think he was singing before I arrived, and I feel bad for interrupting his song.

"Is this you in the photo?" I ask, pointing to a man, also with white hair, in a photo on the wall.

"No, he looks like me, though, doesn't he?" Dave replies.

I ask if he is the priest here. He tells me is not an "official" priest but he is Christian. I can see his faith is strong. Like Gloria, he tells me about Barbara Heck, the woman who created the church. He clearly reveres her as much as Gloria does.

I admire Gloria's and Dave's deep feelings of pride and belonging; Gloria in her town and Dave in his faith. Both are feelings of community. It's something I thought I lacked before this ride. I knew of no one else who wanted to hop on a bicycle and ride thousands of kilometres, camping along the way, over a couple of months. I didn't even know or understand why I wanted to do this. But now, as I am doing what I wanted to do, had no choice but to do, I am finding my community amid all the support of new friends and old. *Just because you're different doesn't mean you don't belong.* As I learn this, I am finally accepting myself. I didn't even know I was lost or searching, but the fact that I didn't know why I wanted to do this tells me I was.

Dave wishes me well on my journey and I continue on my way. I make a quick stop at my happy place, the LCBO, in Prescott. Brian, who works there, is friendly and full of questions: where are you coming from, where are you going, am I doing the big ride that happens after the long weekend, etc. He has mistaken me for a seasoned cyclist. If he only knew.

Because I am traveling along the St. Lawrence River, there is an abundance of historical sites, buildings, forts, and memorials. Donna, one of my best friends and a history buff, would love this aspect of the trip. I, myself, wish I could pay more attention and learn and absorb more from these plaques, mounted on these important places in our Canadian history. It would be impossible to stop and learn all the things and still fit in the number of kilometres I need to achieve each day. This learning opportunity will have to go into the "unfinished business" file, too. And I do not feel upset for not being able to partake. It is okay to have long lists of exciting things one would like to do, then longer and longer lists. No stress. It is simply future wonder that awaits, all this unfinished business. In fact, if one is living life right, the wish list should continue to grow and grow; a never-ending desire and thirst for learning that keeps us alive and moving and always doing, living, learning, and then adding to the list, yet again.

There are a lot of trucks passing along this stretch but they all drive incredibly wide around me. When Dave and I were talking about my ride back at the blue church he said that trucks will drive "embarrassingly wide" around cyclists. He is right.

With twenty-four kilometres left I decide to stop at a Foodland that I happen by. I buy sliced green pepper, red pepper, orange pepper, celery, and broccoli. As I am standing out front of the store, contemplating where I can enjoy my lunch in some sacred spot of shade, a man approaches me. As if reading my mind, without my asking, he suggests I take my food to a beach just around the corner with a shaded picnic area where I can sit and eat. He asks a few questions about my journey, wishes me well, and then goes on his way. I smile to myself. People continue to stroll into my path at just the right moments, offering the exact help or advice I need, or a friendly bit of camaraderie, also greatly needed, and then just as casually strolling away. I head for the beach.

It is called Sierra Club Beach and it is absolutely inundated with wild, excited children. It is adorable and the happy chaos is comical. While I am enjoying their happy madness and eating my veggies, my bicycle falls over.

Fuck.

I realize by how disgruntled and bitchy my inner emotional reaction is to this small hiccup that I am feeling grumpy and am simply in a bad mood. I think it began this morning when I woke and realized that my hammock tent had loosened a bit through the night and by morning I was pretty much touching the ground. Just barely, but touching. It was the realization that I still had not mastered the hanging of my hammock tent that really frustrated me. It's all about the knot. I have to figure out the perfect knot. Also, the trees that I chose were a bit too wide apart, I'm surmising. The problem is I just don't know and shouldn't I have this all figured out by now?

I finish eating and get on my bicycle, only to find that the chain has come off, obviously from when the bike fell. I'm trying to keep my composure, but I feel like having a childish and shameful meltdown that includes lots of fancy language that some people mistakenly label as French they are excusing. I put the chain back on in between scratching my million mosquito bites. The grease from the chain gets all over my hands and legs. I try to resist itching but I don't succeed. I'm a dirty, hot, grumpy mess. Once again, that little voice in my head chirps up: *Welcome to the reality of your little flip-flop fantasy, woman.*

Breathing, breathing.

Once the chain is back on, I twist my body and careen my neck to look at the backs of my legs. Both are positively littered with bites. It must have been that tree I sat under on the grass earlier today. That is probably where the mosquitos were hiding out from the sun, just like I was. Both my thighs are now blanketed in bites and I'm pretty pissed off about it. I still have thirty kilometres to go. The sun is cruel and relentless.

I end up at Upper Canada Camping Ground, which is a private camping ground instead of Upper Canada Village, which is part of the St. Lawrence Parks and my intended destination, in order to partake in their program for cyclists. Clearly I wasn't paying close attention when I punched in my destination to Google Maps. I could just stay here since I'm here now, but Google Maps tells me my original destination is only five kilometres away. I decide to go. The sun continues to beat down, the odometer keeps rolling, and time keeps on ticking. I arrive at Upper Canada Village.

Upper Canada Village is indeed part of the St. Lawrence Parks but there is no camping here. Clearly I confused what Steve told me yesterday. I'm guessing now that he meant that the lady from this park gave him the information about the program, but that didn't intrinsically mean that this park itself was part of it. Who knows? I'm confused but still pretty much unruffled at this point. I think to myself: *I am getting lots of exercise and I am out in the fresh air and everything is fine.* On my phone, I go to the St. Lawrence Parks website and find there are two campsites within a five kilometre radius. I choose the Upper Canada Migratory Bird Sanctuary Nature Campground, another five kilometres away.

The route there takes me along a waterfront trail where I am engulfed by swarms of insects. Thank goodness for my sunglasses and bandanna, both acting as my windshield as armies of different bugs fly right into my face, crash into my sunglasses, and plant themselves on my sun visor.

A deer.

Have I ever seen a live deer in the wild before, asks the city girl? I am in awe. Then I wonder: Do deer attack? I stand there, straddling my bike, bugs all around, deer in front. I Google it and learn: Deer generally prefer to avoid people, although they do sometimes attack during rutting season or if they perceive a human to be a threat to a fawn. Next question: What and when is rutting season? The World Wide Web further explains that a rut is the periodically recurring sexual excitement of deer, goat, sheep, etc. For deer this is between October and December. This gives a wonderful new angle on the saying, "I'm in a bit of a rut," doesn't it? I conclude that I'm safe from the big, bad deer.

Slowly but surely, the city girl is learning.

Finally, finally, finally, I arrive at the Upper Canada Migratory Bird Sanctuary Nature Campground, though I don't see any birds. A man walking his two dogs tells me the office is closed, and I can simply pay in the morning. I thank him for the information. I search around looking for empty campsites that have trees. The trees here are absolutely huge. They are more than a meter in diameter. This poses a problem for me and my hammock tent. The trees need to be far enough apart for the length of the actual hammock but close enough that there is enough rope on each end to wrap around the tree and make a secure knot.

I find two trees that I estimate to be acceptable and begin to set up my tent. I try and try but eventually I realize I just do not have enough length of rope to wrap around these two enormous trees. This day sucks. I'm damn tired and I really don't appreciate so many fails happening all on the same day. I pack everything back up and start roaming the grounds again for a potentially suitable site.

Finally I find one. I hope. Yes. These trees will work. I set up my hammock tent and then, well, I sit at my squat picnic table and just cry. You're optimistic and tough and a trooper until you're not and sometimes a good little cry is what's in order. A hug would be nice too, but for now, weeping will have to do. I call a friend. I relay the day's frustrations. He tells me I shouldn't be upset, that I should expect these kinds of challenges.

This makes me bonkers with anger.

Why am I not allowed to be upset? I know he is trying to comfort me, but minimizing what I am feeling is not the way to go about it. He tells me that I should, of course, foresee moments like this, that I should know that there will be trying and difficult times. Yes. Of course. And now that one such moment is here, I need love and compassion, not logic and dismissal, you bird brain! The less glorious moments are all a part of the story and I will not dismiss them. I'm entitled to them, dammit. I earned these tears.

Associated flashback: Back in Toronto, one day I had become upset at the way two men had blatantly ignored a homeless person asking for money on the subway one morning. I'm not saying they should have given him money; that is a personal choice. But whether you give money or not, you treat a fellow human being with respect. Instead of saying, "Sorry sir, I have no change" the two men just pretended like a live person was not in their presence. They ignored him, went on reading the newspaper, and eventually the homeless person shuffled on. It broke my heart. It made me angry. Like an absolute fool, I posted my feelings on Facebook. This was the day I learned how wise the people who post silly cat photos are as opposed to dumb-dumbs like me who post something emotional or political. All kinds of back and forth comments ensued in response to my post between people who agreed with me and people who disagreed. I had created a bigger mess. Later that day, after the fury on Facebook, I told a friend that I was upset about it all.

What did he say to me? "Perhaps you should spend less time focusing on other people and try to be happy with yourself."

My head exploded.

Excuse my English, but are you fucking kidding me? Is he really saying that I am not allowed to get down? Feel frustrated? Have a reaction? I would be more than alarmed at a person who was one hundred percent happy one hundred percent of the time. Is the goal of life to be unaffected? I think one must and should visit the dark places. It's part of the broad scope of our humanity. Visit, experience, learn, grow, adjust, accept, and then move on. I don't skip steps.

I sit at my picnic table and recover from my rage by reminding myself that this is the same "friend" who told me that I would need something "exciting" to happen during this trip in order for a book about it to sell. "For example, if you meet your husband," he explained to me.

Calm blue oceans, Christina. Calm. Blue. Oceans.

I continue to sit on the picnic table beside my tent for more than a few minutes before I finally have enough gumption to get up and go and have a shower. It doesn't get less shocking; the transformative power of a steamy, hot shower at the end of a long, arduous, sweaty, grimy, frustrating day. It does miracles for the body, for the mind, for the soul.

Baptismal.

I spot some thick, dry branches on the ground that I could have easily collected and brought to my site and made a campfire with. But I simply do not have the energy this time. Although there is no fire ban, there will be no campfire tonight. There will be some wine and perhaps some ukulele, and then an early, long, deep sleep.

Even though this has been quite a trying day, sixty-nine kilometres plus plus plus in thirty-one degree heat under a relentless sun, now that my tent is up, now that I am showered, now that some time has passed, (it is just before ten at night), now that I have spoken to some of my best friends, and now that I have had some wine and a cigarette and a chance to decompress, the now-familiar feeling of accomplishment and happiness is flooding through me again. So far, no obstacle has been bigger than me: flat tires, the physical demands of the long, daily rides, the hot sun, spending countless hours alone, no days off. I make progress every day. Strangers have been kind and helpful, just the way I was, am, counting on. I am doing this thing that I did not understand—that scared me. I am doing it.

I am also beginning to understand it, and to understand me. It's something along the lines of learning who you are, and happily finding you like that person.

"I feel ~~on top of~~ at one with the world."

JULY 13TH – DAY 9

I wake up to the surprisingly loud ticker-tape sound of the chipmunks, the birds chirping, an owl hooting, the loons operatically yodeling, the leaves rustling and the waves lapping. Now that's my idea of an alarm clock. I feel rich, wise, and completely at peace. Yesterday's angst and frustration is all but forgotten. Oh. And the Canada Geese honking. They just went wild with honks. Geesh. It's like they knew I didn't mention them.

I eat veggies and dip for breakfast, but not much. I'm just not hungry. I go to the washroom and change into my riding clothes. I put my shorts on and feel something fall out onto my leg. An earwig. I scream. Although I do greatly appreciate that earwigs are not fast-moving insects, they are rather scary-looking and I abhor them. I was going to comment the other day how repulsive they are when I found a whole mess of them congregating just beneath the tree strap of my hammock tent but I consciously refrained because I did not want to be negative and because it's not their fault they are horrid-looking. But. When I find one of them inside my clothes as I am wearing them, I think I have earned the right to say a little something about it.

I look for the office on the way out to pay for my night stay but I cannot find it. Well, I tried. Thanks for the free stay, Parks of St. Lawrence.

I cannot believe how much garbage there is on the side of the road all along Highway Two. It is the middle of nowhere and this junk has obviously been tossed out of people's car windows as they pass. I'm astounded. Are there really this many ignoramuses who think it is okay to just litter like this? Heathens.

Also, there must be a lot of people who drink and drive because for every Tim Horton's cup, there is also a Bud Light can, almost invariably this brand, one after the other, over and over. I chant this in my head, involuntarily, as I ride along: *Bud Light can, Tim Horton's cup, Bud Light can, Tim Horton's cup…*

I stop in at the Tim Horton's in Long Sault where I have a nice chat with a lovely, older gentleman named Ed. Ed is full of questions about my ride and I am happy to answer them all. We have a great and lengthy conversation. While we are speaking, another self-supported cyclist arrives. His name is Martin and he is riding from Montreal, Quebec to Brighton, Ontario. Too bad we aren't going the same direction. It might have been cool to have some company for a while. Ed mentions more than once how hot it is going to get today. Finally this makes me feel a bit panicked. I bid adieu to Ed and to Martin and I am off again.

A few kilometres before arriving to the campsite I Google LCBO locations. There is one fairly close and not much off the route to my next campground. I buy two bottles of wine, both with images of bicycles on them. Yes, I am a sucker for the marketing. Across the street from the LCBO is a laundromat. Standing out front of it are two young guys, tattooed and not so bad looking at all. They are looking at me rather curiously. I ask them if they know where there's a grocery store. They do and direct to me one. I thank them.

As I am riding away, I say, "Guess what? I rode my bike here from Toronto!"

"NO WAYYYYYYYY!!!" they shout and holler.

I laugh at their awesome reaction. Then I have a little fun with it. I call out, "And I'm riding to Cape Breton to do The Cabot Trail!"

"NOOOOOOOOOOOOOO!!!"

It's only half-past four in the afternoon and my camp is already all set up here at Glengarry Campground. I am halfway through my first bottle of wine. I want to have a shower but it's still thirty-two degrees out here and if I have it now, I will only be dripping with sweat seconds later. I will wait a bit longer.

I sit and I wait, I sip and I play. I am again overcome with gratitude. I also feel damn Canadian and proud of it. What expanses of green and nature and beauty Canada boasts. We are impossibly rich.

Some days, after the packing up camp and the riding and the setting up camp, and the heat and the long roads, I do nothing in the evening. I sit like a zombie and stare off into space to decompress as I sip wine. And some nights I take out my little ukulele. Like tonight.

I sit in the dark. Even long after sunset it is still hovering around thirty degrees. I never make it to the shower. Instead I sit in the dark as these strange-looking insects come and perch all over my hands, my arms, and my mug of wine. Unlike so recently with the common fly incident, I don't mind. Not only does it not bother me, I find it kind of magical.

The city girl has come a long way.

I strum and sing for my little audience of crazy-looking bugs. I'm pretty certain they are loving their private concerto. They don't seem to mind the longer pause before I can switch to the proper fingering to play the G chord. They don't fly away. They are the perfect guests in this magnificent auditorium of still, summer air and starry sky.

Today I rode sixty kilometres in thirty-three degrees with never a forgiving cloud, and no reprieve from the heat, not even now. This moment, pitch black, after this gruelling day, the sweaty hardship, the unprettiness, and though I am dirty, this silence, this peace, the beautiful grit, it's holy, it's perfect. I wouldn't change a thing.

Quebec

"I much prefer to discover than to expect."

JULY 14TH – DAY 10

I hear thunder. There is no rain yet but I better get going.

It starts raining the moment I start riding. Murphy's Law is a bitch. At first it is welcome, light, refreshing. Then it really starts coming down. I look for shelter, even a tree, but there is nothing. Quickly the rain becomes nothing short of torrential. The violence of it is awesome and humbling to witness, but riding in it is cold, and seeing is extremely difficult with so many huge raindrops pelting my eyeballs. Consulting Google Maps on my iPhone is impossible; the phone would become damaged immediately. Finally, on Highway Two, I come to Global RV and Auto. I chuck my bike against the wall and dart in. Sopping and dripping, I tell the nice man at the front desk: "I think you're stuck with me for a little bit."

He laughs and tells me it's all right. We chat while the rain continues to pound to the ground. I am chilled to the bone by their blasting air-conditioning. Finally, maybe twenty minutes later, the rain lets up a bit and I am on my way again.

There is a little bar on the side of the road called Chez Bob. I pull over and walk in. "Is this Quebec yet?"

"Oui," the lady behind the counter says.

I am ecstatic. At just about exactly noon I enter into the province of Quebec. I am stoked. My first big milestone. So long, Ontario.

You know what's an incredibly cool sound? Rain drops falling on a field full of waxy green leaves. There is a massive emerald field spread out before me and it is emanating a soft, percussive symphony. It reminds me of the sound of Quebecois clapping, which is really the tapping of thumbnail to thumbnail. We all clapped like this when my grandma and grandpa walked into a church in Oshawa, arriving at their surprise fiftieth wedding anniversary ceremony where they renewed their vows and were presented with certificates of congratulations from Prime Minister Jean Chrétien, from the Premier of Ontario, and from a number of local MPs from their city of residence, St. Catharines, Ontario, where I was born. My dad, Uncle Roly and Aunt Gisele had bussed in all our relatives from Quebec. They had rented out an entire floor of a nearby hotel to put them all up, with the grand, executive suite reserved for my grandparents. A limo had picked them up in St. Catharines and taken them to this mystery location. When my grandma walked in, we all began tapping our thumbnails together. It is such a subtle, distinguished, delicately enormous sound. Regal. This is fitting for my perfect grandparents. I miss them a lot. I'll never forget that day, that celebration, nor their fairy tale love story. After my grandmother died, my dad and aunt and uncle encouraged my grandfather to date. But he simply said, "No one is as pretty as Mommy." They visited over fifty countries together. I loved them individually and as a couple. I will never forget my beloved grandparents.

And I will never forget this incredible bicycle ride, either.

I am overcome with emotion to unexpectedly be greeted with this old, familiar sound as well as the precious memory attached to it. What a warm and appropriate soundtrack and welcome for my entrance into Quebec.

My sopping wet sleeves have finally dried when round two of the rain comes. I take shelter under the awning of a dépanneur I am passing. A dépanneur is what the Quebecois call a convenience store. I buy a coffee and a little cup of chocolate candies that were my favourite as a kid. I can't resist. They are little chocolate coins, maybe the size of a nickel, with rainbow sprinkles on one side. I love the sweet crunch.

The rain eases up and off I go. I stop and eat breakfast at a little restaurant called Chez Grand-Man. They have mayonnaise packets on the table. That's a first. Here's a little confession: Every time I have breakfast somewhere, I help myself to extra condiment packets for the road. Here's why. I have to travel lightly. I can't even carry camping-sized bottles of condiments. They are too large and heavy. Also, how long does an opened bottle of ketchup keep as it bakes for hours in the heat of the hot sun in my pannier? It is also an accident waiting to happen. I have seen a mustard bottle explode before. The individual packets stay preserved without refrigeration and are compact. I would pay for them if I could, but they are not for sale. So, yes, I "steal" them. I think of all the roadside sandwiches I could prepare with these mayonnaise packets. I can't resist. I take them all.

I am on route five of the Quebec cycling system "La Route Verte." It is absolutely beautiful. The trees here are tall, commanding, and strong. They feel protective, paternal. I feel happy and safe in the embrace of this lush, forested heaven. Ironically, it runs right alongside the highway. Quite the juxtaposition. The cycling routes here are all paved and have rest stops every few hundred meters complete with a bike rack, a picnic table, and a garbage can. Some even have a port-o-potty. I am impressed. Ontario, take note.

Later I am off the trail and riding through the roads of Quebec. I am noticeably in a different province; specifically it's the conspicuous presence of the sideways facing houses and their tin roofs.

About two kilometres before my destination of Parc National d'Oka, at the end of Rue Saint Sulpice, I arrive at a fork in the road not indicated on my Google Maps itinerary. The road to the right is not showing up on the map. Perhaps it is private? The path that seems to be the one I should be taking has a big sign that says, "No cyclists." I stop and stand there, staring at the fork, staring at the sign, processing the facts before me, and deciding what to do.

Who knows why, but there is, at just this junction, an older lady in her car, engine off, just sitting there. When she sees me consulting my phone for so long, she asks me (in French, of course) if I have lost my way. I tell her that I am supposed to go straight but there is a sign saying, "No cyclists." What gives? She tells me that the sign is new and is there because they are improving the path there as it often becomes flooded and is dangerous and also quite bumpy. Oh. So where does that leave me, I wonder. As if reading my mind, she tells me there is a detour a short way back, just past a street or two. These directions sound pretty vague. I think my eyes may have widened at the thought of the impending wild search. Whatever look crosses over my face, it precipitates this from the kind woman. She simply says, "Suivez-moi, mademoiselle."

Follow me, miss. She starts up her car, drives as slow as molasses, checks her rear view mirror every few moments to make sure I am keeping up, and she personally leads me to the divergent path. There are no signs indicating its presence, it is not showing up on my Google Maps itinerary. There is no way I would have known about nor found this path without this wonderful woman's help.

I have entrusted myself to the Universe and it is taking great care of me.

"Merci beaucoup. Bonne journée." I say to this wonderful lady; this helpful, kind soul.

And off I go again.

I take one million photos but still am haunted by the ones I don't take. If I stop to take all the photos I will never arrive. The incredible beauty is ceaseless.

Oh, Canada.

Parc National d'Oka is a natural wonderland. The trees must be sixty, seventy, eighty feet tall. You are truly out in the deep, dark woods. It takes me awhile to get the fire going because all the kindling I collect from the ground is wet from today's rain. I squat beside the fire pit and blow and squint as puffs of smoke sting my eyes. Forever later, a small fire burns. Do you know how I finally get it going? By burning my empty Smartfood bag. Strange, but true.

I stand up, blinking my dry, burning eyes. Looking around, I blurt out in disbelief, "Am I seeing things?"

As dusk is beginning to settle upon the vast woods, the entire forest around me is sparkling. Have I simply gotten too much smoke in my eyes? Trying to see properly, I continue to blink. But the sight before me remains unchanged. I really am seeing what I think I am seeing.

The entire forest is glittering with fireflies.

I have never seen anything like this in my life. There is not a sound, not another soul anywhere around. Just little me, at the bottom of these skyscraping trees, engulfed by this woody sea of tiny, twinkling lights. How blessed am I?

I stand still like that for more than a few minutes. But as the real dark falls, the magic ends—no more fireflies.

All alone in my celebrated "deep, dark woods" and with the comfort of daylight now gone, I suddenly begin to feel extremely vulnerable out here. I have no neighbours close enough to be seen. The odd car drives slowly by. They are most likely trying to find their sites, but my media-drenched, paranoid brain whispers menacingly to me that they are crazed rapists and killers, searching for their next victim. I am a perfect fit, all alone out here, by myself, no one else around. I really start to freak myself out with my crazy thoughts. For the first time since I set out on this journey, I am scared.

Suddenly, there is such a calm that takes over the forest, the stereotypical calm before the storm. Next, the wind swiftly sweeps in like blowing thunder. I know what's next. I have never had the opportunity to really test my hammock tent against a good rain, and barely against a light shower. Now will be that time, it seems. I quickly nestle myself into my hammock tent and wait for the impending storm. I don't have to wait long.

It dumps down in huge, heavy sheets. I have never heard wind like this. My hammock is rocking. Such violent claps of thunder, such dramatic displays of lightning. I wait to feel the dampness start to seep in. The waves keep falling from the sky. I keep feeling for the first sign of wetness leaking in.

But it doesn't. I am dry as a book on a shelf. No leaks, no seeps, and no moisture whatsoever. I am elated. I am beaming because I have proved myself able to protect myself in such fierce conditions. I am so proud and relieved that I begin to enjoy the storm. What an opportunity to experience such a momentous event of nature smack in the middle of it while remaining snug as a bug in a rug. My mind and heart are exploding. My senses and my soul are swept up in this rare and chance euphoria.

The ferocity of the storm actually comforts me. I feel safe from the big, bad boogie man I had created in my mind earlier. I am sure that even a scary-monster-person will definitely be deterred by this weather. The storm has come to protect me. I smile to myself. It is as if nature brought this storm for the sole purpose of taking away my fear.

The storm rages on all night. I can't sleep for the excitement, but it is also the raccoons. They are noisy at work as they tirelessly try to disengage and penetrate my food pannier. The flashlight function on the iPhone is quite powerful. I shine it out, to see if they are having any success with it. What a sight I see. The light makes their eyes glow. There must be a dozen pairs staring back at me. It is like a perfect raccoon family portrait. There are a few raccoons up the trunk of the tree from which my food pannier dangles, and a horseshoe of them around the trunk on the ground. I laugh. I have never seen such a congregation of a wildlife family before. The whole lot of them is out on this mission. The raccoon mafia.

What diligent and assiduous animals they are. They have earned my respect. I have basically accepted that my food pannier will be destroyed and its contents made off with. All the tree branches angle toward the trunk. The pannier lies against it where the raccoons can climb up and access it, though it is at least a bit tricky for them since it will swing away when they lean on it to do their invasive work. I can't worry about it. There is nothing more I can do to protect it. I accept it. They win again, I suppose. However, each time I hear them set to work again, I need to look out and make sure that they have not taken interest in my other panniers. I need those to stay intact to carry my few, essential belongings. There is an open bottle of wine in one and I am paranoid that they can smell it. I am up all night, looking out, making sure it is safe.

This goes on all night. Rain pelting on the fly, raccoons scratching and gnawing away at my pannier, branches spectacularly cracking, falling from trees, and thudding to the ground all around me, and me shining my light out periodically to assuage my paranoia about the other panniers. No sleep at all. None.

I also prepare myself to accept that in the morning I may find that my ukulele is a write-off. It is in a thin, non-sealable nylon bag. I have no idea how it will fare against this storm. I will be disappointed if it is ruined, but worrying won't prevent it. What will be will be.

As the storm dies down and the darkness remains, my fear of the boogie man returns. Please, sleep, save me from my paranoid fears.

It is now 3:55 a.m. I still have not slept. Thankfully the sun will rise soon and put an end to this sleepless, scary soirée.

The rain is pretty much stopped, but gives little last bursts here and there, mild and intermittent. I am beginning to freak out a bit less at all the little sounds and big bangs and cracks and thumps and taps and snaps I hear through the night.

The forest is alive, city girl.

With the first light of sun, I am finally able to fall asleep for a couple of hours. I survived the storm. I survived my silly fears. After two hours I wake, then sleep for another hour and a bit.

When I get up, there is a special treat waiting for me. I beam with victory as I see my food pannier, frayed and a hole chewed into the side, but still hanging and shut with all its contents. They got nothing. I dance, I am so proud and happy. The raccoons may have succeeded back at Sandbanks, but at Oka, it is me who is the victor. That's right, my furry little friends. This time, the city girl wins. I feel giddy.

I begin to take stock of the damage. There are large, fallen tree limbs everywhere. It looks like a tornado swept through. I am in awe. Incredibly, thankfully, my ukulele is just fine. It's still in tune, in fact.

I head for the showers where I undress, shivering, and step inside. I find a strange little box affixed to the shower wall. I discover that it costs four quarters to run the shower for four minutes. This would have been useful to know any time before right now. Ugh. Thankfully I slept in late. The campground's general store should be open already. I re-dress and ride there to get change, then ride back to the showers.

Clean and renewed, I pluck my eyebrows and put on mascara. These two things, plus choosing which flavour of LipSmacker I will use that day, are totally unnecessary and even impractical but are pretty much my only ties to being "girly" right now.

I go back to my site. I am packing up my camp when I hear an acute, loud crack directly above me. Swoosh. Perhaps four feet in front of me, another huge limb, about the length of me and about the width of my leg, heavy with moisture, crashes to the ground. Holy shit. That was close.

Yesterday I rode sixty-two kilometres in torrential downpours in twenty-seven degree heat, followed by a terrifying night of storm and fear. Now that it is all over, I feel elated at what an exciting evening I had, as well as pride and accomplishment. Surviving last night makes me feel as though I've paid some dues, like I'm earning my Girl Scout badges. I feel happy. What doesn't kill you makes you stronger, the saying rightly goes.

My friend Bobby said to me recently, "If you're scared, you're alive."

Damn straight.

"If you love nature, you will find beauty everywhere."
-Vincent Van Gogh

JULY 15TH – DAY 11

I put on my soaked sun visor and dripping wet helmet and set off.

Along the way I stop frequently to check Facebook. It is my link to home, to friends, and to family. It is my connection to support and encouragement. It is also a vehicle for frustration and misunderstanding.

A friend posts on Facebook today that I am brave for doing this bicycle trip in flip-flops and then proceeds to explain to me that I would have a much more efficient pedal if I were clipped in. Clipping in is when the pedal has a mechanism that bolts to a specially designed shoe and "locks" your feet in place. This method allows the cyclist to apply negative or pull force to the pedalling rotation of cycling. Without it, the pedal travels back up as your foot rests on the pedal, unable to contribute any force to the upward motion of the pedal rotation.

I write him and tell him that of course I know about clipping in. I simply did not choose this option. I really didn't choose any option. I started doing my trial runs in the footwear that I already owned, without any thought at all. And it worked. I simply kept on doing what worked. Furthermore, what I am doing is the opposite of a race, the opposite of efficient, and the opposite of fast. It is about going slow, smelling the roses, taking all the pictures, talking to people, and taking my sweet ass time.

He isn't the first to make this sort of comment, he won't be the last, I'm sure, and of course he means well. Another friend replies to the post. He writes simply, "#flipflopfantasy." This is the hashtag I use for all my trip updates. I thank him for acknowledging my little hashtag, for electronically tipping his hat to my method, no matter how mad it may seem.

Almost immediately upon arriving in Montreal, I get my third flat tire. That makes three flats in only eleven days. What the hell is going on? It's alarming. Is it due to all the weight on the back end of my bicycle? It has been my back tire that has gone all three times. What will I do if this happens when I am in the middle of nowhere? I have supplies to fix two flats. Will that be enough? The truth of the matter is I have never changed a flat on my own. Thankfully all three flats have occurred near civilization and help.

Almost immediately, I come to a bike shop called Cyclopathe. Again, I decide I should save my repair supplies for when my bicycle gets a flat in the middle of nowhere where there is no bike shop around. I roll my bicycle over to Cyclopathe.

Here I meet Khalil who works there and Angelo, a regular customer. They are standing out front, talking. They are both relaxed and friendly. When Angelo sees a package of cigarettes in my open front food pannier, he comments, "Oh, you smoke? I love smoking. But I never smoke more than three cigarettes a day."

"That's just like me!" I exclaim.

I tell him how I used to beat myself up about it, telling myself I need to smoke less, I need to drink less, I should this, I should that. But then I turned forty. Best thing that ever happened to me. It took this milestone to make me realize: everything is okay. You don't need to change a damn thing.

"Yeah. Do what you want," Angelo says simply.

Wiser words were never spoken. Charles Bukowski, one of my favourite authors, said the same thing too, though characteristically more succinctly: "Find what you love and let it kill you."

Yes and yes. I love Charles Bukowski and I quite like this Angelo fellow, too.

I leave my bike and all my bags in the care of Khalil and walk to Parc Jarry, just a few blocks away from the bike shop. I sit here with some wine, cigarettes, and my ukulele. It feels bizarre to be in the middle of a big city. It seems I have quickly and fully assimilated to country livin'. I watch two guys and a girl slack lining. Slack lining is the sport of balancing on a rope or strip of webbing that is fixed high above the ground but not stretched so as to be taut. They have a band suspended between two trees about two feet from the ground. I am fascinated. A man comes and asks to buy a cigarette. I give him one; for free, of course. I sit there for an hour or so and people watch. Eventually I amble back to the bike shop. She's all fixed. I cycle the fifteen kilometres to my Couchsurfing host's place in Verdun, a neighbouring suburb of Montreal.

My host's name is Marc Joseph and we actually met through Couchsurfing many years ago. I had contacted him regarding a stay for a weekend visit I was planning to Montreal. He had accepted my request but I never ended up staying with him. I can't remember why. Perhaps I did not end up coming that particular weekend or perhaps someone else offered me a stay first. Either way, we added each other on Facebook and have been in touch through the years there ever since. This is my first time finally meeting him.

Marc meets me downstairs. He is smiley and welcoming. I feel like I already know him due to our long, virtual acquaintance. I suggest that we take up my panniers and leave my bike locked up downstairs.

He looks at me and simply says, "No."

I don't question him, he lives here, and I'm sure he knows best. I begin to take off the heavy panniers. I take one off but he tells me to just leave them on. I laugh. He will change his mind when he goes to lift it, that's for sure. I can tell he is surprised at how heavy it is, but for him, it is no big deal. He carries the heavy bike with its panniers up to the third floor.

Marc proceeds to show me the laundry facilities. He has put out a towel for me to shower. He shows me the futon bed where I will be sleeping in the spare room. He shows me where the spare key is if I need to leave for some reason. He tells me to make myself at home. And then he goes out. Just like that. This is exactly the kind of trust and generosity I am dearly familiar with from being an Airbnb and Couchsurfing host and guest over the years.

Today I rode fifty-eight kilometres under mostly sunny skies in twenty-eight degree heat. There was some cloud, but not nearly enough. Understandably, I crash pretty much immediately since I basically got no sleep last night in Oka. This is my first night in a regular bed since my own back in Toronto.

I am out like a match in the wind.

"If you change the way you look at things, the things you look at change."
-Wayne Dyer

JULY 16TH – DAY 12

I had the naked dream last night. I was completely naked and out in public. This group of young people was looking at me. I just stood there, mortified. Later in the dream I was out in public again. I was naked but this time I had a towel around me. The same group of people saw me and asked if I was naked again. I cried back, "Yes. I expose myself. I don't know why I do this. I'm so fucked!"

What a dream. I think it's a pretty easy one to figure out, though. I felt exposed to and at the mercy of the elements there, alone in the middle of Parc National d'Oka. It shows how vulnerable I felt and perhaps still do, a bit. I need to get my confidence back up after feeling so rattled and scared all night. I do wonder what the appearance of a towel wrapped around me for my second flashing means. Perhaps that I am already recovering?

I also dreamt that my friend Roel was working in the kitchen of some fancy place and that Prime Minister Justin Trudeau was coming to that place around the same time that I would be passing by on my bicycle ride. I arrive and run into Mr. Trudeau almost immediately. I tell him, "Guess what? I rode here on my bicycle from Toronto." I am all excited. He is not. He just looks at me. I am a sopping mess. That is the end of the dream. I am much less clear on what the meaning is behind this dream.

Even though I wake up at five I force myself to stay in bed to catch up on the loss of sleep at Oka. Plus I do not want to disturb Marc at such an early hour. Finally I get up at eight. I make coffee, shower, and do laundry. Marc remains asleep in his room. I charge all my electronics, including my electric toothbrush. Yes, I brought my electric toothbrush. I also empty and scrub down my beat-up food pannier. I thought I would need to buy a new one, but now that it's cleaned up, it's actually not in such bad shape. Plus I'm straight up proud of its battle wounds.

And then I feel those pains that only we lucky women know. Menstrual cramps. Good timing to be in a real house.

Marc gets up and goes out to the grocery store. When he returns, he carries my bicycle back downstairs for me. I really did not get to spend much time with him at all and that is a shame. I am a virtual stranger yet he opened up his home to me and helped me by letting me do laundry and shower and recharge my things and sleep soundly to recharge *me*. He is one of the many wonderful human beings in this world that I knew I would meet.

Upstairs, I announce I am leaving. Marc sweetly looks in his fridge to see if there is anything he can send me off with for my ride. He finds and offers three packets of salad dressing that might be of use to me, on the go as I am. I thank him and take them, adding them to my Ziploc bag of contraband condiments. Downstairs, we say our goodbyes.

"Merci, Marc. À la prochaine."

I set off for the Parc National des Îles-de-Boucherville. It is only twenty-nine kilometres away. I am considering this a rest/treat day. I even wear my orange camping dress as I ride. I just want to. I want to be a girl today.

About seven kilometres into the ride, I come to an extremely long bridge that goes over the St. Lawrence River. It is over two kilometres long. I find that a bit intimidating, for some reason. I begin pedaling across.

What a wonderful view. I stop to take a photo and feel a tickle on my leg. I look down to find about a dozen moths perched there. I scream. Thank goodness nobody is around to witness my embarrassing display of city stupidity. The bridge is called The Estacade but I have officially renamed it, "The Bridge of One Million Moths." They are simply everywhere. I have no choice but to fly into the never-ending wall of them.

At just before three in the afternoon with only ten kilometres left before reaching my close-to-begin-with destination, I finally find what I have been looking for; a picnic table in the shade. I am in Port de Plaisance in Longueuil.

Class is a behaviour and an attitude more than it is a circumstance and today I am proving that. I eat my modest travel provisions in style:

Apéritif: un petit ballon de vin rouge

Amuse-bouche: du fromage

Entrée: un petit pain rustique à la mayonnaise, aux condiments, avec une tranche de la dinde fumée

Plat principale: un deuxième sandwich, un deuxième petit ballon du vin

Dessert: une cigarette à la Belmont Mild

Ha.

Many of the few things I have brought along on this little bike ride have multi-purposes and uses. For example: my camping dresses have also proved to be my post-shower bathrobe, a handy dandy changing tent, privacy for trailside peeing, and a light, cool outfit after riding as originally intended. My hair also serves as a hand towel and a neck protector from the sun. My index finger also serves as a spatula. My forefingers minus my thumb serve as a strainer. Wine serves as both a decompression aid and a sleeping aid. *Baby wipes.* Baby wipes serve as a cool midday face refresher, a dishwasher, a picnic table cleaner, and toilet paper. (I haven't had to take a shit in the woods yet, thankfully.) They also sanitize and leave a fresh scent inside the Ziploc bags where I keep each of my outfits to protect it from moisture when riding in the rain. I give them a thorough wipe when I replace freshly-washed clothes into the bags. Insect repellent can also serve as a fire starter. Bobby taught me this. It is half-past three in the afternoon and I am on the road again.

The cyclist program here in Quebec is called "Bienvenue Cyclistes." It is pretty similar to the program offered by the St. Lawrence Parks Commission. Parks that participate in the program offer a reserved space for cyclists at a discount rate. When I arrive at Parc National des Îles-de-Boucherville, the girl behind the counter tells me flatly that it is full. She has none of the empathy and responsiveness that Steve had over at St. Lawrence Park. She is busy. It is a zoo in here. I'm sure she'd be more helpful if she had the time. In the meantime, I will have to pay full rate for a private lot. That is fine but certainly a much less friendly and welcoming approach than St. Lawrence Park in Brockville that boasts that it will never turn a self-supported cyclist away. Self-supported cyclists are inherently in a more vulnerable and precarious position. I think this stipulation should be a standard part of participating in any advertised program aimed at long-distance cyclists.

I have already taken one ferry to get here to the registration office and now I must take another to get to my campsite.

The discount price for self-supported cyclists is only $7.50. I, however, am paying $30.25 plus tax for this private lot, though it isn't very private. There are no trees. Zero. The lot is one hundred percent gravel. It bears repeating. *The lot is one hundred percent gravel.* I am incredulous. Not a stick of grass. Can this really be classified as camping? The surroundings and park in general make for a beautiful space, albeit a bit too manicured and contrived for my liking, but the campground itself is nothing but a glorified parking lot.

I'm not done complaining, hang in there.

Also, upon arriving, there was some fancy sailboat cruising around, blasting music, with a guy on a microphone calling out to passers-by. I can still hear him and the music now from my site. This park in general is loud and busy with a lot of activities and things going on. I can see its appeal for many people and situations but it is not at all for me.

Happy "rest" day, woman.

Each of these private lots has a bike rack, a picnic table with a sheet of metal bolted on to place your hot pots, and a fire pit. There are lots of neighbours, all highly visible. At least this offers a feeling of safety. This is the polar opposite of the seclusion I had at Oka.

With no trees, I have my first hammock tent challenge. I try using the bike rack and the picnic table as anchors. The bike rack topples immediately and the heights are too low, anyway. There is no possibility for hanging. I would be fine to sleep on the ground for one night but I am afraid that this gravel will tear my tent, never mind be terribly uncomfortable to sleep on. I cannot express enough my dissatisfaction with this place. This is equivalent to sleeping on someone's unfinished driveway.

In the end, I end up laying out my sleeping bag on the picnic table and securing the fly directly over it. A bit claustrophobic but protected, at least.

The glory moments.

I decide to go and check out the area reserved for cyclists at the discount rate. No wonder it is full; it is the size of a thumbnail.

It is later now. Despite all the complaining I have done today about this site, I must say that even though this is not my idea of truly connecting with nature, still, there are no distractions, I have a roaring fire in front of me, a ukulele on my lap, and I am writing my second new song. I would never have done this at home in Toronto, for two reasons; the distractions and the lack of inspiration. Almost begrudgingly I admit that I suppose everything is all right after all. Even here.

A young man from the site across from me comes over. There are three of them over there. They are also on bicycles. He asks to borrow some matches to start their fire. I give him one of my four boxes. He says he will return it right away. I tell him to keep it. I can't help but feel proud and a little smug. Between the three of them, nobody thought ahead to make sure to have fire? Whenever people ask me about my trip and I tell them what I am up to, the second question invariably has been: "Toute seule?" "All by yourself?"

Yes. All by myself. I have to laugh that the three boys have to come to ask Miss Toute Seule for help. I'm more than happy to help, but, it's funny.

Today I traveled a mere twenty-nine kilometres in balmy twenty-five degree temperatures, partly cloudy, perfect bike-riding conditions. Perhaps I should have taken advantage, not had this "day of leisure." The Universe is telling me to go, go, go. And I understand. Why would I need rest from the most moving, emotionally profound thing I have ever done in my forty-one years of life? I hear you, Universe. Thank you for reminding me. I hear your call, and tomorrow I shall continue to follow...

"Her messy hair a visible attribute of her stubborn spirit.
As she shakes it free, she smiles knowing wild is her favorite color."
-J. Iron Word

JULY 17TH – DAY 13

I wake up early in the morning, about quarter to five. Despite my unglamour-ous, wooden bed, I slept soundly. The inside of the fly is a bit damp, which I think is just my trapped breath inside my claustrophobic, makeshift shelter. I get up to shower. Oh joy, another pay shower. A dollar for four minutes. I find this little cash grab annoying. Anyway, I'm getting faster.

I start a fire, make my morning coffee, and have my morning cigarette. Already these little rituals, like the wine at night, have become deeply ingrained and important. They are little pegs on which I hang my day. I am a classic A-type personality combined with a healthy dose of OCD. I need structure. Part of the reason this bicycle ride seemed so appealing is that it gave me a positive, productive, delicious activity to fill my days: bicycle riding. Also, the packing up of my camp is done with care and precision and not performed quickly. These are the things I have control over, the only routine I have. They have become sacred to me.

I pack up and leave. I want to put in as many kilometres as possible today. Yesterday was a bit of a break day. Now I am itching to get back at it.

To be honest I am feeling a bit dejected. I am not finding people in Quebec to be as friendly as in Ontario; not yet, anyway. I certainly haven't had the random encounters with strangers that I had there. Everyone keeps telling me how friendly people are out east. I shall keep that in mind, and as in all bleak moments, know that things will get better. "Not every day is going to be sunshine and butterflies," my friend Bobby reminded me. True.

Although my ten-charge and single-charge units had been fully charged upon arriving at this park, I must have pressed on something during my sleep, inadvertently keeping my phone on all night and using up all the power. My ten-charge is dead. Also, I am stuck here until the ferry starts running at nine.

I am on my way to the ferry and I see a deer with huge antlers. What a marvellous creature, such regal horns. And then a beaver runs across my path. How Canadian do I feel right now? I arrive at the ferry at twenty past eight. I get a much-needed stroke of luck. The ferry is arriving to drop off a worker. I ask if I could please take the ferry across and they say yes. Three cheers for small victories. This ferry is a cable ferry, pulled from shore to shore by a thick wire. I have never heard of or seen one before.

The path from the ferry to the exit of the park is like riding through a wall of gnats. I squint my eyes and purse my lips, all the while also trying to dodge the many snails littering the path. Near the exit, another beaver crosses my path. I arrive at the second ferry, which will bring me back to the east shore of the St. Lawrence where I will continue on my journey. It is nine o'clock sharp. I read the posted schedule. The first ferry is at half-past ten. For fuck's sake. Breathe, Christina. This little "nightmare" is almost over. First world problems. I decide to laugh it off. I have nothing but time on my hands, after all. Poor me: I sit in the warm sun, overlooking the water, pausing. I use the time to do my daily administration. The time flies.

I finally arrive back to my route and get back at it. I am not riding long at all when I arrive at a steep and intimidatingly tall flight of stairs to get up to an overpass to cross a busy roadway. It's quite the challenge, that angle, the weight of my bicycle and panniers, the narrow ridge bordering the stairs for bicycles. I push, grunt, and heave. It's tough, but I get the bicycle up. I feel strong.

At exactly noon I am forced to stop to charge my phone, which is nearly dead. I go to a Tim Horton's in the pretty little town of Varennes but there isn't a single outlet to be found. I go instead to a little pub called Restaurant-Pub Victorin. I charge up all my devices whilst enjoying a spicy Caesar and a bag of jalapeño kettle chips. And then another spicy Caesar. By one in the afternoon I am on the road again.

There is an older couple cycling ahead of me. Eventually I pass them. I stop to take a picture and they pass me. When the path reaches Highway Two, I catch up to them again. They turn around and when they pass me yet again, this time going the opposite direction, the man calls out in French, "Courage." Even this small act of support gives me energy and multiplies my natural but once self-doubting enthusiasm.

After Varennes, it is thirty-seven kilometres of straight riding along the 132 East.

I stop in a little town called Contrecoeur at a restaurant called Au Gueleton to have their all-day breakfast. It is simple and perfect and the view of the St. Lawrence River is stunning. I love these little stops, like at The Mason Jar; these glimpses of other places, other ways, and other people. It's a moment of nourishment, not just for the body but for the mind. I pause my exciting ride and I sit, reflect, bask, and savour. I can't help but smile as I think back to how full of foreboding and misgivings I was about this trip; how much sleep I lost. The panic attacks. The anxiety that robbed me of sleep at night. Now I am glowing. I am indescribably happy. I inhale three eggs, French fries, toast, and a coffee with milk. I charge my phone and my single-charge.

I arrive at the town of Sorel-Tracy, my destination city. I begin keeping my eyes open for places to camp. I stop in at Parc Régional des Grèves, which turns out to be a camp for kids. I pass a few motels then stop at Motel Tracy, which I had actually seen listed on Airbnb. And this is where I meet the warm and wonderful Denise.

Denise is the woman at the front desk and she is bubbly and inquisitive. When I tell her what I am doing, she says, "You know, when I was young, I was quite something, too."

Too. I love this statement. Not only is she telling me I am something special, but also that I am young, bless her. And it is no small thing to be a conduit to happy memories and seeing sameness in each other. I am thrilled to be such a vessel. We continue to chat as she registers me. She hands me the garage opener and tells me I can keep my bicycle in there overnight.

Considering that I slept on top of a damn picnic table last night, staying in a motel, also my first motel stay of the trip, feels like a real treat and I decide to go all the way and order a pizza. I even turn on the TV. I don't actually sit and watch it, but having it on feels strange and ironic, naughty and funny. I play a bit of ukulele, I drink some wine, and I eat the pizza. Today I rode sixty-two kilometres under a twenty-seven degree hot sky. I drift into a sound sleep, like a worm in wood.

"Could a greater miracle take place than for us to look through each other's eyes for an instant?"
-Henry David Thoreau

JULY 18TH – DAY 14

I forgot about my paranoia regarding bedbugs. In the middle of the night I jump up and check the bed, the corners, and the seams. It is totally fine. I turn on all the lights and keep them on as I sleep as Google informs me they are nocturnal. I continue to wake up through the night and check every tickle I think I feel. Isn't it ironic that I feel cleaner and safer and sleep more soundly outdoors?

I wake early and do my daily administration while sipping a hot tap-water coffee. I eat the last two slices of pizza and even play a bit of ukulele. Then, I put on my mascara, and leave.

When I turn in my key and the garage clicker to Denise in the morning (who added me on Facebook the night before, to my delight) she tells me she wants a picture with me and my bike. I am honoured. Then she gives me a warm look. "I see myself in you." she says.

This woman has a way of saying the loveliest things. What a simple and beautiful show of empathy, sisterhood.

My heart and mind races at the sweeping, Earth-saving potential of this comment. Imagine if we could all see ourselves in each other all the time? We would love one another more, trust one another more. We wouldn't have this terrorist business, would we? I read in the news yesterday about the terrorist attack in central Nice, the exact place I spent a week, less than two years ago.

I send a note to Marie-Claude, the kind woman I stayed with there, through Airbnb, only two summers ago. I hope she is okay. (P.S. I tried several times to reach her, with no response.)

I give Denise a hug. I just love this woman. I am off.

As I ride along today my heart is bursting with joy and love. Simultaneously for no particular reason and for oodles of good reasons. It is not just because of the amazing people I am meeting, nor the beautiful Canadian landscape and nature and hot, pretty, peaceful summer country roads and the endorphins of exercise and the smell of grass and manure and dirt cleansing my lungs and brain. It is all of those things. But it is also a simple feeling of pride, accomplishment, and wisdom. Pride for something simple and real and not flashy or superficial. Accomplishment for facing my fears and setting out at all on this wild adventure. And wisdom for freeing myself from so many shackles: possessions, distractions, and judgment, especially the freedom of my own confused judgment of myself. The freedom of the societal lens. This simple living, only what I can carry.

I have to take a ferry from Sorel-Tracy over to Saint-Ignace-de-Loyola on the West Shore. This one is a big one. It is even carrying transport trucks. I go to the upper deck for the ride. There I meet a friendly man named Roch. He asks me about my bike and what I am up to. Of course I am happy to tell him all about my little journey. We add each other on Facebook. He wishes me well, then the ferry docks, and my journey continues.

Something Roch said stood out to me. "C'est un beau défi." he had said.

Even though I am sure he simply meant "It's quite a challenge," I translate this literally: "It's a beautiful challenge." I like the latter translation better. Facing fear is both beautiful and quite the challenge. Both translations are true.

Everyone I pass seems to give me the same look; curious and amused. I dare say, even happy for me. They can't see it beneath my pirate get-up but I am smiling back at them. I always wave, they always wave back, or vice versa. Every one of these little exchanges embolden me.

Everywhere I look it's…bam…beauty in your face. The fields, the flowers, the trees, the sky, the clouds, the country houses. And if not beauty then such immense, open spaces. I am awestruck. I turn onto Highway 138 East. I will remain here for thirty-two kilometres. I like these long stretches of one direction. I can really allow myself to space out and daydream. I can also turn off

Google Maps for a while, which I am sure is burning through piles of dollars on my phone bill for all the data use. (P.S. It didn't.)

Even though the roads and shoulders have all been in good repair today I am still trying to ride exclusively on the white painted line. For the game of it. It's a thing I do when the shoulders are shoddy or when the road is hot. I challenge myself to ride exclusively on the white line where the surface is soft and smooth, and because it is white, therefore cooler. I don't want my tires to heat up and blow out.

There is not a piece of garbage to be found along these highways in Quebec, unlike along Highway 2 in Ontario; a noticeable difference. I am also finding that cars and trucks drive very widely around me, way wider than they need to. It's a lovely gesture. Bless them.

In Louiseville I stop at the Tim Horton's to use the washroom. I get those same looks. Curious. Amused. A man and a woman who are outside smoking stop me as I exit, asking me questions about my bicycle and what I am up to. When I tell them, they both immediately and animatedly extend their hands to shake mine. I am touched. I shake their hands, feeling a bit awkward but happy to meet them.

I end up chatting with the woman, Michelle, for quite a few minutes. She takes my information and tells me she is going to follow me on Facebook. She will turn sixty-one in two weeks. She is warm, friendly, and full of questions. We talk about what most people talk about and what everyone has in common: the opposite sex. Love and sex: the universal languages. I finish my coffee and we say our goodbyes.

I stop to take a couple of pictures of the beautiful church in Louiseville. A man walking by who sees me in my pirate get-up with my laden bicycle says to me: "Soyez prudente. Il y a des fous. Bonne randonnée.» Be careful. People are crazy. Happy trails.

"Merci." I call out.

There is a big, dark cloud that has been behind me for quite a little while. It seems to be catching up. Now I hear thunder. I look at the weather report. They are calling for rain and lightning at three, and it is now ten minutes before. I am pedaling like a demon.

I stop under an overpass, eat the rest of the salad from my abundant pizza order last night, and wait for the rain. It never comes. Murphy's Law, still a bitch. I set off once again.

At the last minute I am backing out of the Couchsurfing arrangement I have set up in Trois-Rivières. Perhaps I am just having a Bukowski moment. When asked if he hates people, Bukowski said, "I don't hate people. I just feel better when they're not around." I think we all feel this way at times. I am just not feeling a vibe with regards to this host. I can't put a finger on it and really there is no need to. I contact the host and tell a white lie, that I did not accomplish the kilometres I intended for the day and I won't be making it to his house. Telling him the truth that I am just not feeling his vibe, can't explain why, and am not in a chatting mood, might unnecessarily come across as rude or hurtful.

Hanging out in a motel room does not sound exciting and decadent when it is the second night in a row, but that is what is happening. Options are limited due to my last-minute change of heart, and due to my lack of skill and experience and innovation with gorilla camping.

Today marks two weeks I have been on the road. Today I traveled a hefty seventy-four kilometres in twenty-seven degree heat with some lovely cloudy periods. For tonight, I have purchased a smaller bottle of wine, just 500mL instead of the regular 750mL. I have never seen this size before. I wonder if that will be enough to relax me and lull me to sleep. It's an experiment.

"Prepare for the worst ~~and hope for~~ but expect the best."

JULY 19TH – DAY 15

I realize more clearly now what was happening last night with regards to my change of heart regarding the Couchsurfing situation. I was confused between the purpose of this trip and what my true nature is as a person. I'm pretty much a solitary soul, but one who ardently believes in the goodness of people. While I love meeting people and having that conversation or that hug and giving testament to their beautiful goodness, at the end of the day, I just want to go home by myself and that's okay. It's a strange mix but I am both a lover of people and a loner. Strange but true. Unique but okay.

I stop in at the post office in the small town of Champlain thinking that they might sell postcards. They don't. I buy some more Canadian and international stamps and ask the lady if there is a restaurant nearby serving breakfast. She directs me to a spot called Manoir Antic and here I am. "Wind of Change" by The Scorpions begins to play. I love this song and at this moment, many of the lyrics ring true. I feel overwhelmed with peace and happiness. I can't wait to get to my campsite.

The waitress who serves me asks if I have come from far. I tell her I've come from Toronto and that I am on my way to Nova Scotia and the Cabot Trail.

"Toute seule?" she asks, surprised.

There's that famous question again. My truthful answer: "Sort of."

Physically, anyway.

Sometime after the restaurant, along my route I find myself on a dirt road through a forest called Rang d'Orvilliers / Chemin Piché. It gets pretty hairy about two kilometres in. When I can find a tire track and follow along in its groove, it is not too bad. But on roads like this, that constant stress of another flat haunts like a storm cloud.

With one kilometre left of this secluded road I see in the distance a minivan pulled off to the side of the road with the back hatch open. There is a man walking around from the front of the van. He has something in his hand— metal. I see him duck into the forest. There is no one else here, just him and me. Every horror film and true crime series I have ever seen flashes through my mind. I involuntarily immediately imagine that he has seen me, and he is readying himself to leap out from behind the bush, to grab me, throw me in the back hatch, and take off with my kidnapped, soon-to-be chopped-up body. In an instant, I have my dog spray in hand, engaged and ready to shoot.

Slowly, I approach. When I get a bit closer, I see his back hatch is filled with pieces of wood. I can see him a few meters in the bush. The metal object in his hand is a saw; he is cutting up logs. My guess is that he is illegally chopping down trees for firewood. He doesn't even blink in my direction. He is probably as nervous about my presence as I am of his.

Wise city girl; prepared, aware. Silly city girl; dreaming up wild horrors.

He is just someone's dad, or someone's son, or someone's kind neighbour, or someone's boring old husband. Any of these scenarios is a billion times more likely than "He is an axe murderer." Or a saw murderer, in this case. It is good to be aware and prepared but it is also good to not let one's imagination run amuck. And it is certainly good to go out and trust that people are good rather than to not go out, let's say, on a long-distance bike ride and experience of a lifetime, because fear and the media and your ensuing imagination got the better of you. Just be smart, prepare, take precautions, trust your instincts, and trust others. When something doesn't feel right, don't do it. And then, bearing all that in mind, get out there and follow your heart.

Rue Nicholas and 3e Rang Ouest are also secluded, dirt and gravel roads. I am forced to go slow as I navigate my path. I have to keep my eyes to the ground. It isn't fun but getting a flat would be worse. In total, there are over nine precarious kilometres. To top things off, when I stop to pee in a bush, I get a mosquito bite...in a place not normally exposed to bites. That should be fun.

At the very end, all at once, there are some hills and some rather strong headwinds. Finally, there is one killer uphill to the entrance to the park.

This park, Camping Panoramique de Portneuf, participates in the "Bienvenue Cyclistes" program. My site costs me $28. They have a section of seven small lots specifically for cyclists. Each little lot has a fire pit and a little picnic table, as well as its own electrical outlet and water tap. I am impressed. It is a grass surface with some trees at the back that align with the fence that borders the park. There are a few that will work for me and my hammock tent. I choose lot T1 of the seven. I am the only cyclist here.

I sit down to eat a snack right away. Today I am hungry. A few minutes later, two other self-supported cyclists, a couple, arrive. They choose the lot directly beside me but then don't say hello or even look in my direction. I find it odd that they would choose a lot this close if they just want to keep to themselves. Whatever. To each their own.

I set up my hammock tent, pour myself a glass of wine, and smoke a cigarette. I go to the washroom and change into my one pair of YOGAJeans and my camping hoodie. It is liberating riding my bicycle around without its panniers on. I feel light as a bird and free as the wind.

I buy firewood. This is a trailer park, I discover. I learn a lot about trailer parks here. There is a part called The Village where people live year-round. The rest of the park is comprised of seasonal trailers. The only camping that happens here is the cyclist section. Learning this makes me really admire and respect this park. They made room for us cyclists even though it is not really a campground. Respect. I give Camping Panoramique de Portneuf two thumbs up for their level of participation in the "Bienvenue Cyclistes" program. Also, the lots directly across from the cyclist lots are designated for motorcyclists. In lieu of stunning scenery from nature I get to see beautiful motorcycles instead. I am looking at three beautiful Harleys right now. It is definitely an acceptable temporary trade-off.

I am having a little trouble starting my fire. Maybe a lot. Enough so that an observant but polite older man approaches me. "There is a lot of wind. You need some dry wood."

You see what he did there. He took the fault for the fire not starting from me and put it on the wind and the wood. Smart man. He has a huge pile of kindling in his hands. He extends his arms. The kindling is for me. I melt.

"Do you have newspaper?" he asks.

"I used it all," I tell him, defeated but smiling.

"I have a lot. One second."

He goes back to his RV where his wife is seated out front. She waves at me. He comes back with a big stack of newspapers. He asks where I am from. When I tell him Toronto, he tells me he lived there for a few years. We chat briefly. I thank him and he smiles. Life's small but important pick-me-ups. No sooner do I get my fire going when it starts to rain. Remember what I told you about Murphy's Law?

I move all the firewood and my panniers to beneath the picnic table and crawl into my hammock tent. I am not in here a minute when another older man pokes his head between the trees. "Bonjour!" he calls.

"Bonjour!" I reply.

He invites me to come keep dry and warm under the awning of the RV, which belongs to him and his wife and is just across from my site. I accept. I laugh to myself. You think everyone is minding their own business, you think you are alone. But you aren't. You are always a part of a community, somehow, some way. It's wonderful. These people have their eye on me, like a mother with her kid at the park. They see my by myself, with my bike, my panniers. They get it. These strangers care. It's beautiful. I love my flagship bicycle for this. I imagine life, after this bike ride, trying to always see people, envision them with a phantom bicycle and heavy baggage floating on their shoulder. We are all on a journey, always, carrying a load, sometimes heavy, sometimes lighter. These people can see mine. Can we always see each other's? We need to. We can if we choose to.

The man who helped me with the fire reminds me a lot of my dad so I decide to call him. I tell him about Oka Park and the forest full of fireflies and the crazy storm and as many other details as my excited breath will allow. He thinks what I'm doing is great and that means the world to me.

I have discovered another double use of my few supplies for this voyage: my bicycle doubles as a firewood dolly. I keep bungee cords wrapped to my bike rack. It is ready to transport logs at any time.

I finish the bottle of wine and I burn all of the firewood. Dusk comes swiftly and silently. I happily and eagerly climb into my precious hammock tent. Today I pedaled seventy-two kilometres in a gorgeous twenty-degree bliss with protective cloud. It was pretty darn perfect. I set up my phone to hang from the cord suspending my tent above me like a mini movie screen and watch the Dwayne Perkins comedy special "Take Note" on Netflix. I fall blissfully asleep like a weary dog on a hot summer afternoon.

"Be a loner. That gives you time to wonder, to search for the truth.
Have holy curiosity. Make your life worth living."
-Albert Einstein

JULY 20ᵀᴴ – DAY 16

I walk over to the RV of the kind man who had given me kindling and news-paper yesterday. I knock on the RV door and give him back the leftover wood and paper and thank him. Again I am struck by how much he reminds me of my father. There is something about the way he smiles, sincerely and with a twinkle in his eye. My father turns seventy this year and that number is freak-ing me right out. My paternal grandfather died at eighty-two. I am already panicking at this genetic math.

Twelve years left with my Daddy is nowhere nearly enough.

I don't own a house or a car. Heck, except for mountains of books, beau-tiful, old-fashioned, paper-bound books, I don't a thing. Once I asked my father, "Daddy, are you disappointed that I haven't...bought a house and... done all that?"

"What?" he shot back, emphatically. "No. What are you talking about? You're doing it right. You travel, you spend your summers in Paris, you lead such a rich, good life. You're always going to have to pay for where you live. No. You're doing it right."

His incredulousness at my question made me feel good. I've never felt like a freak in my father's eyes. In fact I have always felt loved and celebrated by both my parents, no matter what the latest non-conformist thing is I am up to. There has never been a pressure to do anything other than exactly what I am doing. Well. Actually. My mom might ask too quickly and too often if I am seeing anyone. But other than that, they're both pretty excellent at supporting my life choices.

Well, here I am grinning from ear to ear again as I ride. It is always this way in the mornings. I just can't stop smiling. And when I become aware of how much I am smiling I actually laugh out loud at myself. I must look like a complete nutbar to anyone who might be seeing me.

There are more than a few hills today. I have been waiting for them. Every day I remind myself that it has all been child's play and that the hills are coming, the hills are coming. Not once have I settled in and thought, *Okay, I got this.* No. It's the opposite. Every day I think that perhaps today will be the day that I finally battle the real hills. I know they are out there, somewhere, waiting for me. I've been told that the east is extremely hilly. When does "east" begin? Each day, I am on guard, fearful, anticipating, but ready. Today there are some hills, yes, but I know steeper, bigger, more ferocious ones are to come.

Bring it.

I am still riding on the painted white line as much as possible, no matter what the road conditions. It gives me something to do while I ride. I am still making the sign of the cross for every dead animal I pass and, my goodness, there are a lot of them. It's heartbreaking. I keep telling my little friends: "Guys. You have to be more careful." But they don't seem to be listening. Yes, I have begun talking to the animals, dead and alive. A friend tells me that as long as I am aware that I am doing this and think it is funny then I am doing okay, I'm not losing my marbles. Yet.

There is a wonderfully long and steep downhill roller as you enter Neuville that is completely fun to glide down. This is followed by whopper after whopper after whopper. I sweat, I push, I grind my wheels, and I pedal my heavy bicycle up, up, slowly up. I never change my gears when I am riding my bicycle around Toronto but I sure as hell am starting to now. I want to do the work, I am here for the exercise, so I resist gearing down as much as possible. I have been riding steadily at gear five (of seven) but now am forced to gear down to four, even three.

Okay, sometimes the looks people give me are not so much amused and curious, but are more along the lines of: "What the…?" I guess these serious cyclists don't know what to make of my pirate get-up, flip-flops, Paul Frank skull and bones skateboarding helmet and fluorescent, orangey-pink finger-nails and toes; all these strange, silly, atypical pieces of riding gear coupled with the fact that I am clearly packed up for and on a pretty serious, long-distance ride. I had just better be successful or people will have too many points to pick at and say, "Well, duh." or "I told you so." or "What were you thinking?" When you have a big mouth like me and you tell everyone what you're up to, well, that would be quite a lot of egg on my face. I have really left myself no choice but to be victorious in this endeavour.

It's actually a purposeful technique I use. I did it all the time with my marathon and ultra-marathon running. I would tell everyone ahead of time about my upcoming race. Then, in the thick of it, when I was dying and wanted to give up, I would think of all the people I told and I would think about them asking how I did and I would think about how utterly unfun it would be to tell them I DNF'd (did not finish). So I would push on. Yes. Ignorance and naïveté of what I am actually getting myself into are often my two best tools for completing some of these crazy feats. And when those tools fail, pride comes swooping in as a close third. Whatever gets you through.

More hills. It's tough work, but nothing I can't handle. Until Rue de l'Aéroport. Sigh. *Fuck.* I am walking my first hill. I have to turn left onto it at a juncture where the road is already on a steep incline. I have no chance to build momentum. My cheeks burn with shame as I walk and push my heavy steed uphill. I tell myself to get over it and that it is going to happen again and that that's life.

Suck it up, buttercup.

I am now in Quebec City. I am still twenty-three kilometres away from my destination. Today I am going to stay at my friend Éric's house. His will be the last familiar face of my ride. I am excited to see him.

Less than ten kilometres from Éric's, I begin to smile and feel happily lost in the most wonderful sense of familiarity. I remember this path from my walks here last year. I would walk from Éric's house to wherever and anywhere, forever all day. I spent the first two weeks of July here in Quebec City, passing the time as I awaited attending my three-month ultrasound back in Toronto. I was blissfully pregnant, walking all day, totally unaware that my little love had already left me.

This ride was originally planned for last year, the summer of 2015. When I said that this ride was twenty months in the dreaming, did that phrase not strike you as odd? Do you really think I am the type of person capable of planning and waiting twenty months to do something? No. This ride was planned for last summer, just eight months in the dreaming, at that time; forcibly so because the idea came to me (from where?) in November of 2014. I was even more or at least just as confused and scared as I was this summer when I started my training rides. I had just finished my training ride to and from London in May of 2015 when I so happily, though completely unexpectedly, discovered I was pregnant. The bike ride was off, of course, as I prepared for an even greater adventure.

I was overjoyed. The elation was calm and all-consuming. I felt motherly and responsible, changed, immediately. I began writing to my unborn child, one letter each week. I signed up for a website that told me the progress of my little sweet pea, comparing its growth and size to everyday objects. It was a fascinating and wondrous time. By the end of my first week of discovering I was pregnant, I had already figured out daycare costs at the school I teach at and how I would pay for post-secondary education. I shared all these plans in the letters. My little love was going to be taken care of, fully, and with so much love.

But the joy was terribly short-lived. At my three-month ultrasound mid-July, I was devastated to find out that I had miscarried two weeks prior. The pain was crippling. I left the hospital and the world around me looked different. I bought a pack of cigarettes, and a double espresso, not out of desire, but to rub my nose in my new reality, like a bad dog, a failure, a non-mother, fathoms more alone than I was before being pregnant. I dove into the meaningless non-pleasures I could partake in again, seeking some sort of comfort or enjoyment. There was none, both felt toxic. I called my best friend, Darren. I went to his house. I drank a bottle of wine, and just bawled, messily, got drunk. He just let me go on and on, he just listened.

Yes, I remember this route well. I am flooded with emotions. I feel the tears well up. How close I came to meeting the love of my life. It's painful. But I decide not to cry. Instead, I choose to cherish. I will never forget that feeling, my little love. I am forever changed. I am thankful. I would choose that short visit over none at all.

What else can I do?

Éric lives just down the street from the beautiful Les Chutes Montmorency. His house is tucked back from the street amid a small cluster of four houses. There is a long driveway. You pass the house facing the road, then another facing the road, and then there are two houses side by side. Éric owns them both. The house on the left is where Éric's sister, her husband, and their daughter live. The house on the right is Éric's house. Like many houses in Quebec, Éric's house is split in half: one home upstairs and one home downstairs. You never see this in Ontario. Houses are split vertically there, but here in Quebec, they are split diagonally. Downstairs from Éric lives a tenant, also named Éric.

When I arrive, Éric is not yet home. I sit on his front porch, sipping wine and waiting for him. Cars start pulling in and everyone starts coming home. First it is Main Floor Éric and a woman friend of his and two kids. Next is Éric's brother-in-law. Then it is Éric's sister and niece. When she pulls in, Main Floor Éric walks over to her car and helps her unload her things. He takes the little girl by her hand. The cohesiveness of everyone is beautiful. Then the neighbours from the third house come out. Éric's sister goes over with a bottle of beer in her hand. Main Floor Éric, noticing me sitting on the porch up here, offers me a beer but I decline. Instead I sit here, by myself, like a zombie. I realize today that there is a consistent cycle to my daily emotions: I start off in "Ecstatic Monkey," then I transition into a peaceful "Cruise Control" for the day. In the evening, I am "Silent, Wine-Drinking Zombie."

Finally Éric arrives. It is great to see him. He is such a good soul and Earth citizen. He grows his own greens, doesn't waste a thing, composts, recycles, uses environmentally-friendly shampoo and dish detergent, makes all his own healthy food, and is a rock-climbing and canyoning instructor. He, more than anyone else I have ever met in my life, is truly living in synchronicity with his environment. I greatly admire and respect this.

We chat for a bit and share a glass of wine. Then we drive to get more wine. When we get back to the house we begin preparing dinner. When I say "we" I mean "he" and I try to help by chopping some vegetables. Dinner is a homemade pesto. Éric explains to me that a basic, classic pesto is made from pine nuts, basil leaves, and oil. He, however, is making one from sunflower seeds, a variety of different greens including the stems of carrots (he really doesn't waste anything), and olive oil. He says we will put this on top of our salad, which includes carrots, tomatoes, avocado, some type of sprout, and lettuce, all from his own garden.

As we are preparing dinner, the neighbours drift upstairs to join us. Éric is an Airbnb host and a girl from France who is currently staying with him as an Airbnb guest arrives home shortly after, too. Some other colleagues of Éric's also stop by. It goes like this all night, people coming and going.

Amid the happy chaos, exhaustion hits me like a Mack truck. Today I rode seventy-nine kilometres under a mostly sunny twenty-nine degree sky. I silently exit the room and go and lie down on the couch in the front room. I am more tired than hungry, so I lay down and eat nothing. Everyone eventually evacuates and Éric comes and joins me.

He sits himself on the armchair beside me. He puts on traditional Québécois music. He sings all the songs, he knows all the words. I admire this, too: his reverence for local music as well as the fact that he would freely sing along.

'Twas like a lullaby, it seems.

"Riding along, the sun on my face, not a care in the world. These are the moments. This is therapy."

JULY 21ST – DAY 17

I stay in bed until everyone has left and the house is quiet. Another Bukowski moment? Perhaps. It is either that or it is my part in the three bottles of wine Éric and I finished plus whiskey nightcaps. Surprisingly, frighteningly, save for the little extra sleep in, I feel pretty good. I do the dishes, make a coffee (my instant packets with hot tap water), have a cigarette, and fold the laundry (both mine and Éric's).

Last year during my stay here with Éric I went almost every morning to a rustic little restaurant behind Les Chutes Montmorency called "Au Sommet de la Chute." I knew before even arriving at Eric's that I wanted to go there again. And so, without my heavy panniers, I get on my bicycle and ride down to the restaurant. Yet again, I marvel at how weightless and easy it is riding without all the extra heft of my panniers. I feel light as air, like the breeze itself, I'm flying. The light bike is a biological extension of my own body, my wings, I'm like a bird.

I recognize the woman behind the counter immediately. This makes me happy, because a familiar face makes a place feel like home. I ask her if she recognizes me, as well. She says she does but she may just be being polite. I would do this in Paris, too. Anytime someone recognized or remembered me, I would become quietly thrilled. It makes me feel like I have a place there, like I have a small claim to say I belong.

I eat my simple but delicious plate of three sunnyside up eggs, brown toast, and home fries with a coffee.

On a related side note, want to know what really irks me? All these trendy breakfast places in Toronto with long queues. But the standing parade of sheep is not what bothers me most; that part actually makes me laugh. What annoys me is that all these trendy, contrived, pretentious breakfast joints call their eggs "huevos." Huevos. Drives me *mad*. They're damn eggs, plain and simple, no matter what fancy name from another random language you give them. Unless you are a Spanish breakfast joint, then they are simply eggs. Rant over.

I return to Eric's. It is just before noon. I pack up my stuff and ride to the ferry to go over to Lévis. Marc from Presqu'Ile Provincial Park told me that the North Shore is hilly but the South Shore is flat and scenic with farmlands. I had planned for my next stop to be Montmagny, which is, thankfully, on the South Shore. I would have chosen a new destination if it weren't. I vote flat.

Lévis is beautiful with the prettiest, paved trails hugging the stately St. Lawrence. I am already smitten with this humble yet commanding river.

In Beaumont I stop at a little grocery store. I pick up a tub of Ranch macaroni salad, a tub of grilled vegetable pasta salad, and a half tub of yogurt-covered cranberries. I also buy a litre of milk, a 500mL bottle of red, and a small squeeze bottle of mayonnaise. Now all I need to do is find a picnic table.

I stop to use the washroom in a little restaurant in Saint-Michel-de-Bellechasse. Still no sign of a picnic table.

The route is pretty flat, save for one long, rolling uphill in Saint-Vallier.

Then it gets so flat that there is even a long stretch of decline. I basically don't pedal at all in Berthier-Sur-Mer. What a treat it is, rolling downhill through this little town. Then there is one last roller and one little whopper right before entering the Camping Coop des Érables.

This park is half trailer park and half camping and the two are well-integrated. This park, too, has a special row of smaller lots for cyclists. But...there are no trees on those lots. I explain to the nice lady behind the counter that I only have a hammock tent and I need trees.

"No problem. We will just give you a site with services for the same price as the cyclists' lot. These sites have trees."

Just like that, no hassle. I am pleased. Her logic and flexibility are refreshing, human and non-automated. I smile. My hammock tent is proving to be advantageous.

I take a ride through the park to pick a site with two trees the proper distance apart. A man who sees me looking around with the map in my hand asks me if I need help finding my site. I tell him I am all right, actually, and he goes on his way. Then I pass a trailer with a family sitting out on its veranda. A man calls out, asking if I need help. I am in the process of telling him I am okay when two men going by in a golf cart also stop to see if I need help. Bless them all. I go back to the front office to tell the lady which lot I've selected. One of the men from the golf cart is there already. When I arrive he is in the middle of letting them know that there is a cyclist looking for a campsite with trees who needs help.

I tap him on the shoulder. "It's me. I found one," I tell him.

"Oh, good," he says. He looks happy that the "problem" is solved.

As I am setting up my camp, that same man and another man drive by in a golf cart. He explains to me that he works here sometimes and that he has been a permanent resident here since 2011. He tells me he is at lot 141 and he is having a campfire later and I am invited and then they drive off. How lovely, I may just do that.

After my camp is set up, I buy firewood. The man in charge there tells me he will deliver it to me shortly. It turns out to be the other man from that helpful golf cart duo. Even though my pannier-free bike is well-equipped with the sufficient number and lengths of bungee cords to efficiently transport even a large bundle of firewood, I decide to accept the offer. A soothing, hot shower is calling my name.

When I come out of the shower I notice that many of the campsites are covered with Christmas decorations. How odd. I ask a lady who happens to be in the site across from the showers why this is. She explains to me that July twenty-fifth is Camping Christmas, only days away. Every year, on this same day, all campgrounds celebrate it.

"For the kids." she adds.

I had no idea. I am learning a lot this summer, that's for sure. I thank the kindly lady for the information. She responds by telling me I speak French very well. This makes me happy. Actually, a lot of people have said this to me in Quebec. I think that because I am from Toronto, the expectation on my ability to speak French is low. It is one of my favourite compliments.

I am feeling pretty happy. I feel proud that I stuck it out back at Oka, that I didn't let fear beat me. Imagine that. Imagine I'd given into fear and not done this? And look at today: sixty-one kilometres, a high of twenty-eight with a lot of blessed cloud. Not so tough, riding along, sun on my face, not a care in the world. These are the moments. They are all the moments. Every second, shocking, calm bliss.

This is therapy.

Just before dusk, around eight thirty, I start my fire. A man from an RV a few lots down walks over. He has a lawn chair in his hand and he offers it to me so I can sit in front of my fire. He says I can just leave it outside his RV whenever I am leaving in the morning.

I am so not alone.

"Some people feel the rain, others just get wet."
-*Bob Marley*

JULY 22ND – DAY 18

My hoodie doubles as a perfect pillow as I sleep in my home in a hammock like on a cloud. It begins raining down at about one in the morning. Again, I wait to see if the fly for my hammock tent will hold up. It does. I get lost in the soothing sound of the lightly landing rain and the damp smell of the earth and grass. I stay awake for a good two hours. I begin to second-guess these little five hundred millilitre bottles of wine. I think I need that extra two hundred and fifty millilitres to stay asleep through the night. Experiment over.

I get up around nine and pack up my camp quickly and efficiently compared to my normal mode: slow. A man with his two children riding bicycles around the grounds calls out to me to have a safe trip. He is the same man who had asked me yesterday where I got my hammock tent from.

Then the woman in the trailer parked just across from me calls out (in French, of course): "You're setting off? Where are you going?"

She asks me questions about my voyage. We get into a conversation. She tells me about a family that came through this park on bicycles: mom, dad, and five kids whom they were homeschooling throughout their year-long bike trip. Wow. That's impressive on so many levels. If she had just told me that someone she knows has five kids I would have been blown away, never mind the long-distance bike ride and the homeschooling on top. I can't help but again, at this moment, recall how I had felt more than odd and maybe even crazy for doing this bike ride. But now I am out here seeing and hearing about others doing the same and crazier feats. I realize now that there is a community for every oddball, you just have to find it. And once you do, you're not an oddball anymore. You're home.

She offers me a cold bottle of water but I tell her I already have a full water bottle. I don't want to create unnecessary plastic waste.

"Bonne route." she says as she waves goodbye.

I wish her a good day and set off.

After riding awhile, I stop to take a picture of the water, the beautiful St. Lawrence River. A man approaches me from his front lawn, which I am stopped in front of. He tells me what it is I am taking a picture of: L'Isle aux Grues. I tell him he is lucky to have such a beautiful view from his house. He just smiles and goes back to his house.

It begins to rain just before noon. Nothing heavy. At just after one I stop to buy wine for later and to search for somewhere serving all-day breakfast. No luck. I stop at the third restaurant, also not serving breakfast, but I stay anyway, resigning myself to order something else. The restaurant is called "La Libellule." I have a coffee and their "sandwich végé." It is made with Swiss cheese, tomato, lettuce, mayonnaise, mustard, and their in-house made vegetarian pâté. It is to die for. As soon as I arrive, the rain begins to dump down in impossibly heavy ropes from the sky that pelt the pavement like hammers. I escape unscathed this time. I'm staying here until it stops, no matter how long it takes.

The spectacular show doesn't last long. I am back on the road at two with only thirty-eight kilometres left to go.

In Saint-Roch-des-Aulnaies, a man passes me in a car and then spins around and pulls over on the opposite side of the road. As I approach where he is stopped, he exits his car with a basket of strawberries in his hand, extending them to me. I accept, picking two from the top. What a treat, they are sweet and juicy. He starts asking me all kinds of questions: where I have come from and where I am going. He tells me he is also a cyclist and that he is always interested when he sees people doing big trips like this. He encourages me to take more strawberries. I do. His name is Wayne.

"Like Wayne Gretzky," he adds.

I laugh at his unnecessary and funny clarification. We chat a bit, I have a few more strawberries, we say good day, then we each go on our separate ways. Just like that. Yet again.

The whole ride sticks along Highway 132 East until I turn onto Chemin des Berges. Then I follow a hard dirt and fine gravel path right along the St. Lawrence. It is beautiful here, a kaleidoscope of colours cast perfectly by the radiant sun, hues of blues in sky and water, greens of grasses and reeds, and a rainbow of flowers. My love affair with this river deepens daily.

A beaver. I swear animals talk to each other, even between different breeds. I am sure that a bird warned that beaver that I was coming. I heard it excitedly tweeting, and then the beaver scampered away. What a fat little cutie. Then I see the tiniest mouse do the same. I love all the animals. They brighten my days, just like the humans.

I am in La Pocatière now. The head wind is fierce and strong. Even though I am on a decline and am pedaling there is such great resistance that I can barely get any momentum going. It's nuts.

Rain, rain, rain.

I finally arrive in Camping Coop des Érables in Montmagny. This is my first time setting up camp in the rain. All things considered, I am lucky. It isn't raining too hard. Also, I have a somewhat protected dry spot thanks to the tall trees. I'm pleased with the job I do in these conditions. I put up the fly first, then the hammock tent, and then quickly throw in my sleeping bag, almost perfectly dry.

After setting up my hammock tent I go to the onsite dépanneur to buy firewood. Back at my site, I try to start a fire. It's not going well. Almost three weeks in and still I have not earned this Girl Scout badge. It frustrates and disappoints me deeply. I keep trying.

Then something amazing happens. It is like at Oka Park where I just can't believe my eyes. A car pulls into my lot. I'm looking at the driver, wondering what is going on.

Its Éric.

A surprise and welcome visit. He and his friend are on their way to La Gaspésie to go canyoning. I am shocked and thrilled. And they have come at just the right moment. Without my asking, they set to work immediately, gathering kindling to help me with my fire. They gather pine combs, leaves, and sticks from beneath trees. They succeed in getting the fire going, tall and crackling. I am thankful. Another useful double I came up with last night is using my retractable saw as a fire poker.

I give Éric and his friend wine and we three chat for a bit. They can't stay long. After about half an hour they leave. I am overwhelmed with appreciation that Éric made the effort to stop by. What a thoughtful and wonderful treat their visit was.

And fortuitous. The fire.

I take out my ukulele and sit before the sacred blaze and sing and play. A little boy down the road hears me and tugs at his mother's shirt, saying "Maman, regarde." He is pointing at me, curious and wide-eyed. How adorable. The mother and I make eye contact. We laugh.

Today I pedaled eighty-two kilometres in a moderate temperature of twenty-five degrees with rain. I feel spent. The darkness comes, the firewood runs out, and I lay me down in my precious hammock tent. I watch a bit of Netflix on my little mini makeshift movie theatre system, but not much. Exhaustion hits me like a belly flop.

I sleep like a lily pad on a quiet, lonely river.

"Where are we?
What the hell is going on?
...
Spin me around again
And rub my eyes
This can't be happening..."
-Hide and Seek, Imogen Heep

JULY 23RD – DAY 19

I wake with the sun. It has not rained through the night. I look at the forecast and no rain is expected. I burn a little fire in order to make my precious morning coffee. I sit with it and a cigarette, quiet, peaceful, and happy.

I pack up camp quite early. The trees are sappy and the straps to hang my hammock tent have become sticky and gluey. The sap is viscous and gummy and impossible to wash or scrape away. I put Ziploc bags on the straps before wrapping up the tent. I don't want sap all over my tent, too. I cannot express the importance of Ziploc bags (and baby wipes) on a camping trip such as this. Ziploc bags also keep all my individually-bagged clothing dry inside my panniers, serve as a garbage sack, dirty laundry hamper, and more.

I walk over to the campsite across from me and offer my unopened bottle of mayonnaise and a package of Mr. Noodles. I simply have too much food, I tell the lady. She accepts the items. Although I thought I had already learned the lesson of buying only what I want or need to eat immediately, and while I have definitely improved, I still have some work to do.

I pluck my eyebrows, put on mascara, then make my way to the washroom to brush my teeth. I am obviously becoming acclimatized to the bugs. Today as I reach into my pannier to dig out my sack of riding clothes (changing to my second set today; the other set are the epitome of stench) I find an earwig crawling around. With zero emotional reaction, I get a baby wipe, pick it up, shake the baby wipe, let the ugly bug fall safely to the ground, then put the baby wipe back into the package; it is still clean and good for another use.

Three cheers for the city girl.

I leave right after eight in the morning. Of course, at just the same time, it begins to spit. And then there is that hill to tackle that had been deliriously fun flying down when I arrived yesterday.

I determine to ride all the way up, that I can do it. I am going to do it. I want this. After all the rain lately, I need a bit of triumph, a small taste of glory, to even out the emotional score. I give it my all. My legs feel like massive machines and I can feel each muscle grinding like a cog in its axle. I get to the top of the hill, all riding, now walking. Success. And at this same moment, the sun comes out. I laugh and cheer out loud like a happy, crazy person. There are only two words appropriate for this particular moment.

"FUCK, YEAH!

"I hear you, black crow! Hello!" I call out.

It is such a treat to see the birds, the animals. I now always call out to them, talk to them. They keep me company. It would feel rude to not acknowledge them now. We've become quite well acquainted.

The sun is shining beautifully and brightly. I am in heaven. Oh, how after even only a day or so without it, I missed it terribly. It seems a crime to have to cover up with the pirate get-up. But as my skin heats up, I look up and think: *Well, sun, it is a shame. But, even you and I must always wear a condom.*

I call out, "Hi, guys!" to the cows, and, "Hi, guys!" to the horses.

They hear me and they look. They don't look particularly arsed about it but it's clear they hear me.

Today I am not playing the game of riding on the painted white line. Today I am riding smack in the middle of the road like I own the damn thing. Like a boss.

For the first time in my journey I pass some crop circles. Immediately the lyric from Imogen Heep's song "Hide and Seek" comes to mind. I have not listened to a note of music on this trip, preferring to drink in the sounds of nature and the incredible, enormous silence. Music is a fantastic escape, it instantly transports you, spiritually. There is nothing to escape here, but suddenly I want to hear this magical song.

I pull over to listen to it. My stop happens to coincide with where the statue of Dionne le Semeur is located. A motorcyclist happens to be passing at that moment, as well. When he sees me pulled over he slows down and calls out, "Tout est beau?"

He is checking if everything is okay.

"Oui." I reply.

My grin is huge.

The song plays. It is a magical, haunting song. Out of nowhere, completely unexpectedly, I break down into sobs. Heaving, body-shaking sobs. I cry freely in the open space, beneath the sky, among the fields, with not another soul around, to Mother Nature herself. I don't feel sad, I don't know where this rush of emotion is coming from, but it feels cleansing and good. It feels like my spirit is expelling and expunging. But letting go of what? Most likely it is the fear, the heavy anxiety and sleep-stealing self-doubt I suffered through leading up to this crazy ride. It is all emptying from me. I feel lighter. It is the most intense release, a relief, and an unexpected unburdening.

The fields expand before me and this enchanted song grips me, and like a floating spirit I see clearly, objectively, this journey I am on. I have been, I am in, a constant state of awe and incredulousness at the beauty of nature all around me. Away from the rush and stress of the city and regular life, I feel an electrifying clarity. I don't want the flow of emotion to end. It feels like a loving exorcism performed by the Universe itself.

Minutes pass, the song ends, and calmness begins to return. At this point I also remember that I am wearing mascara. I probably look like Alice Cooper after a rainstorm right now. Alas, holy moment over. Slowly I come back down to Earth and wipe away the black guck from my eyes and cheeks. Baby wipes, again, save the day.

There is a path cut into the long reeds leading from the road toward the statue. The grass is cool and dewy and feels refreshing on my hot, dirty feet. I am mesmerized to read the words beneath the statue, they echo the lyrics of the song, and both are in such seamless synchronicity with the nature of my journey. The plaque beneath the statue reads (in French):

"...To all the sowers of ideas, these visionaries who believed in their dreams, in the future..."

I am following my heart, living a dream beyond my imagination, despite my own terrible misgivings and doubt, despite the danger supposedly inherent for me being a woman on my own doing this. I am here. I am doing this. It is all happening; I am making it happen, my incredible, daunting vision. What beautiful irony that I had this emotional emancipation here, in front of this statue. In this moment, I feel the Universe is really winking at me.

I come upon Auberge des Îles where I stop for breakfast. What a lovely view of the river. I enjoy a hearty breakfast in its charming, rural atmosphere. Their only misdemeanour is that their ketchup is served in packets. I have to use one million of these to satisfy my ketchup needs. I use all the packets (about eight) and hide the tightly rolled wrappers in an empty milkette.

Off I go again.

Bonjour. Bonjour. Bonjour. Passers-by call to me, I call to them; them first, me first, on and on, all day long. I can't stop smiling.

A few kilometres outside of Saint-André there is a simple but effective hand-painted sign with a frothy mug drawn on it and the text: "6kms." Then, after another little whopper, another sign: the same frothy mug and "150m." I so very rarely drink beer but I can't resist stopping. I sit on the back patio and look out over the emerald and mint green field, the smudgy light pastel blue river beyond, the low pencil-drawn mountain in the distance, the thick, milky clouds and the uniform blue sky above; all the colours are layered into a beautiful sandwich, a feast for the eyes and the soul.

Another double use for the baby wipes is ashtray.

Five kilometres before Rivière-du-Loup I finally see a picnic table under a tree with a beautiful view of the St. Lawrence River, which I feel very connected to now. She is great company and always there at my side. I sit there and eat my lunch of crackers with peanut butter and jam and a can of spicy Thai chili tuna with a small mug of wine and one cigarette. I am just getting ready to take out my ukulele and play when two couples approach and join me. They ask and encourage me to play for them but I am just not there yet and decline. They are on a motorcycle ride from Gatineau, near Ottawa. They offer me a sandwich but I tell them I have just eaten. After chatting for a short while, I gather my things and continue on my way. They wish me "Bonne route" and I wish them the same.

I arrive in Camping de l'Île aux Lièvres. This campsite is not cyclist friendly. You can lock your bike up at the registration desk but you cannot actually take it on the ferry over to the island. Not doable for me and my heavy panniers. Also, there are only three ferries a day. No, thanks. I am still scarred from Parc National des Îles-de-Boucherville. Back to the drawing board.

I cycle a mere 2.3kms over to Camping Municipal de La Pointe. These grounds do not participate in the program "Bienvenue Cyclistes." That's fine. It costs only $26 for the evening. It's mostly an RV site with about a dozen and a half "rustic camping" sites at the rear of the grounds, none of which have any services. The lots are small and cute with many tall trees and a little picnic table each and big, grey Rubbermaid garbage cans outside each site on the main path. Even though it is "sans services," without services, there is a communal tap and power station with eight plugs available for each of the two rings of campsites. Perfect.

I find it interesting, this camping and RV-ing stuff. The lots are all directly side by side. No real privacy. I wonder what the allure is for this subculture where I am crashing the party but do not feel a part of, per se. This is barely "being in nature."

The community fire pit here gives me the idea that there should be a campers' tradition, much like the Campers' Christmas, where everyone gathers each night, those who want to, to share their stories: where they're from, what brought them here, where they are off to, what they are up to. I bet there'd be some interesting stories.

As I set up my camp, I think about how I have seen quite a number of incredible waterfront properties along my route, and to my surprise, many for sale. I dream of buying one with my imaginary millions, and out back, setting up a ring of trailer tents, the kind that are supposed to hitch to the backs of cars, with a fire pit in the middle. I would put a sign out front saying, "All cyclists welcome to stay for free for the evening." I would feed them and let them do their laundry and hear their stories and recharge their phones and share a drink over the night campfire and just spread the love that bursts in my heart and ask them to do the same always. *Be the change.*

I play the ukulele and drink my wine and eat my bun with turkey pâté and roasted red pepper hummus and Camembert. Today I rode sixty-eight kilometres under a kind sky bearing down only twenty-three degrees of sweet heat. But, still. Darkness falls and I obediently head to bed. Netflix. I fall asleep, deeply, like a wood frog under a pile of rocks in the dead of winter.

I awake at three in the morning. My body just automatically wakes up after five or six hours sleep and with going to bed at dusk, three in the morning already makes for a solid six hours of sleep. I look at my route for the next few days, I check Facebook. And then I feel something.

I feel an animal poking from below, its back rubbing along the bottom of my hammock tent as it passes beneath me. I freeze. Actually, this isn't the first time I have felt this, and like last time, I can't be sure if it's actually happening or not. The last time I felt this I concluded I must be imagining it. But this time I am pretty sure that some sort of animal, most likely a raccoon, is indeed bumping me from below. I don't know what to do.

So I just wait and fall back asleep.

"I'm dying. Then again, I've never felt so alive."

JULY 24TH – DAY 20

Brrrr. Second chilly morning in a row. Fourteen degrees. I slept in my YOGAjeans and hoodie again. It is my only warm outfit. I may have to buy some socks for sleeping. I wish I'd bought those ugly slippers at Camping Rivière-Ouelle. They reminded me of the ones that Grandma Laflamme used to knit. Good ugly. Homely. *Homey.*

The Free Hugs Guy is back at it; I saw a new video of his circulating on Facebook. See. That's exactly what I've been talking about on this trip. I'm doing the same thing, really, just in a way more chilled, drawn-out, Canadian kind of way. But I'm out here just believing in the goodness of people, putting myself in their care, proving the world is a good place, that a woman, a wee "toute seule" like me can be safe and secure out in our world on her own. We just need to spread the word, believe it absolutely in our hearts. It's about per-spective. About choice. About seeing ourselves as part of a bigger community, always. Again, as the Talmud says, "We do not see things as they are, we see things as *we* are."

We need to tell the good stories. Louder and way more often.

Even though I know I will have to change almost immediately, I cannot bring myself to change out of my warm clothes as I begin riding. I'm just too cold. I pluck my eyebrows (there's no better light than the morning sun to do this) and set out. I get as far as the washroom before changing.

There is a whopper of a hill immediately as I begin. I smile. It is the road's way of saying: "Welcome back." Me climbing it and feeling amazingly about it is my way of responding: "Thank you. It's wonderful to be back." And, so, another glorious day begins.

When will this honeymoon phase end? Will a day come that I begin to second- guess this trip? Or will it just continue to be incredible day after incredible day after incredible day?

If my emotion cycle each day has been ecstatic monkey, cruise control, zombie, today I have skipped right to cruise control. I'm still happy, but I'm scared. In two days I will be in New Brunswick. I don't know New Brunswick. I went once as a little kid. I was about eight years old. I remember nothing. It is completely foreign territory. It is where the hills will really begin. It has all been a picnic. The real work, the real test, lies just ahead. I think. I know nothing.

At just about seven kilometres into my ride I stop at Resto Pub d'Antan for my sacred breakfast of eggs, homefries and toast. The waitress smells like the perfume Grandma Laflamme used to wear. I ask her what she is wearing. She tells me it is Opium from Yves Saint Laurent. For some reason I feel that it is unlikely that this scent, named after a serious mind-altering drug, is what my sweet, old grandmother wore, but why not? It has been a wonderful surprise how much I have seen and felt my paternal grandparents and my father here throughout Quebec. It is like I am found and belong here, though I am a stranger in my own home. Can I miss a place I've never lived? It's what it feels like. I'm so frequently overcome with nostalgia.

At L'Isle-Vert, I turn inland from the St. Lawrence. Until now I have had long, rolling hills, whoppers, even elephants of hills. But, here, immediately, things are different.

Within the first kilometre that I leave my faithful river companion, the landscape changes. I see in the near distance a hill so steep I laugh out loud. I think of those Saturday morning LooneyTunes cartoons where cars drive up an impossibly steep hill and then just flip right over. This is that hill. As I near it, it does not visually flatten as most hills, quite graciously, do. I feel like I am in the Twilight Zone. Is this a real thing I am seeing?

I give it my all. I gain as much momentum as I can, then my bicycle angles up, my heavy load dragging behind. I start to weave across both lanes of traffic, side to side, to reduce the dramatic angle of the incline. It's not the wisest decision as a car could come barrelling over the top of this monstrosity at any moment. I trust my ears, though. The coast is clear. I'm making progress. Up, up.

A third of the way, I have to jump off the pedals. I say jump because with so little forward motion happening, simply stepping down is not possible; I would topple over for the lack of balance. Think of trying to stay upright on a non-moving bicycle. I'm sure seasoned Toronto bike couriers could swing it but not this non-cyclist and her super-heavy, loaded-up bicycle. I stop, I heave, and I heave, struggling to catch my breath. I am incredulous at the angle of this thing.

After I catch my breath, I try to continue. Do you know how difficult it is to begin riding with a bike this heavy on an angle like that? I grunt and inch my way up some more. My quads feel like cannons, like meter wide iron clubs, like weapons. I can feel every nanometer of every muscle in my legs engaged, clenched, fighting. I have to stop again.

Heaving, gasping for more breath, I realize it would probably be faster and certainly easier to dismount and push my bike up the hill. If I have to, I shall. But not yet.

It isn't a pretty show, but I do it. I ride all the way to the top. I am beaming. That wears off quickly, though. Dread sets in and fast. Is this what the rest of the trip will be like? I realize that this journey really only begins today. Rue Notre Dame has more of the same and then so does Chemin Denonville. Giant, unforgiving "hill" after enormous, unmerciful "hill."

It's on.

I stop for breath again. The work is relentless. All day long: straight up, straight down, straight up, straight down, straight the hell up, then straight the hell back down again. I grow to seriously loathe the downhills. They just feel like the undoing of all my hard work, my guts and soul being tossed back into my face.

I enter Saint-Paul-De-La-Croix and the road flattens for a few precious meters. There is a dépanneur. I have a coffee and an oatmeal chocolate chip cookie. The nice man behind the counter also fills my water bottle for me. I have used this same water bottle for the journey so far. I am consciously not creating a trail of plastic.

I sit on the porch of the dépanneur and enjoy my snack and rest. Michel, a sixty-eight-year-old local, stops to chat with me for a bit. He asks about my bicycle. I tell him it is nothing; a cheap, basic model. It has only seven gears, cost me only three hundred dollars. He tells me about his. His has twenty-one gears. We chat a bit then he goes on his way. I continue to sit. I am somewhat in a state of disillusionment at the terrain I am experiencing today. I am already whipped; a shell of myself. I have travelled only thirty-nine kilometres.

Just as I am about to continue on, a van pulls up. A man jumps out. He comes right over, says hello, and tells me he passed me earlier, on those horrid hills. He begins to pepper me with questions: where did I start from, where am I going. He offers me some advice on different routes and tells me about some things I might see on each of the routes. It is too much detail and information for my hot, tired brain. I smile and nod. He wishes me well and goes back to his van. But then he comes back.

He has more questions: where did I learn my French? We chat a bit more, and then again we say our goodbyes. He almost makes it into his van this time but again he comes back with yet more questions: "Why do you wear all this?" He is referring to my pirate get-up. I tell him it is to avoid the sun, the dust, and the bugs. This time, he actually makes it back into his van. But…he springs back out, one last time. "Wait. Just in case." He writes out his name and phone number and the name of the city. "Just in case." he says again.

His name is Anicet. This time he successfully gets into his van and pulls away. I am moved. I carefully place the number in the inside pocket of my food pannier and continue on my way.

The hills begin again, immediately and cruelly. Add to this a wonderful sign reporting gravel roads ahead. So it's like that, is it? I'm starting to get angry, to toughen, I am rising to the occasion.

Bring. It.

As the brutal roller coaster begins again, I can't help but think to myself: it is a *damn* good thing I did not know what I was getting myself into with this whole east coast bike ride idea. Three cheers for blind courage.

I re-name the route along Route de la Station, Rang A, Route du Cap, and Rang Grande-Ligne, through the string of small French towns L'Îsle-Vert, Saint-Paul-De-La-Croix, Saint-Clément and Saint-Cyprien, the Road of Hell. Or: Cyclists' Nemesis.

About mid-way through Saint-Clément there is finally some reprieve. I come upon a long, fairly flat stretch of the QC-293 South. It takes a while for me to rid myself of my "game face" attitude, to simmer, to quiet the battle spirit and feel gentle, open, soft again. Saint-Cyprien, too, starts out flat and downhill. That doesn't last, though.

As I ride along this stretch, I see this guy doing an extended pop-a-wheelie on one of those ATVs which I have seen dozens of out here in the country. Ha. He looks like he's having fun.

I am starting to get nervous about where I will sleep tonight. Unlike when I was following along the St. Lawrence, I have not passed any motels or Bed & Breakfasts or camping grounds. I have no Internet connection. There is nothing much here except distant, intermittent farmhouses. It is almost five o'clock. I suppose I will just have to keep going for now.

At some point in Saint Cyprien I stop by the side of the road to eat under the shade of a tree on someone's lawn. The house has no cars in the driveway. I figure nobody is home and I am not bothering anyone. I use my bicycle panniers as my table (yet another double use). I make myself a sandwich with the last of some turkey pâté and roasted red pepper hummus. I can only find room to eat half. My panic about accommodations for the evening is slowly mounting and my gumption for tackling these never-ending hills is waning. There is another disgustingly steep and tall hill right in front of me, waiting with resounding patience and smugness.

Except for stopping to take breaths on some of the hills, I have managed to stay on my bicycle and ride not walk all of the hills today. I am damn proud. I feel like a warrior princess.

At the top of the hill is another house. This one has a few cars out front. And two dogs. They come bounding out at me, no leash. Each time this happens, the intense and immediate terror is heart-stopping. The threat I perceive is sudden and ferocious. I am now quite adept at fishing out and engaging my dog spray in milliseconds, without thinking. The problem is that I don't want to use it. I don't want to hurt the dogs. They are house pets. When I was told before this trip that dogs would chase after me, I thought they meant wild dogs. A wild dog I think I could spray; it has not been taught boundaries, it has not been tamed. But a domestic dog? I can't do it. And so, with dog spray in hand, I don't use it and instead cry out in panicked English, "No! Please don't come here! No!"

Hilarious. Yes, that should do it, Christina. Your polite little plea, barely squeaked out above a whisper. Well done, dear.

They come right up to me, barking, snarling, but not attacking, of course. Then a man from the house comes out, laughing a little as he quiets the dogs and calls them off. Who knows what my face looks like, but he asks, in English, "Are you okay?"

I tell him yes, I am fine, but ask him if he knows where a motel or campground is. I tell him I have been looking for quite a long time now and have not passed any accommodations along my route and that I am starting to panic. This is when my voice cracks and the tears well up. I struggle to keep my composure. I can't let a few hills and a bit of desperation get the better of me. Not yet. There will be worse days, this is nothing, you can't fold already, I tell myself. I hold the tears back.

I have been travelling nearly three weeks now and each day there has always been an abundance of options for shelter; numerous motels and campgrounds. This is the first time that I have not passed a single opportunity for accommodation. Of course it happens on the day of brutal, never-ending hills. Today I set out from Rivière-du-Loup with a destination one hundred five kilometres away: Parc National du Lac Témiscouata. I knew I most likely would not make it all the way but I would set out and I would simply stop when I needed to. I assumed there would be as many choices for accommodations as there had been up to now. No such luck.

Screw Murphy and his stupid Law.

When the man sees my emotion he gives me a warm smile and tells me not to worry. He tells me that "just down the road" there is an "Éco-Site de la tête du Lac Témiscouata" with eighteen camping spots. He tells me the woman who runs it is named Colette and it is open and it is quiet and safe and secure and I am "very close" and I will be fine there. He says if there is any problem I am welcome to come right back and there is plenty of room here for me. I am flooded with relief. I thank him with the deepest sincerity. I feel fifty pounds lighter. He offers me some dinner but I graciously decline. I need to know where I will sleep tonight first. I continue on.

It is important to note that when people use relative terms like "just down the road" or "very close" they are speaking with their car brain. Also, when people give distances in terms of minutes: same deal. Sigh. I ride and ride. My panic begins to mount again.

But alas, there is no need to fear. After five more kilometres of QC-293 South, all of which were on a slight but glorious decline, I come to the QC-232 East junction. I turn left. After half a kilometre, I see it: a sign for the Éco-Site. My hellish, nine-hour day of riding straight up and straight down hills is finally coming to an end.

I go up to reception. Closed. The grounds, frankly, look abandoned. And spooky. There is no one around. There is one truck parked near the entrance. The door to the bathroom/shower, in the same building as the office and around the side, is open. The worst-case scenario is I shower and wild camp here. I can just crash on a site and pay in the morning. But why is there nobody else here? Where are the other campers?

There are two signs; one says "Plage," and the other says "Camping." With my bicycle in tow, I walk the camping grounds. There isn't a soul here. I'm starting to get pretty creeped out. Wild, crazy thoughts start seeping into my brain again, like when I was alone at Parc National d'Oka, or on that stretch of wooded road when I encountered the man with the open back hatch. *What if the man directed me to this deserted place so that he can come and find me here and...* Ridiculous. Those would be some pretty incredible odds, that I would stop at the very house to ask for help of one of the microscopic percentage of humans who are capable of harming another innocent human. But that's just what happened to the two girls whose car broke down in the woods in that disturbing movie "Human Centipede." That film...I am scarred forever. Or what if some other nutbar is here? I keep my wits about me, but again I have to forcibly coax my sensible, rational side to take control of my irrational thoughts and overblown fears.

I continue to walk, deeper into the campground, checking out the sites for appropriately-spaced trees and any sign of human life. There are trees a-plenty but not a single person to be found. I am simply unsure if I have the fortitude to stay on this seemingly abandoned campground all alone, *toute seule*.

Then I find one tent, beside a smoldering fire. I call out a hello but there is no response. I don't know if the presence of whoever's site this is will be comforting or will freak me out even more. I continue my walk-through. I come back to the entrance. I leave my bicycle leaning against a fence and follow the path to the beach. I walk the last step of the path, and then I step out into a magical world, a natural wonderland of mountain and lake, immense and breath-takingly gorgeous, and dazzling with sheer, deafening silence. I am stopped like a statue.

This is Lac Témiscouata.

It's like I've stepped into a mythical, enchanted kingdom. *Queendom.* What massive beauty, I am crushed by it. The mountains draw a thin, eloquent line between the bottomless lake and the never-ending sky. All one million shades of blue, from a navy black to a powder white, weave themselves across the water and through the air and between the clouds. Can a lake be this still? Like a piece of glass. A mirror. Not a soul around. Just me and this colossal, humbling beauty. The mountains are so perfectly reflected in the water that I cannot tell where the land dips beneath the surface and becomes only an impression. The clouds are like little snagged cotton balls. The perfectly clear and motionless surface of the water is like a portal between universes: the great sky and the mysterious depth of the sea, reality, and dream. I just stand there. I am captivated, I forget my fear and panic. I go ankle deep into the water, flip-flops and all.

Then I spot two people walking along, a ways down on the eastern shore. I know it must be the people from the empty campsite. I wait.

Indeed, they are the lone campers, Sylvie and her chum Egide. I ask if they would mind if I set up camp right beside theirs as I was "toute seule" and I would feel safer if I were close to them. Yes, of course, no problem, they say. We talk about what a wonder it is that there are no other people here partaking in this incredible beauty. Sylvie invites me to join them at their campfire later on. I thank them. I am boatloads relieved. I fetch my bicycle and head to set up my camp.

I choose site 16. The sites are set up in a horizontal figure-eight pattern with the southern edge of each loop sitting on the lake. These two prime spots, the edges of each loop, even have their own little path that leads to the water's edge. I am on a separate loop but still right beside Sylvie and Egide. It is perfect.

The two trees that I use for my hammock tent are the perfect distance apart from each other; the most ideal distance yet. I have become so confident in my knot tying that I am almost forgetting to test the knots after setting up. Dusk is approaching quickly. After my seventy-seven killer kilometre day under a blazing sun, tired, catatonic, I take my mug of wine down to the water and just sit there. What a day, what a day. I am thankful. Thankful for the man telling me about this place, for Sylvie and Egide's presence there, for the warm shower I just had, for this immaculate lake and majestic mountains, for making it here, and for doing what I'm doing. I feel like I am under a magical spell, incredibly, unwittingly, one I cast upon myself. I sit and I stare and I sip and I sit and I stare. I am in the sweetest stupor.

I finish the wine as the last light creeps away. I don't go to Sylvie and Egide's fire. I crawl into my cradle. I am asleep before my eyes close, deeply, like an old penny, wished upon long ago, tossed with hope, and still sitting, working magic, at the deep, murky bottom of Lac Témiscouata.

New Brunswick

"The journey of a thousand miles begins with one step."
-Lao Tzu

JULY 25ᵀᴴ – DAY 21

I awake just before sunrise. I have to pee something fierce but it is still too dark and too cold for me to even consider getting up to go relieve myself. Through the mesh window of my hammock tent, to my left, a thin line of bright red catches my eye. *What am I seeing?* Groggily, I squint through the mesh window of my hammock tent. Is that the black and red-checkered blanket I had seen draped over the picnic table at Sylvie and Egide's site? I squint some more, and then with a start, I check the time: it is quarter to five. That is the sun coming up.

Suddenly it is neither too far nor too cold for me to get up. I bolt out of my tent, I have the longest pee of my entire forty-one years of life into a bush, I grab my iPhone, and I rush to the water's edge.

Oh, my. Indescribable beauty. The sky is on fire. The lake is on fire. Long flames of red cherry and purple wine quietly, in slow-motion, erupt. Fingers of amber and blades of strong steel illuminate over silver sky and tumble down into an endless black lake. There is no Earth, there is no divide. Below and above are seamless. There is not another soul around to witness this miracle. Sylvie and Egide still sleep. I am the richest girl in the world.

I stay like that, under a timeless hex. Whenever later, I wake from the holy hold this sacred scenery has on me. I walk to a short length of old, dead log, I sit and breathe it all in, snapping photos with my iPhone all the while. An eternity passes, but in a moment. And then, after allowing itself to be beheld by my eyes and drunk by my open, thirsty heart, the sun tucks back beneath the billowy clouds. They are like a soft, patchwork quilt, coming apart at the seams from so much use and love. I go back to my cradle and snuggle in.

I don't rest long. Soon something else catches my eye. A double sun. I recognize and understand the strange sight I am seeing immediately. It is the sun poking its head out again, but this time, at this angle, it is perfectly mirrored in the lake. Once again, I bolt. I bust out of my hammock tent in a flash. In seconds I am again at the water's edge. My soul drinks again. The flames have been soothed and cooled by the crisp, shiny deep sky blue. Same sky, same sun, completely different mood and skyscape. There is nothing to say and nobody to say it to. This silence, this void of any need of words, is perfect. What electric peace.

Egide is up and has a fire going already. I approach.

"Bonjour!"

I ask if it would be possible to boil some water on his fire to make a coffee. He tells me he has boiling water already and sugar and milk and, yes, I am welcome to come partake. I grab my orange, plastic camping mug and my instant coffee packets.

Egide and I sit chatting while Sylvie sleeps. He asks me to guess his age. I say fifty-two.

"Sixty!" he tells me proudly.

He is a carpenter, retired. Sylvie is his boss, he tells me. He offers me yogurt. I decline. I have so much food, too much, I tell him. It feels good, peaceful, sitting and chatting with my neighbour.

Sylvie gets up at seven. I stay and chat a bit longer, then leave them to their privacy. I sit by the lake for another hour. It is the calmest bliss.

Then Sylvie comes out. She says Egide is hurt in the groin and cannot go out in the canoe with her. She asks if I would like to join her because the ride requires two people. Um…does a bear shit in the woods?

"Oui!" I tell her excitedly and immediately.

I pack up my camp and walk my fully-prepared bicycle over to their site. Then, off Sylvie and I push off into regal Lac Témiscouata. She is a wonderful companion and guide. Sometimes we sit in silence and just let the canoe drift. Other times she points out different animals that she sees or names the others we can only hear. She tells me she is native to these parts, that she has spent the last thirty to forty years watching these lands change. She points to some of the fallen trees and tells me how that area had become flooded and that all this water was never there before. She comments on the magnificence and majesty of the beauty. I can't agree with her more. I gush out a thank you for the canoe ride, basically out of nowhere, simply swept up in the moment. She gives a little laugh.

After about an hour and a half we bring the canoe back. My chance and sacred experience at Éco-site de la tête du Lac Témiscouata is coming to a close.

I walk my bike out to the front entrance, pay the sixteen dollars for my previous night's stay, and sit at a picnic table and eat. I haven't even begun my day's ride and I am feeling tired. Perhaps it is time for a day of rest? But I need to get somewhere where I can charge my ten-charge and my single charge, which are dead. My phone is also nearly dead. The nearest town is Cabano. I need to get at least to there. And then, you know how it is; if you can get to point A, you are probably also capable of getting to point B. The trick is to keep your points close together, create a series of small goals in order to achieve a big one. Like I did at my first ultra-marathon. Off I go…

Eight kilometres after leaving Éco-Site, I stop outside of a closed inn in Cabano, called Gare de Cabano. I look for and find an electrical outlet on its exterior walls. I plug in, pull up a chair, and chill as I gorilla charge my electronics. It takes more than an hour and a half, but I don't mind the rest. In that time, I complete my daily administration. I also drink down the delicious mango passion fruit juice that Egide gave me for my travels. It is delicious. I don't normally drink juice at all, except for that fermented grape one, of course.

I begin on the Trans-Canada Trail. I am to stay on here for twenty-six kilometres. About one kilometre in, I am revelling in how flat it is. I see the cutest little brown bunny. I call out a hello. I have seen deer, chipmunks, beavers, rabbits…the only thing I haven't seen yet is a moose. For that I keep hope.

So far today everything is as I need it to be; cloudy, flat, and the beauty redundant. There are not a lot of demands from the scenery to have its photo taken. There is just a beautiful, therapeutic repetitiveness and melodic monotony. Along this part of the route, the Trans-Canada trail is unpaved but it is made of hard-packed dirt and fine gravel. It is not bad at all.

Although I started the day in an uncharacteristic flat and even mood, at only eleven kilometres into today's flat Trans-Canada Trail, I have definitely made the transition into my ecstatic monkey mode once again.

With less than six kilometres left on the trail, I stop off at a rest stop and have a little meal of Camembert on an olive ciabatta bun, a tin of spicy Thai chili tuna with a packet of mayo, a few sips of Australian Barefoot Shiraz from my Cranks water bottle, and a cigarette. A few drops spit from the sky as I set off again at four-thirty.

Just before six in the evening, it starts to rain. At quarter after seven, it starts to pour. I keep on riding. I am so close to New Brunswick, I am too excited to stop. I pull over under a big pine tree and have some sips of wine. I wait a bit, listening, watching the rain come down. It shows no sign of stopping. I set off again.

Welcome to New Brunswick. I love that I actually have to pass under the overhead sign, an actual threshold to this next milestone of this transcendental voyage.

After a sixty-kilometre day, I am staying at the Ritz Motel in St-Jacques. It is cute and only $55 plus tax. Emotions are soaring. I have made it to New Brunswick. I order pizza. It is disappointing, just like last time. I watch a bad movie about a religious cult. The "comforts" of fast food and mainstream entertainment are not comforting at all. I don't drink wine or play ukulele. After tossing and turning for what feels like forever, I fall into an eventual sleep sometime after midnight.

"Wonder awaits those who wander."
-My friend Kirsten

JULY 26TH – DAY 22

I wake up at half-past eight. I had such trouble getting to sleep last night. I was agonizingly awake for hours, uncomfortable in a bed. This morning, my back is sore. I'd rather have slept in my hammock tent.

I get up and give all my camping cookware a proper wash as I boil water. Then I sit myself on my front step and have my morning coffee and cigarette. It has stopped raining but it doesn't look like it will hold off for long, the skies are a solid grey. I check my phone. Sure enough, it's calling for rain, all day long.

I'm feeling a bit deflated and like a weirdo again. I'm forty-one years old and spending my summer playing with my "toy bicycle." Fran Lebowitz, one of my literary crushes, said once in an interview that "bicycles are just toys, really." I was a bit deflated that my idol could say something so stupid. But she did, and it's in my head as I ride my silly little toy all day long as I wear dirty, stained clothes and steal condiments from restaurants and pee on roadsides like a stray dog. My hair is fried from the sun. I am covered in mosquito bites. I have one look every day and that's a scary, dirty mess. Then I look on Facebook and see all my friends having fancy cocktails and meals in exotic places and passing their time with large groups of friends in extravagant cottages. Why don't I crave to do something like that? Why was this the only thing that felt right to do? Why am I the only person I know doing something like this? Why am I so different and such a *freak?* I'm going to be single forever.

Today my destination, as I continue along the Trans-Canada Trail, will either be Saint-Léonard at sixty kilometres or Grand Sault at seventy-two kilometres, depending on the topography. There are campgrounds and motels available in both. For once, I checked ahead.

I really need to do laundry. The trail is dusty so my panniers and I got quite dirty yesterday. I can't bear to put on my damp, dirty riding clothes. Instead I am wearing my last fully clean outfit (my second of two sets of capris and tank top). It is perhaps a bit foolish but it's what is happening. I unplug all my pluggables and get going. Everything is fully charged except for me.

I stall leaving. Can you believe that I am actually afraid that my outfit is "too sexy?" The last thing I would want to do is attract any attention. Or if anything were to happen to me, they would say, "And what was she wearing?" I keep looking myself over in the full-length mirror. Well. I don't really have much choice. Anyway, it's a Lululemon tank top and MEC capris. You're being paranoid, I tell myself.

And as much as I didn't really drink wine last night save one lone mug, I take one big swig now as I'm leaving. I just feel like it. I can do whatever I want, right? I'm wearing flip-flops to ride across the country, for crying out loud. It›s quarter to eleven. Here I go again.

About a kilometre or two into my ride I come to a barrier. The path is closed off for some reason. Since I am stopping anyway, I have a second swig. I rejoin Rue Principale. Maybe I will pass a dollar store where I can get more baby wipes and Ziploc bags. They must have dollar stores in New Brunswick. Penny pinching is universal, right?

A kilometre or two later I make a quick stop for a final third swig. Oh, what would "they" say if they saw me day-drinking like this? *Who cares?* More glory moments.

In Ontario, the liquor store is called the LCBO. In Quebec, it is SAQ. What magical acronym do I look for in New Brunswick? I message my friend Amanda on Facebook Messenger since she is from here. I eagerly await her reply.

I was less than cheery about setting off today due to my lack of sleep, but there is no choice in the matter, you have to go. You do what you need to do. But now, not long after setting off, I am rather enjoying myself. As a matter of fact, these clouds are ideal, protective from the unforgiving sun, the temperature is perfect, I have drunk just the right amount of wine, and so long as the rain holds off, I actually feel my ecstatic phase coming on.

I marvel at what a drastic and elevated difference in mood I have undergone. Riding a bicycle is magical that way. It seems that I have taken to being depressed indoors, drinking in the morning, and only being able to get a good night's sleep in my hammock tent. I am beginning to worry about how I will assimilate back into my regular life come September.

An older gentleman passes me as I am stopped to have a cigarette. He twirls his umbrella as he walks along. He smiles at me and says hello. I melt. I, just like my father, get sentimental when I drink. I love any similarity I have with my father. It is a gift and an honour.

I pass some graffiti; the classic "fuck off." What a shame. A giant waste. That person had a platform and an audience and that is what he or she chose to say?

I come across a Dollarama. Yahoo! I buy: baby wipes, Ziploc bags, socks for those cool mornings in the hammock tent, lip smackers (I am down to my last one), travel size toothpaste, sesame snaps, a can of Alpha-Getti for lunch later today, and two small bottles of 50SPF spray. I have 85SPF spray but it is like spraying on that fake snow they decorate windows with at Christmas time. I want to offload it but can't bear the thought of just throwing it away, of wasting. My little shopping spree at Dollarama feels luxurious and fun.

I don't ride much farther before I stop at a neighbourhood restaurant to use the washroom, change into shorts, and, oh, well, sure, have a glass of wine. For such a casual place and such a low price, the wine is actually pretty palatable. I don't wince when I sip it. I also order a small plate of onion rings to accompany the conspicuous glass of mid-day wine.

The entire ride is flat with the occasional mild rolling hills; a smooth, peaceful glide.

After riding seventy-three kilometres, I arrive in Grand Sault. There are signs for camping at "Les gorges et les chutes." It sounds heavenly. I direct myself there. On the way, I pass the gorge. Its incredible depth and natural cavernous architecture are simply awesome.

If there is a truly bilingual place in Canada, it is New Brunswick. As soon as you cross the border into this province, all signs, even every street sign, is posted in both French and English. It seems that everyone speaks both languages completely comfortably and interchangeably. Although I just fell in love with Quebec, I am already being unfaithful. I love it here. You feel the difference in the province's personalities immediately. It's strange. Just by crossing an imaginary line. Both are wonderful but each is definitely unique. Here, the beauty is kept secret, tucked away, raw and unadultered. It is humble, rural loveliness. And way less religious.

Pat, at the front desk of the campground, is kind and caring. He wants to put me in a site directly beside the office building where he normally puts women who are alone for safety and security reasons. But I did not come all this way just to hide or cower. I tell him I need trees and that I am not worried about safety and security. He says he will come for a walk with me to pick out a site that will work for me. There are only three lots that sit right on the edge of the gorge, where one can see the falls and hear them, too. Well, guess which lot I get? I am beyond thrilled. I am maybe ten meters from the falaise. I can see the gorge and waterfalls even from within my hammock tent. I will hear the falling water all night long. This is unreal. How was this prime spot not gobbled up already?

When you follow your dreams, when you follow your heart, magic ignites, and hidden riches manifest.

Pat asks me why I have not brought a friend along.

I tell him, "Oh, you mean someone else who has the entire summer off and thinks that riding a bicycle from Toronto to Cape Breton is a good idea?"

We both laugh. Pat is darling.

Sure, I could wait to do this bike ride until I have someone to accompany me. I could wait until it is a safer world. I could wait until I have more money. On and on. There are plenty of reasons why I could or "should" wait to do this bicycle trip but none of them are any good. From what I gather, you only get one life and it's happening now. There is no wait.

Delivery! Pat comes with a wheelbarrow full of wood and his niece atop. I show him my hammock tent. He is fascinated. Oh, we have it all and know it all in Toronto, he says. I tell him I bought the hammock tent at MEC and it is also available for purchase online. I'm surprised he has never seen one with all the campers coming in and out of here. His delight and enthusiasm are infectious.

I drink wine, saw wood, and update Facebook. There is something uniquely satisfying about watching a post blow up with likes and comments. I drink more wine and work diligently at starting a fire. No dice. I feel like crying. It is dark. My immediate neighbours' fire roars away as they sleep. It makes my frustration multiply and my shame burn deeper. My neighbours from one lot over are still up and sitting at their fire. With some hesitation, I approach them.

Their names are Ed and Pauline and they drove here from Ottawa for Pauline's daughter's wedding. She beams with pride as she tells me this. They tell me the wood they bought from here is wet and they weren't able to start a fire with it either. That makes me feel better. They give me a couple of pieces of the wood they bought in town and a piece of cardboard to fan it. How kind of them.

I finally get my fire going. I sit in comfortable numbness, intoxicated by the wine and the fire and the sound of the waterfall and woozy with the satisfying fatigue of pedaling seventy-two beautiful kilometres. I go to bed.

I am out like the power in Toronto on August 14th of 2003.

"We do not see things as they are, we see things as we are."
-The Talmud

JULY 27ᵀᴴ – DAY 23

Last night on Facebook I posted a photo of my left arm tattoo. It is the first line of my favourite poem from Emily Dickinson, a poem I have concluded is about the forgotten wisdom and pure joy of riding a bicycle. My tattoo reads, "My wheel is in the dark."

I wrote, "Emily Dickinson, tonight my wheel is *not* in the dark. Tonight it shines. I am so happy. I am thankful I just keep following my heart, despite my head sometimes."

This is wiser than I meant it to be, I wrote this without thinking too much. It is a constant battle, though, isn't it? Or tug of war. An everlasting negotiation between the two. If the heart wins more often, I think it's a good life.

I wake just after eight and make myself a cold coffee, which really isn't bad at all. It is my second one like this thus far this trip. It just takes a little bit of work to dissolve whatever is in those Nescafé Sweet and Creamy instant coffee pouches. Ed walks by and we chat a bit. He is a down-to-Earth and genuine man. He, too, is curious and impressed with my hammock tent. He leaves and I pack up all my stuff, then wait around until ten when the office opens and I can buy laundry soap. The wash cycle is thirty-six minutes. I walk over to the washroom and take a thirty-six minute shower. It is glorious. I leave my 85SPF spray can and 70SPF lotion in the washroom. I really hope someone takes and uses these.

My neck is covered with welts; huge mosquito bites. I even have mosquito bites on my face. Ugh. I am quite the glamour girl these days.

I debate for a good long moment about going down the four hundred and one steps to view the gorge that Ed had told me about. In the end, I decide against it. The road is calling me. And this is a vacation; a time of peace, no stress. There is no way I can do all of the things. I am doing so many of the things and I am doing the main thing and that is riding my bicycle from Toronto to Cape Breton. That is a big thing. No need to feel pressure or upset that I cannot do it all. It is a long life—I can come back. I won't go down the steps, I want to get going, and that is perfectly okay.

As I am leaving with my loaded bicycle, I call out a goodbye to Ed and Pauline. Both call out a goodbye, and then Ed adds, "Be safe!"

There is something in the way that he says it. A heartfelt sincerity rings, it is not just some automatic parting phrase, I can see it in his eyes, too, and this moves me.

I will, Ed, I promise.

I quickly duck into the washroom on my way out. I change into my riding clothes, pluck my eyebrows, and put my mascara on. Off I go.

I had no idea before this trip that bumblebees make a clicking sound. I think it is the bees? Every time I hear the sound there has been a large bumblebee flying around. It sounds like they are loudly tap dancing on the air. I am confused, though. I have seen many bees in my life and have never heard this sound before. But I keep hearing it and it really seems to me that it is coming from the bees. I Google the sound and find an identical one but it is that of a katydid. But everything I am finding about katydids seems to say that they only come out at dusk or in the dark. All the times I have heard this loud clicking sound have been during the day. I'm confused.

The city girl will have to do some more investigating.

At exactly two in the afternoon, and five kilometres into a twenty-four kilometre stretch of the NB Trail, I stop. I visit nature's toilet, wash my hands with a baby wipe, and then stand and eat a can of Alpha-Getti. Believe it or not, I am actually looking forward to this meal. It was one of our favourites as kids and reminds me of another of our favourite snacks, crackers and honey. I drift into a memory… Angela wasn't born yet, it was just Carolyn and me. My mom was crying in the kitchen because she had nothing to feed us. We said,

"Mommy, we can have crackers and honey." I can still picture it perfectly; the big red box of Premium Plus saltines in the brown metal cabinet in our dining room, the squeezable bottle of Billy Bee honey in the kitchen cupboard.

My mother cried, "I can't feed you guys crackers and honey for supper."

We said: "Yes, you can! We'd love it!"

We were overcome with glee at the prospect of having this for dinner. I can still see her face, her eyes, as she watched us gobble down our favourite snack. She was mortified. Carolyn and I were ecstatic.

I drift back into the present and eat a packet of sesame snaps for dessert, concluding my lovely little lunch and melancholic reverie here under the shade of a tree alongside the trail.

My childhood wasn't perfect. But this trip is calling up much of the lost loveliness of it. The Talmud is so wise.

Later in the ride I arrive at a strange clearing of bulldozed gravel. It is unclear which way the path continues. While trying to evaluate the scene, I stop and eat another can of Alpha-Getti. A truck approaches with two men inside. I should probably mention now that since entering New Brunswick, I have not passed any cyclists on the trail. Zero. Nor are there any walkers. Just me, alone, all day long. I have encountered more than a few ATVs, which is ironic since all motorized vehicles are forbidden from the trails. I passed a car when arriving to this clearing. And now a truck.

As it comes near, I call out, "Excuse me!"

The truck slows and rolls its window down. I point straight ahead where there is a semblance of a path/road and ask if the trail continues this way. To my surprise, they tell me it does not. They point to a huge mound of gravel, about eight feet tall, and tell me it continues that way, up and over the pile. I am in disbelief. Yet another hilarious blemish on the NB Trail.

"Good thing you came by." I tell the men.

They ask me if I will be able to get my bike over the huge pile. I tell them I will be fine, yes, I'll manage. I am actually excited by the hard work it will be to get my bike over that little mountain. The route has been so flat that, incredibly, I feel like I am not getting enough exercise.

We start to chat. They ask me where I am from. I tell them Toronto, and that I rode all the way here on my bicycle. I am proud. They are impressed. The driver tells me he used to work in Toronto when he was sixteen years old.

He helped build the Don Valley Parkway. I tell him that we Torontonians call it the "Don Valley Parking Lot," because it is always maddeningly congested with traffic. We all laugh. I ask what is going on with this strange clearing of bulldozed gravel. They explain that there was a flood recently. They add that if I can't get my bicycle up over the embankment then I can follow the path I was originally going to mistakenly follow and that would take me to the road and eventually the road would meet up with the trail again. I thank them both for the chat and the advice.

"Good luck on your travels." the men tell me. I thank them again, and they drive off. It is now twenty after two.

I grunt and heave and push and drag and sweat and laugh and I get my heavy bike over the mound.

The NB Trail has turned out to be full of surprises and quite the obstacle course today. First, there was a stream crossing. Yes, the trail literally just goes through a little crick. Then there were the bulldozed hills of gravel. There have been fallen trees that I had to either move or walk my bike over. And now, quite unbelievably, I have come to a complete dead end at the edge of a small cliff. There is a huge gorge, maybe fifty feet across and fifty feet down. I can see the trail continues on the other side of the gorge. There is a sign here, right at the end and not before, that says: Trail Closed. Thank you, Captain Obvious. This same sign a little farther back would have been super helpful. I can see the same sign on the other side, too. Unbelievable. Too funny.

I turn back. About half a kilometre later, I see a little dirt and gravel path leading down a steep hill to a road. I carefully walk my bike down it. At the bottom there is a house and there is a man outside it, working in his garden. He tells me that the trail is closed and that the army has promised to come and fix it. He says that the gorge I just encountered (or perhaps the missing bridge that used to go over it?) has only been there for about a year. Perhaps this also has to do with the flood that the other man told me about? He asks where I am from. I tell him Toronto and that I cycled all the way here from there.

"Wow, you are quite the classic lady," he says to me.

Hmm. I'm not sure I understand this compliment. Maybe he meant that I am *not* a classic lady; the ornamental, less capable, stay-at-home, tucked-away-from-the-world type. Maybe he meant that I am a classy lady? I'm not too sure but I am sure that he meant something nice.

I join up again with the NB Trail on the other side of the gorge. It is lovely and definitely interesting, but it is sand and gravel and stones and makes for slow going. I weave along from side to side to find a smooth line. I constantly slip and slide as the back tire inadvertently slips on large, smooth rocks. Thankfully, this is not a race.

One! Two! Three! Three huge dogs come tearing out from a house along the path toward me!. I immediately stop my bicycle. Without thinking, I call out, "No, no, no! I'm okay! It's okay!"

I have the dog spray on hand but again, these are domestic dogs. Even though it is still an utterly terrifying experience, somewhere in the recesses of my logic and instinct I know that they won't actually attack me. My heart is pounding through my chest. They retreat, and I get back on my bicycle.

It's half-past four and I feel my mood begin to turn foul due to the terrible state of the NB Trail. I awkwardly meander my bicycle around yet another huge puddle surrounded by mud. I am slipping and sliding on the rocks at the side of it as I try to get around it. At just the same moment I hear yet another motorized vehicle coming from behind. It is a motor bike. It passes and I make it past the mud puddle without falling in. I return to the middle of the trail when I hear yet another motor vehicle right behind me. Again I move off to the side and wave him past. I'm trying to be polite but actually I am quite annoyed. This second motorbike passes and he is followed by an ATV that I didn't notice, and it almost runs me over as I angle in to rejoin the path. It also kicks up a lovely cloud of dust for me to ride through. Thanks for that. I still have almost nine kilometres to go on this forsaken trail. I have only traveled twenty-one kilometres and it has taken me forever.

Oh, look. Here they come a-freakin'-gain.

Two motorbikes and an ATV come from the opposite direction and pass me. I continue down the road. Not long after, I see an ATV up ahead of me, pulled over to the side of the path. I see a guy sitting in the flatbed at the back of the vehicle and another guy sitting in the driver's seat. What is going on here? I am immediately on guard. I take out and engage my dog spray. I continue toward the vehicle, slowly and cautiously. The path is secluded and, as I said, there are no other cyclists or pedestrians around. It would be incredibly easy for a motorist to attack me or snatch me up or rob me. I really don't think this is the case here, but it is only wise to be prepared for anything.

As I get close, I call out, "Is everything okay?"

"Flat tire. Help is already on the way," the guy in the back replies.

On this trail, that explanation makes total sense. In fact, I am more than shocked that I have not had a flat here myself. I pass the stopped ATV without incident.

After I've passed, the guy in the back calls out, "Thank you, anyway."

I wave, sheepishly.

At around six in the evening and with twenty-five kilometres still to go, I decide I have had quite enough of the damn NB Trail. I change myself into a car on Google Maps and pull onto the road.

At half-past six, I hear thunder.

Litter along the side of the road seems to be picking up again like back in Ontario. Bud Light can, Tim Horton's cup, Bud Light can, Tim Horton's cup. There are also bags of fast food garbage and the odd plastic soda bottle half-filled with a yellow liquid. I'm pretty sure I know what *that* is. I am incredulous and annoyed and disappointed and a bit shocked about all the garbage. I guess people are drinking and driving. I guess truckers are pissing into pop bottles. Okay, I get it, you need to pee. But then throwing it out the window? Really?

A trucker toots his horn when I wave hello. I love this. I remember when we were kids, being in the backseat of a car going on a trip somewhere. Carolyn and I waved like mad at the truckers and pulled our fists down, mimicking a horn toot, trying to get them to honk their horn for us. Oh, and when they did, what a sense of accomplishment and sheer joy. I may be forty-one years old, but it is still just as thrilling. I mean, it's not something you do driving a car, right? Or at this age. But when you're on a bicycle, it's totally normal. Different rules. Better rules.

It is after eight at night. I only have an hour before sundown. I am two kilometres away from my destination. There is a restaurant and I stop at it. I have fish and chips.

"Where did you ride from?" the waitress asks me.

"Toronto." I tell her.

She bugs her eyes out at me. "Wow," she says solemnly.

My self-created label of misfit disintegrates a bit more.

I arrive in Riverside Country Campground. Kenneth, in the office, is sweet and helpful. I tell him I need a site with trees for my hammock tent. He gives me a funny look, pauses for a second, then says, "Don't worry. We'll make sure you are taken care of."

I notice on the campground map that there are three cabins. "Oh, you have cabins, too?" I ask.

"No, no, I got rid of those a long time ago. That map is old," he says as he fills in my registration slip.

Then he stops. He looks up, looks at me, and adds, "Well. I do have one. Let's go have a look."

Exciting. I have never stayed in a cabin and the prospect of a new experience thrills me. "Well, how much would it be?" I ask.

"A campsite is thirty dollars. I can give it to you for fifty," Kenneth says.

"Okay. Let's go look," I reply.

It is darling, the cutest thing ever. I tell Kenneth immediately that I will take it. He explains that his mother actually lives here but she is away and it won't be a problem for me to stay one night. How lovely of him to go out of his way to make this available to me. Kenneth leaves and I begin removing my panniers from my bike and bringing them inside my adorable digs. Soon enough, Kenneth is back to deliver some free firewood. This is standard practice for this campground. What a sweet perk. The people from next door come and give me some kindling. They tell me that if I need anything at all while I am here to just come knocking. They also tell me that I am welcome to use their steps that lead down to the river, but I need to be careful as they are steep. I am touched by their kindness and thank them. All this warmth and generosity is a welcome ending to an otherwise frustrating day on the trail.

I settle in, and then go and shower. (I have my own toilet in the cabin but no shower.) I return to my little lodge, pour myself a glass of wine, and sit in silence on the porch. It is pitch black out. I sit and I sit, then I sit some more. There is no stress, no worry, just a resounding internal equilibrium that allows me to just be. No ants in my pants, no anxiety. Just warm, fresh country air. It permeates my nostrils, eye ducts, ears, through my hair, and every pore of my skin. It holds me in simple happiness. It is therapeutic for me to do this. Staying still for me is usually a huge challenge. After today's eighty kilometre ride in twenty-eight degree heat on a disaster of a trail, it is easier. I simply revel in the calm and the nothingness. It is needed, appreciated, correct.

My dad had a funny little plaque hanging in his place when we were kids. It read: "Happier than a pig in shit."

Agreed.

"The best thing we can do to make this world a better place is to lead by example and share the story."

JULY 28ᵀᴴ – DAY 24

I wake up around eight and make myself a coffee. I use the neighbours' stairs, as offered, and take them down to the river to drink. It's calming and soul-soothing just to be near any natural body of water. It feels balanced, all of life in sync, like home.

Some of my friends have been encouraging me to take a day of rest. The thing is that I rest every night. If I felt I needed one, I absolutely would take one. But I feel fine, energized, ready and eager to ride each morning. I'm happiest when I'm on my bicycle, just riding along.

I stop in at the office to thank Kenneth, and off I go.

Just inside Florenceville-Bristol, the French fry capital of the world (who knew?), there is a bridge going over the St. John River. It has two narrow lanes; one for each direction of traffic. It has a paved shoulder maybe half a meter wide. I decide it is safer to ride up on the cement curb that the guard rail is attached to instead, since it is almost a whole meter wide. However, once I get up there, I discover that on my bicycle I am taller than the guard rail. I can see right over it and into the water. I think about the strong backdraft that happens when trucks pass me. It is sometimes so strong that it forces me to hold on tightly to steer properly. I think about potholes and rocks. I really start freaking myself out.

I cross the bridge without incident but riding up on the curb like that was dangerous. I won't do that again.

In Florenceville-Bristol, I stop at a pizza place for lunch. It is the same pizza company I had ordered the second disappointing pizza from on my first night in New Brunswick at the Ritz Motel. But there is no other option. I have been craving a plate of pasta, and they serve pasta here. It looks like this chain pizza company will get a second chance to make a good impression.

I order the seafood pasta in a mushroom cream sauce. I am the only customer here aside from another table of two ladies who chat pleasantly the whole time.

The two ladies finish their meal. As they pass my table, the shorter lady asks me how my pasta is.

"Not great. Bland," I tell her. "But not too bad."

I hate being negative. The irony of hating to be negative is funny. The two ladies leave and I leave shortly after them. They are in front of the restaurant, taking a selfie of themselves.

"Would you like me to take a picture of the two of you?" I offer.

"That would be great! Thanks!"

I take a photo with each of their cameras. When they see my bike parked just behind them, they begin to ask me questions. When I tell him what I am up to, they become excited and start asking more questions.

Their names are Sharon and Pat. They are cousins. Pat is a retired high school English teacher. Sharon is a retired registrar from the University of Maine. Both these ladies are full of energy and smiles. I am sure it would be a hoot to hang out with them for an afternoon. Sharon, the shorter lady who spoke to me earlier, tells me that she thinks that what I am doing is wonderful and brave. She asks if I am on Facebook and if I would mind adding her so she could follow my journey. I tell her I would love that. I add both Pat and her. I take a photo of them and tell them what a pleasure it is to meet them.

I have met countless wonderful women on this trip. Every single one of them has become excited when I tell them what I am doing and has been sincerely if not passionately supportive and encouraging. They tell me I can do it. Not one of them has thought that what I am doing is silly or too dangerous. It means the world to me.

I am not some weirdo—I am brave and adventurous.

Like has often been the case this trip, it begins to rain just as I begin pedaling. That darn Murphy guy again! It changes from soft rain to hard rain, back and forth, for the rest of the afternoon.

Next I reach Hartland, home of the world's longest covered bridge. It is one thousand two hundred eighty-two feet long. I had no idea this was even a thing, covered bridges. They are cool looking and certainly a token of nostalgia. It opened in 1901. I take a picture. At this moment, it begins to pour down…and hard. There is a gift shop beside the bridge. Finally, I am sure to find postcards for all my non-Facebook friends. And shelter. I go there.

I walk into the gift shop. As I am entering, there is a couple exiting. The man stops when he sees me. "Hey! We've seen you before!" he says.

I look back and forth from his face to his wife's, trying to place them.

"We were at Camping Chutes et Gorge. We were behind you in line in the office. Remember? The man sent us to the other campground where he told us it would be nice and quiet?"

I squeal. "Oh my goodness, that's right! Yes! I do remember you guys!"

I have met many kind and caring people along this ride. It is pretty awesome. But what I don't get to experience much during this trip is being recognized. Someone who knows your face. Familiarity. I love the exploring, the learning, the newness of everything and everyone. I love it. But how wonderful, the joy of recognition. It's a sense of community and belonging.

We stand there and chat. The man tells me that the other campground was lovely and quiet, as promised, and that they had really enjoyed their time there. They too are from Ontario. When I tell them what I am up to, the woman tells me that she had biked PEI by herself before. I am thrilled to hear this. She says that when she did it she took her sweet time. I tell her I am doing exactly the same thing. It is such a thrilling surprise to run into this lovely couple. Their names are Jim and Marlene.

The rain continues to pour, ladle after ladle, the air is pure soup. I wait outside the gift shop for it to calm. After a short while, it slows a smidge. The ants in my pants have won the wager against my no-rain-gear, cold-fearing self. Time to go.

All day I have caught glimpses of the NB Trail, which basically runs alongside the route I am taking; the 105 South. The trail definitely looks flatter than the road. But every single section I have seen looks as rocky and gravelly and puddle-filled as the horror that I endured yesterday. I definitely made the right choice in acting as a car today and taking the road. The only major drawback to the roads is the dogs. I pass a house with three little doghouses in front. Immediately my anxiety skyrockets and I try to keep as quiet as a mouse. I pass another house where there is a dog lying down out front. I break out into a sweat and hold my breath and make it by unnoticed.

At a quarter to four, the rain stops and the sun comes out. I am glad that I won't have to set up my camp in the rain. Except for a mild case of rain at Camping Rivière-Ouelle back in Quebec, which already feels like a lifetime ago, I have never had to set up camp in the rain, never mind a heavy one. Likewise, I still have not yet had to have a cold shower or shit in the woods. Life is good.

With ten kilometres left to go, I spot some antique Esso gas pumps. I stop to take photos.

A man from the house next-door sees me. "Hey. If you like that, I'll show you a few things."

He comes over and opens the massive door to the garage behind the pumps. He invites me in to have a look. I follow him inside.

There in the garage is a tremendous collection of antique signs, cars, bicycles, sewing machines, trucks, and all kinds of miscellaneous, cool rarities. Standing among this precious, aged collection makes me feel like I am stepping back in time. It is magical, nostalgic, and fucking cool. I take one million photos. There is a beautiful Harley Davidson motorcycle. And then. There is an old Chevy truck he is rebuilding. It is sexy. Not a bad hobby, this kind stranger has. We chat for a bit. He has a really adorable little chuckle. I tell him I am headed to Cape Breton.

"Our daughter goes to university right there. It's about a six-hour drive from here. You've got a bit to go, still," he tells me.

Ha. Yes. That's an understatement. I like how he said "our daughter" and not "my daughter." I bet he's a good husband. He wishes me well on my journey, and as I am leaving, somewhat out of the blue, he calls out to me, "Life is good!"

I love this. I tell him I agree. It is. I tell him I have that exact little phrase written in plastic letters on my fridge at home.

"Life is good," he repeats.

Yep. And indeed it bears repeating. And so are people.

I stop at a Tim Horton's in town just before arriving at the campground to buy a sandwich to bring to the park for dinner. I think this may be the friendliest town I've been to yet. The man behind me in line strikes up a conversation about my bike trip. He tells me about his cousin, a woman, who had biked from the west coast across Canada with different friends along the way. The boy behind the counter chimes in and tells me he is more of a runner.

"Me too, actually. Have you run a marathon yet?" I reply warmly.

"Oh, not yet, I need to quit smoking first."

We laugh. I tell him it is great that he is running and good for him. Then I say to the boy making my sandwich, "Can I please have a lot of ketchup packets in the bag?" I say this with a big, sheepish grin.

He grins back. "Sure." He puts a handful in.

I smile bigger, lean in, and press him. "Can I have more?"

I see he is amused. He smiles larger, too. His eyes are wide as he puts another huge handful in.

My eyes light up. "Thank you." I croon.

We both laugh. I don't think he knows what to make of me and my big helmet head and goofy grin and obsession with ketchup. That guy has a really wide, sincere smile. How contagious it is.

Sixty-three kilometres of pedaling has landed me at Yogi Bear's Jellystone Park. It has water slides and mini golf and bouncy castles and loudspeaker announcements beginning with, "Attention, all Jellystone campers." There are just loads of kids and families. And me. The thunder begins to sound and the wind picks up minutes after I finish registering and finding my site. I race to get my hammock tent set up before the rain comes. Miraculously, I do.

A dad and two kids from across the road, which is ever so cutely called Picnic Basket Lane, come over to ask questions about my hammock tent. We have a good little discussion. The kids are friendly, sweet-faced, well-behaved, and polite. The dad tells me about tree tents and shows me them online. Very cool. He tells me if I need anything at all to just come on over. I melt and thank him. Then the rain begins to come down, down, down.

I climb into my hammock tent and watch the first episode of *Stranger Things*. There is free Wi-Fi here. I am instantly addicted. The rain eventually stops. I get up, eat a bit, and then go and buy firewood for something to do. When I return, a little gang of five-to-ten-year-olds have stopped their bicycles behind my lot and beside where my hammock tent is hanging.

"Cool tent!" one of the kids calls out to me.

They're adorable. They are all looking, fascinated, at my flying saucer-like accommodations.

"Thanks, guys!" calls back the forty-one-year-old woman.

Too funny.

I have trouble starting a fire, yet again. I am a terrible Girl Scout. In desperation, I throw in both bandannas from my pirate get-up to start the fire, hoping for the same magic that the Smartfood bag held for me back at Oka. No such luck. I am crushed. I drink milk and a Gatorade G2. I'm thirsty, and quite the anomaly, I don't feel like drinking wine.

Maybe it's the rain, maybe it's my continued failure at being able to start a fire, but I feel fed up and grumpy. Maybe the novelty of all this is simply finally wearing off. Maybe I'm just tired; mentally, not physically. I actually love the hills, which seem to be steadily increasing. I want the challenge and the exercise. There has been nothing I can't handle. So far. But I have had all this gumption and enthusiasm and passion coursing through my veins. "It's at least fifty-one percent mental," I've always said about my marathons, specifically, but also about any challenge in general. If my enthusiasm begins to wane, will I have enough energy, fire, and determination to make it to the end of the Cabot Trail?

With the campfire finally roaring, but with my own spark snuffed and cool, at quarter to eleven, I crawl into my hammock tent.

JULY 29TH – DAY 25

I wake up just before eight. I can't get a fire started, shockingly, but the embers
from last night's fire are still hot enough for me to heat up the water in my
small metal pot to almost boiling. Along with a cigarette, I enjoy the coffee
that, may I state proudly, is too hot to drink immediately. I pack up and get
on the road. I am no longer acting as a cyclist on Google Maps itinerary as it
keeps leading me to the NB Trail, which is unrideable, to put it kindly. I am
taking and following the 105 all the way to Fredericton.

No sooner do I start out when I come face-to-face with my favourite
terror; an unleashed dog barrelling toward me with a vicious bark and a menacing snarl. Instinctively I reach for my dog spray, but I realize I brought it
into my hammock tent with me last night, as always, but forgot about it and
left it there where it remains, wrapped up and bundled away inside my tent in
my back pannier, completely inaccessible. I have no choice but to continue on,
unarmed, in the direction of where the dog is waiting for me. Eventually the
dog retreats to the house without event. I am sure this will always be the case,
but until the dog's withdrawal actually happens, the confrontation continues
to petrify me.

I have only just begun and already there is breath-taking beauty to behold.
My sour mood from last night lifts from my shoulders and evaporates into

the clean, crisp, country air. My regular feelings of bliss and gratitude return in tidal waves.

My little game of riding along the white painted line is out the window in this province. Cycling in New Brunswick, certainly along the trails but even along the roads, is more like mountain biking where you are constantly navigating to find your line; a path suitable to travel along.

I stop at the Irving in Meductic to use the restroom. There are a couple of gentlemen, one younger, one older, sitting at the back of the store, having a coffee. There is an older lady serving at the counter. The older gentleman gets up, comes toward me, mid-store in one of the few aisles, and asks where I am coming from. I tell him I rode here from Toronto. All I see is the lady's face popping into sight from back where she is, like she has a projectile head, Inspector Gadget-style. "My word!" she exclaims solemnly.

I can't help but laugh.

The three of us strike up a conversation. They tell me that the old highway, which is what I am travelling, is going to end soon. I will either have to go down to the walking bridge or up to join the Trans-Canada Highway. The younger gentleman has joined us now, too. He shows me on his iPhone using Google Earth where the walking bridge is that, he tells me, the government spent a million and a half dollars to build. The old bridge got flooded out when they built the dam, he informs me. I am learning a lot about this bridge. These people seem pretty stoked about it. Then the younger gentleman shows me Google images of the bridge. It does look pretty. It's a suspension bridge. My only hesitation is that I would have to follow the NB Trail for a bit to get there. Oh, man. I mull it over as I eat some baked chips and salsa and drink my coffee in front of the Irving. The woman from the front counter keeps coming out to tell me more things; what a scenic ride I will have through New Brunswick and Nova Scotia and what sights I will see. She is excited for me and my trip. It melts my heart. I decide that I need to see this bridge. Wish me luck.

Before reaching Richy Road, the road that the super friendly crew from the Irving gas station told me I need to take to get to the bridge, I pass my first cyclist! This is the first cyclist or pedestrian that I have passed since entering New Brunswick. I'm not kidding. When he sees me, he glides over to my side of the road and asks where I have come from.

"Toronto," I tell him.

"And where are you biking from?" he clarifies.

"Toronto," I say again.

"Wow!" he says. "Where did you start from today?"

"Woodstock," I reply.

He tells me, like my friends at Irving just a few minutes earlier, that this road will be ending and that I need to take the Trans-Canada Highway. I ask him about the suspension bridge. He says that the highway will be much faster. I ask him if the bridge is something that I should perhaps see since I can take the Trans-Canada Highway anytime in a car.

He thinks for a short moment. "Yeah, maybe you should take the bridge."

His name is Bob. He tells me he lives around here and that if anything goes wrong on my route I am welcome to come stay at his house. Just like that. Yet again.

I turn down Richy Road. Hallelujah, Bob was right. The NB Trail actually *is* paved on this section. "Nineteen sixties pavement," he had told me. I can see that it is in some disrepair and I understand his lament but I am nonetheless thrilled. Woot! Woot!

Short-lived "woot, woot." The paved surface ends just before the suspension bridge and it turns back into the NB Trail I know and loathe.

Sigh.

However, would you look at that...

A wide open lake roofed with exclamatory clouds bursting from an unknown heavenly vortex just beyond the blanket of deep green pines bordering and perfectly reflected into the unbelievably still waters. The sapphire sky too, is dancing on the water, echoing the enthusiasm of the clouds above, and without even a ripple. Such wide open space but not a sound in the air. There is only resounding calm, piercing solitude, and this lovely little lake. Like so many of these moments, there isn't another soul around, all this beauty and serenity is just for me. I can't resist stopping to drink it all in. I pour myself a glass of wine and light a cigarette and sit on a large piece of driftwood.

Uh oh. Next thing you know, I am earning a new Girl Scout badge: my first shit in the woods. Yes, the glory moments. Thank heavens for baby wipes. I text my friend Kirsten immediately to tell her. She understands the hilarity of this rite of passage. I've earned this badge, now if I could just perfect my fire-starting skills...

In my empty chip bag I deposit my garbage of a cigarette butt, three soiled baby wipes and a granola bar wrapper. I fold the chip bag and tuck it into my pannier. As I begin to ride along, I remember that I have a sandwich in the pannier, too. The folded chip bag is right beside a sandwich I bought earlier and was hoping to enjoy later. Oh, man. Yes, folks, that's what we call roughing it; your ashtray and toilet garbage side-by-side with your next meal.

The suspension bridge is modest and pretty. I ride over it and beyond. My head is in the clouds. I am loving every moment, every pedal, every tree, every bee, every cloud, and every absence of every city sound. I am near giddy with the simple joy of riding my bicycle. I am carefree and happy as a child. I could be in the *Guinness Book of World Records* for being the oldest girl in the world. It's how I act and how I feel.

Yesterday I noticed I have a rash behind my armpits toward my back on both sides. It must be a heat rash. The other thing I'm noticing this morning is that I'm feeling quite sore *down there* quite early into my ride as opposed to only near the end of a day's ride. To help remedy the pain, I shift my weight. It is then that I realize I have been "left lip favouring." So now I am on the right. I will have to keep *lip shifting*. So that's a new brutal reality. More glory moments. My poor vagina.

Thanks to the wine, I soon stop to pee. I remember being a little kid, maybe five years old. We were at Sears. My mom was buying me new underwear. It was a package and each pair had a day of the week on it.

"Mommy, why do we have to wear underwear?" I had asked her.

She thought for a moment, then said, "To catch the drips."

Well put, Mom. Now, more than ever, she couldn't be more right. That's exactly what it's for when you are peeing in bushes all across the country. I get back on my bicycle, also my one-walled washroom stall, and carry on.

Unexpectedly I see a sign for camping in five hundred meters. It is only two in the afternoon. I look on Google Maps. I have traveled only forty-two kilometres. That means that there are still sixty kilometres to Fredericton, my next destination. It's perfect, I decide. I am lightly day drunk, the sun has come out, there really isn't much thinking needed. Although I have not taken a day off yet, a mere forty-two kilometre ride is like a day of rest and today I think I shall just call it quits and relax the rest of the day. After a full day of rain yesterday, I could use it.

I pull off and register at this mostly deserted campsite called Sunset View Campground in Hawkshaw. The peace and privacy is just what I need. I will play my ukulele and even go for a swim in the pool.

As always, like a good Girl Scout, the first thing I do is set up my hammock tent. Every setup is unique. This one is on a steeply sloping small hill. I am in the first lot right beside the office building and I have zero neighbours. Since there is no view from any of the sites, none are near the water, any site is as fine as the next, unlike back at Camping Chutes et Gorge. One must cross the road to see the beautiful Saint John River. I hang my tent at the highest height yet. I have to manoeuver skilfully to jump up and in. I take a nap. It is such a rare treat to enjoy some relaxation during the daytime instead of sweating and baking in the sun or being rained on.

I go for a swim. Incredibly, it is my first time with my head under water all summer. It feels damn good, cool and refreshing, easy. My weightlessness is shocking. I still need to skinny dip at least once. Not here, not now, but some-time. I thought about it back at the suspension bridge but decided against it since there was a mass of reeds blanketing the shore and also I could not see the bottom of the water.

After my swim, I take a shower. Then I just sit at my little picnic table and write postcards. My more than thirty dollars' worth of stamps are caked together from being rained on. I carefully separate them from each other and borrow some tape from the office to attach them to the postcards. Other campers begin to arrive. Later I will go to the riverside with my ukulele to watch the sunset.

As I am about to leave to do exactly that, Doris, an older woman I had met in the washroom earlier, comes by my site with her husband, Harold. She had told him about my bike trip and wanted him to meet me. I feel honoured. They are from Maine. We chat a bit and they wish me well on my journey.

The sunset is stunning; the colours, the reflection in the still water, and nobody out here to see it save for me. Not a single other soul as far as the eye can see. Incredible. What could be a better thing to do than witnessing this, I wonder? Where is everyone?

I come back to start my fire. It's plain embarrassing—troubles again. An adorable, blond-haired little boy approaches me somewhat timidly and offers me his help with the fire since, he proudly explains to me, he went to outdoor camp and has learned some tricks. How precious. I melt.

"I would love your help since I am not talented at starting fires whatsoever," I tell him.

Then a little girl and her mother approach. I assume the boy is her son and I explain to them that he must have noticed me having trouble starting my fire because he has come over to help. Well, before you know it, I have the whole family there, mom, daughter, two sons, and father, all collecting kindling, fanning, blowing, trying to get the fire going. It's both touching and absolutely hilarious. Mom and Dad are Kristen and David; the blond-haired boy is Cailin, his sister is Eden, and his brother is Dawson. They are a beautiful family and they come from Guelph, Ontario. Between the six of us, we finally get the fire going. I thank them, especially Cailin.

The fire is still roaring now as I lay in the cocoon that is my hammock tent. I am imagining my apartment back in Toronto, trying to deduce if there are properly-placed beams behind the drywalls for me to set up my hammock tent there. It would certainly be a unique set-up, one I would probably only use if I have no Airbnb guests as it would be just a little odd but oh, so comfortable. I honestly don't know how I'll ever get to sleep in a regular bed again.

JULY 30TH – DAY 26

I wake an hour before the sun. I ride down to the lake to see the sunrise but only stay a few moments as the sky is dull and lackluster, hidden by a solid sheet of grey cloud. I gather kindling like Outdoor Captain Cailin taught me to do and begin attempting to restart my fire. Success! I make my morning coffee and have a cigarette. It is truly the perfect recipe to ensure that all important washroom visits happen before leaving instead of later on, potentially on the side of a road. No need to earn that Girl Scout badge again. I begin to pack up my camp.

As I am doing so, shy and helpful Cailin saunters by again. He calls out a hello. It's pretty endearing to witness his obvious internal battle of wanting badly to help with the fire and his shyness. He comes over with some cardboard and begins to fan my fire.

"I think it's out for good now," I say.

"Yeah," he agrees.

He ambles off. Then, just before I am leaving, he comes back over again. "Do you want this cardboard for some other camping you do?" he offers.

I melt into a puddle. "That would be great." I tell him.

I don't really have room to pack up thick leaves of cardboard, but how on Earth can I say no to this sweet, helpful little boy? I pack Cailin's cardboard in my pannier.

I am on the road before eight. It is chilly. I wear capris with a tank top and a hoodie instead of my regular lighter riding gear. Of course, before long, the work from the pedaling warms me, and the sun gets brighter and warmer. I take off the hoodie.

When I get to the little town of Lake George I see a sign on the other side of the highway I am travelling beside that simply says: "RESTAURANT." It has been a long time since I have had a delicious egg breakfast. I detour. There is also an ANBL sign (the blessed abbreviation that Amanda informed me of, Alcool Nouveau-Brunswick Liquor, also a completely bilingual acronym) beside the restaurant sign. It's perfect.

Four eggs, in-house made whole-wheat toast with butter, peanut butter and jam, baked beans and coffee with milk. It is called Acorn Restaurant and the atmosphere is lively. I like it. I can tell from the amount of traffic and high energy of the patrons that I am near a major city. Fredericton is close. After my meal, I go next-door to the gas station and buy a bottle of red. It is called "Smoking Loon" and it has a bird on it. I laugh and think of the Portlandia skit "Put a bird on it." Great show, hilarious skit.

I tuck the bottle of wine into my pannier, put my helmet on, and am getting ready to leave when about a dozen bikers, all dressed in black leather and club jackets, pull up. I notice a patch that says "Mississauga" on one of the men's jackets.

"Are you from Mississauga?" I blurt out.

"Yep," the burly, bearded biker replies.

"Oh! I'm from Toronto! Did you guys ride all the way here?" I ask excitedly. It's somewhat of a stupid question, I recognize.

"Yep, did you?" the man asks.

By this time most of the other guys have gathered and are listening to our exchange.

"Yep," I reply.

"On that?" he asks incredulously, looking at my bicycle.

"Yep," I say proudly.

Next thing you know I'm chatting it up with this group of bikers. Like everyone I've met along this journey, they ask, "By yourself?"

"Yes, by myself," I tell them with confidence.

They tell me that I am brave. I can tell I have impressed this group of large, tough-looking men and I just love the irony. And am I really so brave to venture out into a world where I have met countless kind, caring, friendly souls? Am I brave now, amongst these dozen sweetheart bikers full of smiles, encouragement, and warm wishes? The only thing I am brave enough to do is to believe in the goodness of people.

The whole lot of these tough-looking men are kind and lovely. Someone suggests we get a photo. I am thrilled. I am beaming. This is so cool. We take the photo. Before I leave, I shake the hand of each member. The handsome president, Roger, suggests that we add each other on Facebook, and we do. As I ride away I cannot wipe the smile off my face. I love Harley Davidson motorcycles and feel an acute affinity to the sub-culture of motorcycle clubs.

I am riding down French Village Road, a quiet, low-traffic road, near Fredericton. A car passes me, pulls over about thirty meters in front of me, and a man hops out. He is flailing his arms at me. As I get closer, I see he is waving a water bottle and a package of trail mix at me. "Here! Take this! I got it for you! I think what you're doing is great!"

All that in the first sentence and one breath. I laugh. "What is it I'm doing?" I ask him.

He replies with a question. "Are you from Fredericton?"

I tell him I am from Toronto, that I rode here from there, and that I am on my way to do The Cabot Trail.

"See! You're cool," he croons.

He tells me that he and his wife (whom he has been with since she was sixteen years old, he adds proudly) are teachers; he has just retired and she has one more year to go. He assures me he isn't flirting with me, he just thinks that people who do the kind of thing that I am doing are awesome. I'm flattered. I also understand his need to clarify that he is not hitting on me and I really appreciate it.

He tells me about a German couple who are RVing it (and the RV is designed by the engineer husband) across Canada for a year and a half. He met them in much the same way he is meeting me now. He befriended them, and then brought them a crate full of vegetables from his garden to take with them on their journey.

This man is happy and enthusiastic. I love his energy. His dog, head hanging out the window, is named Parker, and his own name is Bruce. He tells me he saw me a little ways back, and he rushed to the store. There was a line-up, he lost track of me, he looked for me again, he found me, and voilà. What a doll. I am moved by his thoughtfulness and effort. I thank him sincerely. And actually I am out of water. We add each other on Facebook, and then go our separate ways.

As he is driving away, he calls out his car window, "I love you!"

And there is no misinterpreting his meaning. He means it in the sweetest, purest way. What a beautiful thing to say.

"I love you, too!" I call.

And I mean it.

I am so not alone out here.

At two in the afternoon, after sixty-six kilometres in sunny twenty-seven degree heat, I arrive at Christina LaFlamme's house. Yes, you read that correctly. Christina is my name twin and we have known each other through Facebook for the past few years. Our "cyber paths" crossed due to our having the same name. When Christina saw on Facebook that I am doing this bike trip and that I would be passing by so nearly, she invited me to stop in. We would finally meet. I accepted graciously and immediately.

When I arrive, her husband Mathieu is in the driveway. An absolutely adorable little boy, Félix, comes to the front door, excited at my arrival, inviting me inside. Then out comes lovable little Annabelle, and then, finally, Christina.

She has the kindest eyes and prettiest smile and I love her immediately. Félix and Christina help me carry my stuff downstairs. Their house is huge and gorgeous, including their finished basement. She shows me the luxurious bathroom I will have all to myself. It is swankier than any hotel washroom I have ever seen. She has already set out a towel and washcloth for me. Then she sets up the laundry machine for me to do any washing I may need to do.

"Félix, come upstairs, let Christina settle, she'll come up when she's ready," Christina says leading adorable Félix upstairs by the hand.

I admire her wisdom in recognizing I might be tired. I am.

As I sit alone downstairs, decompressing, hearing Christina, Mathieu, Félix, and Annabel carry on as they were, I marvel at the beautiful reality of this situation. Christina and her husband have invited me, a stranger, here to share a night with their family. Will people believe these never-ending acts of human kindness, trust, and generosity when I tell them?

Félix speaks both French and English and switches back-and-forth between the two languages effortlessly. As does the rest of the family, including little Anabelle. Félix is only five and Anabelle is only two. It is truly impressive. I have already said it but it bears repeating: New Brunswick is, by far, the only truly bilingual province in all of Canada.

I shower and throw on jeans and the smock-style shirt that Darren bought me as a gift for this trip. It looks like a huge potato sack on me, but it is the only acceptable "dinner wear" I have for a social setting. I present Christina and Mathieu with the bottle of Smoking Loon. Christina and I drink it. Mathieu has a beer. We all sit outside on the back porch. We look at maps and at the LaFlamme ancestry book that Christina has. She spells her name with a capital "F" and I do not but we discover that we both have Quemeneur as a common ancestral last name. We decide that we are sure we are related and the case is settled. I have a new cousin. The family tie is confirmed when she suggests we open a second bottle of wine.

We have chicken wings on the barbecue and a salad made from greens from Christina's friend's garden. We also have marinated potato slices, also done on the barbecue in tinfoil. For dessert there is a pie and Christina makes fresh homemade whipped cream to put on top. I am full but can't help myself from partaking in each new offering. I am bursting. It is a wonderful meal and I truly feel at home.

I am so full that my stomach hurts. To be honest, I also feel a little drunk. I have surpassed my very exact personal consumption limit of one bottle of wine. Even a glass more is too much, and coupled with the generous meal, I really need to lie down. The plan is to take a walk after dinner, but I tell Christina I need to have a nap first. When she comes down to fetch me, it is useless. I am done, and it's a terrible shame. My friend Daniel once said about me: there is no dimmer switch with me: I am either full of energy or sound asleep. No in between.

He is right.

"A candle loses nothing by lighting another candle."
-James Heller

JULY 31ST – DAY 27

I had trouble staying asleep last night but this time it wasn't because I was in a bed. In fact, it was dreamily comfortable as I lay buried in the coolness of the sheets. It was a futon, which I did not unfold—I tucked myself in it like a wiener in a bun. And the pillow is made from hulled buckwheat, Christina had explained to me. It was like resting my head on a firm, jelly donut. The only reason I couldn't sleep was because I had crashed so early. Six hours is the maximum I need. My body is a precise machine.

In the morning, Christina, Mathieu and I enjoy real espressos. What a treat. Mathieu busies himself looking at my routes and suggesting stops.

"He's a planner," Christina tells me.

She makes buckwheat crepes for breakfast. They are delectable and I have three. Then, sadly, it is time to go.

Christina and Mathieu help carry out and attach my four panniers to my bicycle. I say goodbye to my new cousin and her amazing family. Félix and Annabelle say goodbye as they watch television together, as adorable as can be. I set off minutes before nine.

Au revoir, ma cousine. À la prochaine.

Along the Valley Trail in Fredericton I spot a man picking berries. I saw people picking berries along the trail yesterday, too. I ask him what kind of berries they are. He explains to me that they are choke-cherries and that they are edible, although dry and bitter. He says they are best used to make jam.

He tells me that at The Pumpkin (Moxon's Country Pumpkin) up ahead, there are jars of choke-cherry jam for sale. I am thrilled that this man is so knowledgeable. I will keep my eye out for The Pumpkin. He hands me a little branch of the cherries. I put a couple of the berries in my mouth. He's right. They are quite tart but I can imagine that the sugary jam would be delicious. I wish him a great day and we each carry on.

Another flash lesson for the city girl.

I stop at an Irving before exiting Fredericton and stock up my food stores with a tuna sandwich, a salmon sandwich, and half a liter of milk. I also buy a coffee with milk.

"Nice day for biking," the sweet, young girl behind the counter says to me.

"Yep. You'll never guess where I've biked from," I reply.

"Where?" she asks.

"Toronto," I say.

"*Get! Out!* That is the *best* thing I've heard all day. That is the best thing I *will* hear all day. That's *amazing.*"

Seeing these incredulous, happy reactions never gets old. I feel fortunate that I have this awesome conversation starter and smile-infector to share. She asks me if I feel in better shape than when I started.

I tell her, "Actually, no. I feel I'm in the same shape as when I started; stronger, yes, but visually, overall, basically the same shape."

I don't tell her that I know exactly why that is, but it can be summed up in four words: daily bottle of wine.

Her co-worker approaches and the girl turns to her and exclaims, "Do you know where she just biked from?"

I am thrilled at how excited she is for me and about my trip. I pay for my stuff, and we say goodbye.

I look back as I walk from the gas station with my bicycle, drinking my coffee. I see her looking at me, giving me the biggest grin and the most enthusiastic thumbs up through the window. I can't help but crack up laughing. Her energy is fantastic. I love sharing the joy of this special journey with others. It is like the flame of a candle; it loses nothing of its light by lighting another candle. Likewise, the joy and wonder of this ride I am doing seems to be contagious and as it spreads I am lifted higher and higher.

To start my ride today, I decide it is safe to take the trail since the conditions here close to Fredericton have been favourable. Wherever the trail crosses a road, the drivers invariably stop and wave me to cross first. Even when I have already come to a full stop because they arrived before me, they still wave to me to go first. Little gestures like this do a lot for the soul, I tell you. I hereby declare it my continued duty to carry on this small, important work once I'm back in the big, busy city of hungry, neglected souls. A tiny pebble can stop a huge machine, and a smile, a small act of kindness, can save someone's day.

At half-past ten, I stop along the side of the trail to eat the second half of an old sandwich that I bought at an Irving two days ago. I dress it with one of the three salad dressing packets that Marc Joseph had given me for my travels way back in Montreal. The creamy, rich dressing turns my old, dried out, mediocre sandwich into something pretty darn tasty. I love that Marc's small act of generosity endures, continues, long after he gave. A cyclist passes and, seeing me stopped, asks if everything is okay.

Like always, I melt a little. "Yep," I reply cheerily.

I never want this bike ride to end.

After my sandwich, Google Maps tells me to continue following the NB Trail for thirty-six kilometres. Choosing to be optimistic, I decide to give it a shot. I pray it remains in good repair.

Fifteen minutes later I stop my bike along the trail. When I arrived in Fredericton yesterday, there were finally other trail users: cyclists and walkers. Now it is back to normal: just me. Period. *Toute seule.* All day long. With no fear of being seen by anyone, I pull over to use nature's toilet and change into shorts.

Throughout my ride, my path gets darted across by quick, scampering little chipmunks. Sometimes I have to slam on my brakes for fear of running one of these too cute little guys over. Sometimes I only notice at the last minute that I have narrowly escaped squishing one beneath my heavy bicycle. It happens again. Just now. A chipmunk darts into my path but way too close for comfort. Without thinking, I cry out, almost angrily, "That was way too close, Mister Chipmunk!" I've addressed the chipmunk as *mister*. Those were my exact words. I said this out loud. Even more so now, I am seriously fearing the re-assimilation process come September.

Farther on, I see a Loblaw's and a sign on the side that says, "Breathe... wine is sold here." I'm breathing, baby. I am more excited than I care to admit at this surprising find. Do grocery stores now sell alcohol? I try not to get my hopes up but it is useless. I'm hoping. I veer off the path and circle around to the front of the store.

A small, older lady walking through the busy parking lot starts waving her hands at me. I slow down and stop in front of her.

"Oh, you're reminding me of my bicycle in Germany."

She has a heavy German accent. She goes on, "You know I learned to speak English just by watching TV."

And just like that, with no hello to begin our conversation, she begins chatting with me. She tells me her bike had a sloping crossbar instead of one going straight across like on a men's bike, like mine. She asks me my name. I tell her. She tells me hers is Helga. Then just as abruptly, though not unkindly, she bids me a good day. I bid her one back and she walks off.

I enter the huge grocery store and ask the stock boy with chosen calmness, "Do you guys sell wine here?"

"Yes," he says. He leads me to the wine section.

"Have you always sold wine or is it a new thing or what?" I ask.

"It has been about a month," he tells me.

How thrilling. I learn that Ontario is going to follow suit in September. It is the best news I've heard this summer.

I decide I will no longer buy wine based on theme or picture. I just can't palate it anymore. I buy a dry New Brunswick wine: "Richibucto River." I also buy Alpha-Getti, it has just become a thing with this ride. I also buy matches, and more Starbucks instant coffee packets.

As I start piling up items in my arms, that same stock boy who helped me with the wine approaches me with a basket.

"Would you like a basket?" he asks simply, with a smile.

Am I turning into a big wuss? I find his attentiveness touching. It may be a small good deed, but it's thoughtful all the same. He could have easily done nothing without anyone noticing but he chose to care. That's what makes it special. It's how we will save the world, one little good deed at a time, done "just because" and not for any return. I accept the basket, and I smile and say thank you. Sometimes I wonder if I over-celebrate mediocrity, when I become so happy at these "little things." But every time, I come to the same conclusion: Nope. These little things are great.

I am in Oromocto and it is half-past twelve. I get back on the trail but almost immediately it returns to its characteristic deplorable state. At least I got a good fifteen kilometres out of it today. Time to turn myself into a car on Google Maps and take to the roads.

At half-past one in the afternoon, I pull over. There, on the shoulder, I eat my tuna sandwich and drink some water.

Today is an easy ride. After a fifty-seven kilometre journey, I finish early at quarter past three. My campsite at Coy Lake Camping and RV Park is ideal. It is pretty secluded, tucked away behind the entrance and away from the rows of RVs. There is even a bit of forest for me to nestle my hammock tent in. I find two trees that are exactly thirteen heel-to-toe steps apart; the perfect distance. I arrange two picnic tables in an L facing my hammock tent. I have created a cozy, outdoor bachelor apartment. I love it.

For already a few days now I have stopped wearing bug spray. I also wear hardly any sunscreen. When I am hot and sweaty and dirty all day, and then I finally have a shower, it is a pretty challenging task to willingly re-soil myself by spraying on chemicals and alcohol and greasy liquids. I'd rather be eaten alive. And that is exactly what is happening. Sigh.

I sit and have a snack of baked potato chips, salsa and queso, and a glass of wine. Then I crawl into my suspended tent and have a short snooze. I wake up just after seven. I have a shower. Then I pack up my ukulele, the rest of the bottle of wine, my stainless steel wine glass and my cigarettes, and I make my way down to the water's edge of Coy Lake to watch the sunset and play a few songs. Elaine from the front office told me there is a little path that will take me there where I can have complete privacy and solitude.

She is right. Yet again, I have a beautiful landscape of intense colours and melting, piled, fluffy cloud and eerily deep reflection and tranquility, and all this splendour there for my eyes only. Nobody else from the campground has come here to witness this.

Unfortunately I did not recork the wine properly. It has spilled and drenched my cigarettes and soaked my ukulele. What a waste, what a mess. I pray I haven't done any permanent damage to my ukulele. I quickly snap a few photos and then make my way back to the campground. Elaine sees me and asks how the water's edge was. I tell her it is stunning but that I have spilled my wine all over my ukulele and cigarettes.

"Do you want me to run you down to the store? Ex-smoker here. I don't mind," Elaine offers with enthusiasm.

I am a bit stunned for a second. Perhaps I should stop being surprised at people's kindness and generosity, but it continues to bowl me over each time. A cigarette with the wine would be delicious but I also don't want to put this sweet woman out. After a few moments' reflection and Elaine assuring me the store is really not far at all, I accept. Elaine and I get into her car and off we go to get me cigarettes and her to get milk and the newspaper for her mother.

"See, she needs milk. It all works out."

Elaine rocks.

Upon returning to the campground, I thank Elaine, say goodbye, and then go off to my campsite to start a fire. I collect a lot of small branches for kindling, just like Éric and his friend did for me back at Camping Coop des Érables and how Outdoor Captain Cailin re-taught me yesterday, too. As luck would have it, the eight-dollar bundle of firewood I bought comes with newspaper and kindling, too. The wood is dry. Today the fire-starting luck is in rare abundance. I have noticed this trend or coincidence on the ride: the days I am best prepared are the days I need it least. Fortune favours the bold, as the saying goes. And the wise, it seems.

Quickly and easily I have a roaring fire ablaze. I feed and feed more firewood, letting its flames burn free, rising and falling with ferocity; it is a huffing, roaring tangerine tiger standing on its hind legs. I sit mesmerized. I am proud.

I call my older sister Carolyn. Through Facebook she has been enthusiastic and supportive of me during this journey. Every day she makes all kinds of comments about how she admires what I'm doing. She private messages me to tell me that she wants to do what I am doing. Her attention and remarks have been non-stop and I feel deeply her support and presence throughout this trip.

We have a great chat for half an hour. She really understands my mindset, purpose, and philosophy about this trip; the simple living, the belief in the goodness of people. It doesn't take a great person to do a great thing. It takes doing a great thing that makes a great person. I am actually paraphrasing her here. And one thing is certain: I feel great. I am happy to share this moment with her during this sacred time of self-affirmation. I am not changing, I am just gaining strength and confidence in who I am, who I've always been. Finally, at forty-one years old, I get me, I accept me, and I really like me. What a load off. Doubting oneself is taxing.

With the fire still roaring, I crawl into my sacred cocoon and watch episode two of *Stranger Things* as I munch on the last of some liquorice. My own private movie theatre. I love my little viewing set-up. I feel accomplished and fulfilled. My days are long and purposeful. My evenings are relaxed and in nature. I am blessed by so much kindness, love, and support, from strangers as well as from my loved ones at home. There is momentum, always. It's like Albert Einstein said, "Life is like riding a bicycle. To keep your balance, you must keep moving."

Well said, Al. Well said.

"What a wonderful life, associating vulnerability with strength and joy rather than with weakness and fear."

AUGUST 1ST – DAY 28

I awake in the morning to the chattering of a chipmunk and the cock-a-doodle-doo-ing of a rooster; the best alarm clocks ever. I eat a can of Alpha-Getti for breakfast and half a liter of 2% milk. Freezing, I climb back into my hammock tent. It is not yet eight o'clock. I have to get going early today. I have my longest ride to date planned: ninety kilometres, and I am a little nervous about it. I don't want a repeat of day twenty when I was panicking at the end of the day about finding a safe place to sleep for the night. Just a few minutes more, then I will get up and start packing up and get going. Just a few minutes more...

As I am packing up my camp, Elaine comes walking over with my fully-charged single-charge battery, which she charged in her cottage overnight for me. She offers me a cup of coffee. I haven't saved any wood from my fire last night, plus I need to start being more open to people's acts of generosity and kindness, so I accept. I love this woman. As we chat over coffee, I tell her I am planning to travel ninety kilometres today to my next destination of Sussex.

Elaine gives me an odd look. Then she says, "You're in my backyard. I think I can find you a better route."

We go to the office and she pulls out a couple of different big, paper maps and gets to studying and pointing. I am touched. And find me a better route, she does.

Even though the route she shows me follows the Trans-Canada Highway for thirty-six kilometres, I actually don't mind at all. I haven't ridden along a major highway as of yet and would like to explore what it's like. Even if it proves to be unenjoyable, it will at least be a unique and novel experience. And to be honest, I could also use a break from taking photos of the beautiful scenery that constantly demands its magnificence be captured in a picture. I'm certainly not bored of the beauty, I am simply in a mood to hustle. I thank Elaine for her kindness and thoughtfulness. Off I go.

I cross two bridges. The first takes me over the mighty Saint John River, the second over the Jesmeg River. Before each of these bridges, I see the same sign: "No bicycles" and "Cross wind." Well, what the hell do you do? I can't turn back. Well. I suppose, in fact, one could. But how is it that a highway can just suddenly kick you off? It isn't right, I tell you. So, in defiance and disregard for this unfair though surely safer ban on cyclists, over I go. I hold on tight and am watching carefully down the road to see if any trucks are approaching. I don't want to battle a backdraft while I am perched high above the guardrail, with a clear view over into where I could fairly easily tumble under certain conditions. I pedal, I try not to look down, I watch for trucks. There is no moment of fear or panic. All goes just fine.

About twelve kilometres into the day's ride, I stop along the side of the highway to use nature's restroom. I have to shield myself with only the low steel guardrail; there is no bush to tuck into. The traffic is shooting by fast enough that it is not a big deal. I also eat half a salmon sandwich and change into shorts.

After another twelve kilometres, I stop and eat the other half of the sandwich and have a swig of water. Then, perfectly timed, I see a sign advertising that in a mere four kilometres, I will reach exit 365, and a restaurant. I can feel myself go dreamy-eyed. I imagine that my eyeballs actually transform into two sunnyside up eggs as I ride along, fantasizing about my favourite meal of the classic all-day breakfast. It's a much looked-forward-to highlight and feast for me along this ride. A simple breakfast feels to me like a royal repast. Thankfully, exit 365 is also the cut-off for the Highway 10 East junction, which I need to take. I would have turned off anyway, but this scenario, which includes no extra kilometres or backtracking, is perfect.

Today the clouds are beautifully woven and intricate like the scales of a fish. I can't take many photos because I take the fact that I am riding on a major highway with utmost seriousness and focus on safety. This means no taking photos while riding, and no stopping to take photos, either. With the speeds the vehicles are going here, there would be no such thing as a minor accident with one. I want to keep my time on here as brief as possible.

It is twelve-thirty when I order four sunnyside up eggs, home fries on the grill with onion, and whole-wheat toast and coffee with milk at McCready's Restaurant on Coles Island. I have travelled only twenty-eight of the seventy-eight I need to do today, shortened thanks to Elaine.

As I am sitting, enjoying my delicious breakfast, I think about my journey and realize that I am more than halfway "there." By day's end I will have travelled about 1 637 kilometres. A straight route from Toronto to Baddeck, my scant-planned destination and starting point of the Cabot Trail, is about 2 120 kilometres. However, I have not been travelling a perfect line. It will end up being more kilometres than this.

I have purchased a train ticket online. I will catch a train on August twenty-eighth in Halifax, bound for Toronto. That much I now know. From now until then, I will continue to take things day by day.

At the restaurant I meet another woman who is cycling. She started in Vancouver and she is on her way to Newfoundland. She is riding with a girl-friend, who is about an hour behind her, she tells me. I thought perhaps she was going to be the first long-distance solo female rider I have encountered along my own epic journey. But alas, no. She has a riding partner. I don't know if I feel disappointment or excitement to still be the only solo female rider I know. I don't want to be the only female doing something like this on her own. I want to encourage other women like me. I want to find like-minded others. At the same time, I am enjoying how special I feel, being the only one, too. This is my moment. Usually "being the only one" or "different" has made me feel like I don't fit in, or even at times, like there is something wrong with me. Out here, on this epic journey, it has made me feel special, celebrated, power-ful, and inspirational. I never want to lose this feeling. I vow not to.

As I am putting my helmet on and getting ready to go, I meet Dale and Murray, two gentlemen on beautiful Harleys. We begin chatting. They are from Barrie; fellow Ontarians. They aren't on Facebook so we exchange numbers. We agree to get together and go for a ride once we are all back home. They wish me well and tell me to be safe. Off I go.

Off I go in the wrong direction. I forgot that I am acting like a car today. The directions I just followed on Google Maps were for a cyclist and took me two and a half kilometres west on 10 to join up with the no-thank-you-NB-Trail that then angles back eastward. What I actually need is to be going east on the road. I finally realize this after five kilometres out. *Fuck.* I turn around, and carry on. Going the wrong way was still exercise, at least. Ten whole extra kilometers of it.

The last thirty kilometres are brutal. Before this, the day had consisted of long, steep roller after long steep roller. But now, it is whopper after whopper after whopper. Up Gibben Mountain, down Gibben Mountain. Up Mount Middleton, down Mount Middleton. I have even swallowed my pride and have hit an all-time low gear of two. Even on two, I am going in such slow motion up these mountains it is like I am not actually moving at all. It has been a long, tough day.

I arrive at the Town and Country Campground in Sussex, New Brunswick at almost six in the evening after a healthy seventy-eight kilometre (plus ten.) ride. They have a drive-in movie theatre here. Very cool. Unfortunately, they only show films Thursday to Sunday. I check my phone. Today is Monday.

The campsites are in a neat row along the perimeter of the grounds, tucked behind all of the trailers, which encompass the entire center grounds. My site has two perfectly placed trees, almost exactly thirteen heel-to-toe steps apart. There is a picnic table and a fire pit that I can't use; there is yet another province-wide fire ban on. I have a quaint little view of some green open space and some trees. It is certainly not deep-woods camping, but there are a lot of neighbours and I feel safe. And no matter what the scenery, or lack thereof, it is always good to be outdoors.

Even before setting up my hammock tent, I sit and eat the rest of my home fries from lunch and drink my Californian Barefoot Pinot Noir like it is water. I write this on Facebook: "Today at noon I reached the halfway point in this incredible journey I quite naively undertook. I find it hard to process...on so many levels. I can't thank enough all of you who have been following me along my way. Your "likes" of my photos, your comments, your private messages of encouragement, and the friendship requests of your significant others all carry me in ways I cannot express. I am overwhelmed with the love and support from all of you I know, and all of you I've met along this transcendental way. THANK YOU."

And I mean it from the very bottom to the tippy top of my overflowing heart. People are wonderful. Why doesn't the news speak of them more often? One "feel good story" to entertain us at the end of a depressing, sensationalized string of "feel bad" or "feel scared" stories just isn't cutting it.

I set up my hammock tent. A little girl and her mother walk by. The mother asks me about my hammock tent because her daughter is curious about it, she tells me as the little girl remains shyly quiet. I show and explain how it works.

The little girl is fascinated. "I want one," she whispers to her mom.

Adorable.

Then I pack my toiletries pannier onto my bicycle and make my way to the showers. This is where I meet Tori and Hannah. Both showers are being used. I wait there in the washroom where these two young girls are hanging out.

"I like your top," Tori says to me.

"Thank you," I say. "It's from Lululemon. Do you guys have Lululemon here?"

They do, she tells me. And just like that, I am chatting with these sweet, lovely girls while waiting for the shower. I think about telling them that I am a teacher and asking them what grade they are in but decide against it. I don't want them to see me as an authority figure in this moment, just as a fellow human being.

By the time I am done showering, the sun is setting. I play a bit of ukulele and then go off to bed. I watch some of episode three of *Stranger Things*, and despite how much I am loving it, I fall asleep almost immediately. What a life I am leading this summer; meeting so many kind strangers, being vulnerable yet taken care of, and, stunningly, associating vulnerability with strength and joy rather than weakness and fear.

What a wonderful life.

"You don't just lie down and die and let life pass you by because there is danger out there. You prepare, you stay aware, you stay smart, you trust your instincts, and you go."

AUGUST 2ND – DAY 29

The rain awakes me at three-thirty in the morning and I am not able to get back to sleep until sometime beyond quarter after five. I rise around seven-thirty and have a breakfast of a can of Alpha-Getti and a coffee made with hot tap water from the washroom. And a cigarette. I begin packing up my camp when I hear a sweet, friendly voice call out good morning.

It is pretty, seventy-seven-year-old Lonny from the trailer one over and to the south of my lot, number twenty-six. She is holding out a bag of home-made chocolate bark, which she has brought out to give to me. "For energy," she says simply. My heart swells. Although we haven't exchanged a word yet, it is clear she understands what I'm up to. I am on a long, physically-challenging endeavour, and she is providing some delicious nourishment to help me. I am moved.

We chat for a good little while. She tells me about her son and his second wife and how they are doing a three-week bike tour with twenty-nine other people in Cambodia to raise money for brain cancer research. They are doing this because their own child died of brain cancer. I feel shattered. I can't imagine the pain those parents went through.

Then Lonny tells me that two children at this campground also have brain cancer. The one girl is doing really well. "Though," she adds, "it is still only a matter of time."

The crevice in my heart deepens. These poor children. The reality is awful but Lonny's empathy is beautiful. My heart is saddened at these awful tragedies, but I am glad that Lonny is sharing her heavy stories with me. Sharing pain lightens the load and it is my honour to take on this labour of love. I thank Lonny for the chat and for the thoughtful, delicious gift of the homemade chocolate bark.

The first part of today's route leads me along a ten-kilometre stretch of Waterford Road. It is a beautiful but incredibly hot, sunny day. As I near the end of Waterford Road, on the left-hand side, I see a beautiful creek leading to a deep, blue-green, crystal-clear pond of crisp, clean, delicious water—heaven on a hot, sticky, sweaty day such as this. Furthermore, the pond is bordered by a wall of handsome, cavernous rocks. Lightly flowing and trickling into the pond, there is a story-book babbling brook that cascades down long rock steps that are, quite perfectly, crowned with a little waterfall. I can see to the very bottom of the pond; it is that clear and clean. It has a pebble bottom; not a speck of reed or sand. In fact, it looks so clean, cool and inviting that I decide immediately: I am going in. I may have decided against going into the water back at the suspension bridge, but the desire to swim, and when I say swim I mean skinny-dip, at some point this summer, burns on. I think this is my chance.

I take a look around, evaluating whether attempting a skinny dip is safe and reasonable. The road is not desolate, but it is extremely low-traffic. I won't need to worry much about the seclusion or privacy of the spot being upset. There is a house on the other side of the road, maybe a hundred meters back from the road. There are two people sitting on the porch, but my newfound little piece of paradise is sufficiently far and hidden from their view. I feel comfortable and safe that civilization is both close enough for safety and far enough away for privacy. It is likewise very, though not completely, hidden from the view of passing vehicles. Though perhaps a bit visible, I am likely to go unnoticed. I will be a quiet, small speck of black tank top and black shorts until I will be only a little head in the water, just another rock. I stash my bike behind the guardrail and go for it.

I carefully climb down the boulders and dirt path to the water. I take many, many photos. My heart is pounding, erupting in delight here in this tiny cache of natural beauty. I wade over to the other side of the pond to the stone wall.

A car passes but doesn't even look my way. So does another in the opposite direction. Same thing. I feel affirmed that I am adequately far in distance and inconsequential in clothing and size that I am easily overlooked.

I take off my shorts and underwear under the shield of my long tank top. I have become an expert at changing while completely keeping all private areas concealed. My pulled down tank top with elasticized bottom looks like a 1920's flapper-style bathing suit. If I feel comfortable enough once I'm head under, this will come off, too.

The water is shockingly, impossibly crisp and cold. It is gorgeous and calling to me clearly. What a find; a true oasis. I can't wait to be head under. I am moving slowly, savouring every moment, easing myself into the fabulously freezing water. It is going to take a bit of time. It is *that* cold. I get waist-deep. With each centimeter deeper I venture, I am filled with excitement and exhilaration.

A third vehicle passes by. It is a truck. I see the driver, a man, notice me. We make brief eye contact as his truck whizzes by. He is out of my sight, but I hear his tires screech to a stop.

Buddy, what are you doing? I think miserably to myself. I know he has stopped because of me. I know he is going to re-manifest any moment. I am alone and I want to be left that way. I am on guard. I stand there, freezing, waiting.

I hear the truck door slam and then from behind the bushes I see the man, who looks to be in his early fifties, walking fast and purposefully, bounding excitedly toward the pond. He pulls his shirt off and says, "You're going about it all wrong."

He hops the guardrail.

"Oh," I mumble. "And I guess you are going to show me the *right* way?"

My voice is reluctant, unenthusiastic, my face glaring of consternation. But he isn't receptive to any of my body language, just like he isn't perceptive of the environmental cues, a strange man approaching a lone woman in a desolate area, like Bruce wisely was that day outside of Fredericton.

The man ambles with agility down to the water. In half a second, he dives into the water. I see him swimming toward me under the water. Lacking any regard for spatial respect, he surfaces directly beside me. He is at most a foot away. I am in shock. I can't believe that this man could be so ignorant to how uncomfortable and unsafe coming this close to me would make me feel; *is* making me feel. And since he is, whether ignorantly or purposefully, blind to all these cues and norms, I can't help but begin to fear what line he will cross next.

He stands there beside me, strikes up some small talk, asking me where I'm from, telling me he swims here all the time, telling me there is another such pond not too far away, and that we should go there. I decline but partake in the small talk out of obligation but also not knowing what else to do. I am also acutely aware that I am half-naked. He can't tell this due to my long, elasticized-bottom tank top, but should he try anything wanton, he wouldn't have much trouble.

His name is Andrew. In his acute lack of wisdom and sensitivity, still standing a foot away from me in the water, he suggests that we go to his house "for a smoke." I have never heard this particular phrasing. I assume he means marijuana.

"I don't smoke," I tell him flatly.

He persists. "Come on, we'll just go for ten or fifteen minutes."

All I want is to get back up onto the road.

"I'll follow you on my bicycle." It is a lie. I figure once he is in his truck, I can turn into the house across the road and explain to the people on the porch that I feel unsafe.

"Oh, no. There are too many hills. Just come in my truck with me. I'll take you there and drive you back. You can trust me."

I can't believe what I am hearing. Can he not hear himself? If you need to use the words "you can trust me" to coax a woman to go with you, you're out of line and need to leave. Immediately. Can he not read the weariness and disinterest and anxiety written all over my face? How is it possible that he is not picking up on the flatness in my voice, the heavy cloak of disinterest? I can't imagine that he thinks that I would go off with him after already saying no more than once. I respond sternly. "I am not leaving my bicycle."

It is my lifeline, my everything, and in this case, perhaps my anchor to safety.

Finally, he moves away from right beside me. I exhale. A little. He climbs up onto the opposite bank. It looks like he wants to take another dive in. I still really want to go head under and I don't want to let this ignorant asshole steal that opportunity from me. Now that he is a normal, respectful distance away, I quickly dunk my head. The water is beautifully cool and refreshing on my hot head; baptismal, though rushed and tainted. Now that I have done what I came to do, at least in part, and now that he is far enough away from me that I feel I can move, physically react to the situation, I begin to actualize my desire to leave as quickly as possible.

I ask him if he can give me some privacy for a moment. I look toward my small pile of clothes on the rock ledge.

"Oh, sure. Sorry. No problem. I just thought we were chatting."

Like his phrasing "go for a smoke," I again don't quite understand what "I just thought we were chatting" has to do with my request for privacy but I don't care at all and don't bother to clarify. I am enormously thankful that he is finally being receptive, that he seems capable of a blatant verbal cue, and is being decent about the request. He turns his back, I climb out of the pool, and carefully put on my shorts and underwear in one fell swoop without "showing any skin," just in case he turns around, which he does not.

I make an attempt at de-escalating the intensity of my fear. "I should have had you take a photo of me in there," I say. I am trying to be casual, polite, and nonchalant.

"Get back in and give me your phone. I'll take a photo of you."

I almost laugh out loud. The last thing I am going to do is get back in and give this guy my phone. I regret my poor choice of words in making my forced, insincere small talk.

I wade over to the roadside bank, where he is. I have no choice. He is where the path to "out" is. I desperately want to leave this situation that feels like it is dragging on forever. I think of the shame and stupidity I would feel if anything were to happen here. They would say:

"She was alone?"

"What was she thinking?"

"What was she wearing?"

"*Where* was she?"

"Why was she there?"

I am scared but I am also angry. I am angry that he has stolen my moment. I am angry that he is allowed to be here alone and I am not.

I am angry that I feel scared!

I am angry at his lack of empathy.

Creepy Andrew extends his hand to help me up. Reluctantly, I give him my hand. I begin climbing back up to the road, Andrew right behind me. As we ascend the short, steep slope up to the road, he again suggests that we go to his house "for just ten to fifteen minutes." I understand perfectly what he is suggesting and cannot believe his persistence.

"I think I am just going to get going," I tell him.

I am less afraid to be firm with him now that I can see the house across the road again.

Andrew then begins asking me what route I am taking, completely ignorant to the fact that me telling him my route would be against all basic and logical safety precautions a woman might take while travelling alone.

I spit out short, angry sentences. "I'm not sure. I don't know."

"How can you not know?" he asks.

"I use a GPS and I just do as it tells me." For the most part, this is actually true.

"Show it to me. Where is it?" he presses me.

My patience is waning and my anger with this *fucker* is intensifying. "It's on my phone," I tell him. "I don't know the next direction until I come to it. I have four kilometres along Creek Road. That's all I know."

I can't believe what I just heard myself say, divulging the next part of my route. I'm spiralling under the pressure of this surprise, unwelcome, and intense situation.

"Oh, yeah? Then what? Shepody?"

I am about to crack. I tell him angrily, "I honestly don't know." I completely change the topic and ask, "Are you on Facebook?"

"No," he mutters. He looks disgruntled.

"Well, nice meeting you," I say, forcing cheeriness.

I begin to make the motions of leaving, unpropping my bicycle from off the guardrail, swinging my leg over the cross bar.

"See ya," he says with rancour.

As I ride by his truck, I make note of his license plate number. I immediately text this information to my friend Tony, the last person with whom I had been texting, the person at the top of the list of my sent texts. I also include his name and the make and colour of his truck, a blue Ford.

I continue down Waterford Road. Andrew passes me. He doesn't wave. I'm not surprised. I feel fairly safe here where there are intermittent houses. I think about tucking into the house across from the pond, telling them what transpired, telling them I feel unsafe, asking if I can wait a bit there, or even if they could drive me to the next major town. But I don't. I'm afraid I am being dramatic. I am afraid of being a product of the very media I criticize and from which I want to rise above. I don't trust my own judgment. Perhaps I am making a mountain out of a molehill. I don't want to come across as ridiculous or crazy or seeking attention. I ride on.

I keep my eyes peeled to the road ahead, looking for Andrew's truck, pulled over somewhere, waiting for me as I take a slight left onto Creek Road, the road I astonishingly told him I would be taking next. I am on high alert. My eyes are darting left and right, straining down the road in the bright light, searching non-stop. I am scanning the surroundings so carefully that even the thick arm of my Harley Davidson sunglasses is too much of an obstruction for me. I remove them and tuck them into the bungee strings of my top back pannier. There are fewer houses around now. My heart is racing. He did pass me, he does know this first street of my route. I am incredulous and angry at myself that I buckled under my fear and leaked this bit of information.

Then I get to the next turn, Phil A. Munroe Road. I hesitate before turning. The condition of this road is atrocious. I can't even call it a road. It is gravelly and dusty and pockmarked with ruts and potholes, uneven and straight up. I need to travel four kilometres here. Ugh. I would normally just reroute myself as a car in this situation but I realize I have no reception. Google Maps will continue to function under the current, already-loaded itinerary, but I can't change it without Internet reception. I realize at this moment that not only can I not reroute myself, but also that the text I sent to Tony did not go through. Nobody knows where I am or what is happening to me. I feel a chill go down my spine and shame flush my face.

But then, a mental silver lining appears. It occurs to me that this road looks so horrible and unrideable that there is no way this Andrew character would guess I would turn down it. *Therefore I want to turn down this road.* And that is what I do.

It is terrible-going from the get-go. Rocky, dusty, slipping backward as I walk and push my bicycle straight up an immediate hill, short but steep. I arrive at the top, and since I am finally off the road that I told him I would be on, Creek Road, I finally feel safe enough to pull over for a moment. I continue to dart my eyes and turn my head in all directions, scanning my surroundings as I dig into the side pocket of my back pannier and pull out my bear spray. It is still in its cellophane wrap, which I take off immediately. I look around. I tuck the garbage into my food pannier, and then read the instructions. I check out the lever carefully and decide that I understand how to use it. I tuck the instructions into my food pannier. Then I hoist the bear spray front and centre from my handlebars. I feel worlds safer with this weapon on hand.

I have my speech prepared should he present himself. "Don't fucking come any closer. I have already texted your license plate to a friend and this spray will fucking kill you."

My alarm bells are still ringing like mad. I am a bundle of nerves and scared as hell. I may have kept my cool in his presence, but now my nerves are unravelling. His ungodliness has stolen the wind from my sails, that is certain.

It is extremely slow going on the four-kilometre stretch along Phil A. Munroe Road due to the terrible conditions of this "road," as Google Maps calls it. This is *not* a road in my opinion. This is a temporary, use-at-your-own-risk detour lane at best. Furthermore, this route is completely and dangerously desolate. Not a single other soul around. There isn't a single house, business, cottage, shack, or abandoned piece of farm equipment, nothing; not any sign of life whatsoever. I am the only one here on this desolate path lined with a never-ending, tall-treed forest. It's just me and the deep dark woods. And perhaps Andrew, lurking in the bushes.

At one-thirty in the afternoon, I decide that this road is too ridiculous to continue on. There are signs for Adair's Wilderness Lodge. I decide to go there instead. Hopefully there will be Internet connection and I can reroute myself as a car. I detour from my itinerary and head for the lodge. However, about a kilometre and a half later, unbelievably, I change my mind. I can't see the end of Phil A. Munroe Road on my Google map. I am fearful that I will go several kilometres and find myself at a dead end. If I go back the way Google Maps is telling me to go, and even if the whole twenty-four kilometres that are left of my day's planned journey are as treacherous and slow-going as these four kilometres have been, at least I will know for certain that I am headed in the right direction and will definitely arrive somewhere other than a dead end. I can't believe I have created three extra kilometres of hell for myself. I backtrack the kilometre and a half and search for my next turn, eerily named Dark Hollow Road.

After what seems like an eternity, I finally approach Dark Hollow Road. Like textbook pathetic fallacy, the sky rushes with ill-intention to cloud over and darken and encourage my fear. I turn down the road, full of trepidation. About four hundred meters in, I come upon a lone house, on the left. It is the first I have passed since leaving Creek Road, already an hour ago. It looks empty. I can't believe what I am reading—a sign on the front says, "Nuts Landing." I am somehow riding on the set of a bad horror film. *Nuts Landing*. Really?

Two kilometres down the road I realize I am not on Dark Hollow Road at all. I am on, quite unaptly named, Pleasant Lake Road. I am absolutely baffled at how this has happened. This road is the only cut-off there is for several kilometres either way on Phil A. Munroe. I came to this road at the exact point where the itinerary told me to turn. What the hell is going on? When are today's nightmares going to end?

Dumbfounded, defeated, miserable, tired, and still petrified, I turn back. Again. I return to Phil A. Munroe Road. I am bewildered and unhopeful as I turn left and search for some other road.

About fifty meters down from Pleasant Lake Road, I notice some faint tracks leading into some overgrown grass and bush. There is no way that that is a road. I am about to discount it and carry on searching, but decide to stop and pull the overgrowth back and peek in. Just in case.

It is definitely a path of some kind, actually. I look at it, and then back at my itinerary. I think I feel as stupefied by the state of the path as I did by Andrew's selfish and ignorant behaviour. I simply cannot believe it, but the reality starts to register. *This is Dark Hollow Road.* I am now full-on angry. Are you kidding me? This is not a road. It is barely a path, one completely invisible from the other hellish road. This route sucks. These directions are hideous and dangerous for cyclists. I have just spent hours travelling along stupid Phil A. Munroe Road and now I have to travel another three and a half kilometres on this spooky, dodgy semblance of a path? I am exasperated and fed up and very pissed off.

I yank my bicycle through the straggly resistance of the overhang and overgrowth that curtains the dismal way. Riding is not possible, even though it is flat. I walk and trudge and push and drag my bicycle along. It gets worse. Then the "road" goes straight up; like *straight the hell up*. I think this was perhaps once a stream that dried up. It is steep with huge rocks and boulders and crevices for its surface. My anger is skyrocketing. I push my bike up, wheel width by wheel width. My journey along Phil A. Munroe and Dark Hollow is taking hours. There is only deep, quiet forest as far as the eye can see on either side of me. To add to the misery of the day, because I am completely enshrouded by trees, there is no sunlight at all and I am cold.

Let me be clear here. Hills, even the mountains I've been waiting for, I am fine with. I welcome. I appreciate the hard work it takes to climb up them on my heavy bicycle. However. Dark Hollow Road, with its shitty, loose, deep, gravel; its treacherous, lopsided, unkempt, boulder-ridden, dirty, sandy, slippery, dusty poor-excuse-for-a-trail filled with holes, gaps, fractures, and ruts going straight the hell up for over three kilometres that Google Maps has the audacity to call a road is not cool and *that* is what I am angry about. And all this, out in the middle of nowhere; not a single other soul is to be seen. Not in a car, not on a bicycle, not on foot, not on some distant worksite that is at least visible from afar, not a single house to pass (unless you count Nuts Landing on the wrong turn). This "road" should not be promoted as part of a bicycle route by Google Maps. It is desolate and dangerous and unfit for bicycles.

Breathe, Christina, breathe.

Fuck that. I'll breathe later. Right now, I'm *mad*.

At quarter to four, finally, finally, finally, I emerge from the thick of the forest to a wide, blond-sand, dusty, out-in-the-open, gravelly, flat road. Hallelujah, hallelujah! I could cry for joy. Almost simultaneously, the sun comes out from behind the clouds, full strength. Murphy's law: cloud and cool weather while I am protected by the cover of a sea of dense trees, and then just as I exit the shelter, the hot, burning sun returns. Of course. There isn't a curse word strong enough.

I look around. This might be some sort of construction site? Wide-open space, cleared land. I look on my itinerary, and nearly drop my phone for the shock. Just as suddenly as I had felt relief for being out of the scary, desolate forest and finding a flat, open road, the terror comes sweeping back with ferocity. Andrew had asked me about one road and one road only; he wanted to know if I was taking Shepody Road. My itinerary shows me: that is exactly where I am now.

I am on Shepody Road.

A sudden flush of heat spreads throughout my body from head to toe. I feel like I could pee my pants. I was probably completely safe and fine the whole time along Phil A. Munroe and Dark Hollow Road. It's Shepody where he will be, if anywhere.

Well. I have fucking had it. Enough of this shit. Something just snaps in my brain. I switch from afraid to *ferocious*. I am exhausted physically, not just from the gruelling route but from the crippling fear. Enough. I am so damn angry by this point that I think:

LORD HELP THAT FUCKER IF HE CROSSES MY PATH NOW.

Alas, my fury is stronger than my fear. And so, in this case, I view my anger as a gift.

Shepody Road is gravelly, rocky, and unbelievably dusty, but at least it is a real road. I will follow it for eight kilometres before reaching highway 114 East. I hope with all my heart that the 114 will be paved. I am covered in dirt. My panniers are covered in dirt. I am out of water. I stop and literally drink a can of Alpha-Getti and then have a cigarette. Then I carry on. I have no choice. Up, down, up, down. It is a modern-day miracle I have not had a flat.

The first ray of light: the 114 is paved. I'm elated. I glide along, relieved, but in an almost catatonic state after everything I have endured today. It has taken me all day, over seven hours already, to travel just under forty kilometres. I have no words. Complete exhaustion on every level.

I arrive in Fundy National Park pretty much right away despite the fact that Google Maps tells me I still have about twelve kilometres to go. It's because that is the distance to the center of the park rather than its entrance, I happily realize. I pay my entrance fee and camping fee and set off to find my site. Well. It turns out that my troubles aren't quite over yet.

Of the nine lots still available, and quite unbelievably amid this massive National Park, dense with gigantic, sky-scraping trees, none of the available lots have trees. There are a few coniferous trees, planted as borders, around the lots, but their trunks are unreachable for tying my hammock tent to without chopping branches which I would never do, plus I'm sure is illegal.

I don't understand what the idea of camping is if you just pull up to a square of grass, or, in some cases, a square of gravel. Despite my fatigue, I backtrack back to the entrance to get a refund.

I start to travel the fourteen kilometres through the center of Fundy National Park, destination unknown. Here there are some major whoppers, let me tell you. Big, steep hills. But. They are on paved roads, I shan't complain. Pavement is my new best friend.

What a day. I am numb, in a daze. I get to the top of one of the many dramatic uphills within the park when I notice something out of the corner of my eye. It is a small, acute patch of blue, a different, unique blue, whispering to me in a different voice than the St. Lawrence and the St. John had. I am tremulous. It is in the shape of an upside-down triangle, a sapphire wedge beyond some far-off mountains. Oh, my goodness, oh, my goodness. It isn't river blue, it isn't lake blue. I am swooning, I am gasping. In a moment, the day is a flush and my heart begins to race. Is it what I think it is?

It is ocean blue.

I pedal with fury. Emotions rise. Despite the day, I suddenly have bounding energy. I can't help but be carried away with the realization, seeing the map in my mind, imagining a little dotted line from Toronto…all the way, here, now, to the East Coast. That blue is the Bay of Fundy and that is salt water from the Atlantic Ocean. It's getting closer. I see now a little upside-down parallelogram-shaped azure patch between walls of trees and at the vanishing point in the road ahead of me. I ride and I ride, I race toward that little spot of blue as it keeps getting larger and larger, immense, grand, so expansive, that, catch my breath, it swallows me whole. My chest begins to heave, and, finally, tears come.

I am overcome with humility and respect as I behold the magnificent site before me.

The Bay of Fundy.

I am incredulous and proud that I have arrived here, by myself, on a bicycle. Only now, at this moment, more than one thousand seven hundred kilometres of riding, only now do I realize: Woman, you are doing this. You got this. This view. This majesty. This accomplishment. I accept now that a lot of the unknown is now known, that I wasn't wrong to think I could do this. I've learned it again: fear of the thing is always way bigger than the thing itself.

Now that I have reached this magnanimous milestone, my mind allows me to finally release some of the stress, terror and torment of the day from within. I sob softly. I feel better, a little catharsis. Like another little flash of the exorcism at the statue of Dionne Le Semeur, I feel lighter.

There is a lookout point with oversized Muskoka chairs. I get a grip on myself and approach. I take photos and have a cigarette as I sit in one of the four Adirondack chairs. I just sit, drink in the view, and breathe in the moment. A man and his dog approach me.

"Where did you ride here from?" he asks.

"Toronto," I say without emotion. I'm just too exhausted to be any bit exuberant.

"I'm surprised to see you having a cigarette," he says.

"Yeah," I reply.

I don't have the energy to offer any justification or even make a joke. Also, there is no point in making excuses. Smoking is stupid. Even I am surprised that on a trip like this my smoking has increased. His wife walks up and he tells her where I have ridden from.

"Wow," she says. "Safe travels." Then she adds: "*Enjoy* your travels."

I admire her reflection and addition.

I get back on my bicycle. A couple take two of the four chairs in my place. They call out to me, "Did you ride your bike here from Toronto?"

They must have overheard my conversation with the couple.

"Yeah," I reply.

"We're from Ontario, too," they share.

I like how finding any commonality bonds complete strangers. We often talk about how we must accept and celebrate our differences but we mustn't forget to find and celebrate how we are the same, too. We are all one. Fellow Earthlings, that's all we all are. They are from Brampton. They wish me luck and off I go.

Just before reaching this beautiful look-out point there was a sign that said, "Steep hills, sharp turns for the next 4 kilometres." I had thought to myself: *Ha! As opposed to what!?* But moments after leaving the look-out point, I soon understand. It is all steep *downhill* for four glorious kilometres. What a wonderful denouement to the climax of the Bay of Fundy.

I am nearing the end of the immense forests of the park. There is a sign for motels and chalets. I can only fathom how expensive they probably are. But. If ever there is a day I deserve some creature comfort and care, it is today. More importantly, I think of the view I would have. I have already passed the turn to the first motel by the time I decide to splurge on a motel room. I cross the lanes and drag my bicycle across a grassy, hilly median to the small downhill that leads to the office. I glide smack into a sign that says: NO VACANCY.

I feel the tears well up.

"Don't worry, dear. You're really close to town. There are many motels there." the lady at the office says comfortingly.

I feel somewhat relieved but not too much, because, like always, I know that "really close" is a relative term she means in car distance. It could be far for a weary, worn cyclist like me.

I get back on my bicycle, pedal up the small hill, rejoin the main road, and continue the glide down and out of Fundy National Park. "Welcome to Alma," the sign reads. Just beyond it I see a busy little street full of restaurants and stores, beached boats and motels. It looks positively charming. Thank goodness. It is half-past seven.

First, I go to the general store and buy two bottles of wine, some snacks, and some postcards. I ask the man at the counter if there is a motel nearby. He tells me to go to The Alpine Motel. I do this.

Again: NO VACANCY.

This town appears to be a major tourist hub. I ask the father-son duo behind the counter if they know of somewhere else that has vacancy. They tell me that they have just been on the phone looking for a vacancy for someone else and were able to find one room and that that was the last one. Who knows what my face must look like at hearing this news, but the father suddenly says to his son, "You can try calling again."

The son gets on the phone although I can see on his face that he knows it is futile. He calls a few numbers but with no success. The father and son look at each other. I must look really desperate and pathetic. The father then looks at me. "Do you have camping gear?" he asks.

"Yes!" I say with a new glimmer of hope.

"Well, we have three acres of land just back there." He points out the window. "If you can find someplace suitable, you're welcome to camp there."

"Thank you so much!" I say with enough gratitude and earnestness to fill The Bay of Fundy.

Off I go, north on School Road, steeply uphill, of course. I get to the plot of land the father had pointed out. I have to fight my way through some bush. Then I get to a small forest of tall, skinny trees. There are two trees perfectly distanced for setting up my hammock tent. I stand there, hemming and hawing. I see an old, empty, discarded beer bottle on the ground below where I am planning to hang my tent. I think of Andrew. I think of how dumb people can be when they are drunk. I am just not feeling comfortable in this secluded little forest after the day's events and the empty beer bottle on the ground. My spirit is shaken. I decide against staying, though the sun is setting quickly and I have no idea what I am going to do. When is this insufferable day going to end?

I go back to the Alpine Motel to let them know I am going to move on and look elsewhere. I begin riding slowly up the one street that runs through this small town, suitably called Main Street. I am scanning people's front lawns and trying to see into their back yards, looking for and evaluating trees. I enter a shop selling live lobsters. It has a massive tank in the middle of the store with all sizes of lobster. I ask the man behind the counter if the trees on the side of the store belong to this property. He tells me they do not; they belong to the house next door.

As I exit, there is a man approaching the house. I say in an unconfident and weary voice, "Excuse me, can I ask you a question?"

"No!" he says sternly and looks away.

I have no energy to have any disappointment or emotional reaction to his unfriendly, one-word answer. I simply turn my bicycle around and keep looking.

I continue riding up the road, which quickly leads me away from the populace downtown area and into more unknown. I feel uneasy leaving. At this late hour, despite the seeming lack of possibilities for shelter here, I think that I better stick around, close to civilization. I have no idea what awaits me if I carry on. At least here there are restaurants, shops, blind hope of something turning up. I turn back around again. This time I see a white sign for a Bed and Breakfast. There is a woman sitting on the porch of a big, white house in front of which the sign is perched. A glint of hope ignites.

"Any vacancy?" I call out.

"Sorry, no." she replies.

"Would you happen to have any trees in your backyard that I could hang my hammock tent on? I'm happy to pay."

"Have a look around back," she says.

I walk my bicycle around to the back. There are three trees there in a perpendicularly perfect "L" shape. I measure with my heel-to-toe footsteps. Both two-treed arms measure exactly thirteen steps apart. I go back around to the front of the house. Hoping against hope, I ask her if she would mind if I camped here tonight and I would pay her.

"Of course."

I burst into tears.

"Oh, dear, you've had a long day. It's okay. Go on and get yourself settled," she says compassionately.

Although my ride only amounted to fifty-six kilometres today, she has no idea how dead right she is.

"Thank you," I manage to squeak out as I attempt unsuccessfully to hold back my sobs.

I understand exactly what is happening to me. The day is finally over. The last problem is finally solved. Now I can break down. Some survival instinct inside me kept it together while I needed to. But now. This day. The nightmare is over. I am safe from Andrew. I have somewhere safe to sleep. It all comes rushing out of me like Niagara Falls.

I set up my tent. I pack the empty pannier that had held my tent and sleeping bag and bike repair gear with a bottle of wine and my ukulele. I ride out to the bridge that goes over Salmon River as you enter Alma from Fundy National Park. There is a little takeout place, fittingly named Fundy Takeout, tucked beside the river on Fundy View Drive. I order fish and chips. I sit at a picnic table overlooking the beached tugboats, the setting sun beyond the mountains somewhere behind me. I eat the fresh, delicious meal as I sip my wine. My chest feels like an impossibly small cage for my heart inside that is flooded with emotion, inundated with relief, and overflowing with achievement and pride.

Today, I truly surmounted, succeeded, overcame. I could have been vanquished by fear but instead I conquered. I could have been defeated by obstacles and exhaustion but instead I triumphed. And this is how horror turns into beauty. With perseverance, strength, and time. I sit here, but my soul is soaring high in the sky.

I want to share this moment with a friend and call my buddy Vince. He isn't home and I leave a message. I get on my bicycle and pedal to my little hanging home in some kind stranger's backyard for the evening. I think of Mary from Bath. I think of Bruce from Fredericton. I think of my many guardian angels who have helped me along this incredible journey.

And I think of Andrew. His ignorance. His selfishness. His lack of sensitivity. He stole my day and shook my spirit. Like a prayer, I look up into the big sky, out into the Universe, and I exchange my anger and fear for hope. An earnest hope that he learns what the world is like from a woman's perspective, and about empathy.

I crawl into my cozy palm-of-Mother-Nature's hand, without a shower, without an underwear change, without even a tooth-brushing, but safe.

"Fear of the thing is always way bigger than the thing itself."

AUGUST 3ᴿᴰ – DAY 30

I awake at just after four in the morning. I feel guilty for doing so but I pee at the back edge of the back yard. I have no choice. I climb back into my hammock. I check Facebook. I drift back asleep. At six I get on my bicycle and leave to go and watch the sunrise at Salmon River.

I prop my bicycle on a bench overlooking the Bay of Fundy and set out on foot, walking the ocean floor. *I am walking the ocean floor.* There is no one else out here. I could just stare out into the never-ending ocean forever. It is mesmerizing. I try to make a short video but my hand is shaking from the cold. It is thirteen degrees. I walk back, sit on the bench and wait patiently. Finally, just before seven, the sun peeks out from behind the mountain. Like I now talk to the animals, I am also talking to the sun. Quietly I say, "Hello, there, sun."

Just look at all this. I am the richest, wisest, happiest girl in the world.

I make my way to "An Octopus' Garden Café." I have a double-long espresso and an orange juice. Then I have three eggs with toast and jam and home fries. And a second long espresso. All the while, I write and I write. I strike up a conversation with the girl behind the counter. Her name is Rochelle. I tell her about my bike ride and she freaks out. We add each other on Facebook.

A table of five young, good-looking men come in which prompts me to have some consciousness of what I might look like. I go to the bathroom and I cannot believe what I see in the mirror. This time it's certain: I look like Alice Cooper after a torrential rainstorm. Because I was so dirty yesterday, and because I cried, and because I was wearing mascara, and because I had not been able to have a shower last night, my face is streaked with black and brown. I laugh out loud. I guess Rochelle was too polite to tell me? Wow. Yet another glory moment. I clean myself as best I can, return to my table, and continue writing. I stay there two full hours.

I go back to Cleveland Place, the bed and breakfast place where I am technically staying. I am packing up my stuff when the lady from the porch comes out back. She hands me my single-charge, which she charged overnight for me. She asks me how I slept and I told her I slept like a pea in a pod. She says, "Look. You can even have breakfast."

She pulls a cherry from a branch of the tree where I slept and eats it. I slept in a cherry tree. I love this. I ask her if I can pay her and she refuses. She tells me she is going out now. She wishes me well and we say goodbye. I don't even know her name.

Last night in my hammock tent I had an epiphany. I texted my niece Abby and told her that I was buying her a bicycle.

"Why?" she asked.

I told her it's because I want her to know the joy and wisdom and freedom of riding a bicycle. The same goes for her brother, my nephew, Mathieu. I also have a nephew, Colby, in British Columbia and a niece, Maya, in Alberta. Since they have been born I have been trying to think of a way to have a connection with them. Bicycles. That is how. I call my sister Nicole and tell her that I will be buying Colby his bicycles for life; his first and every time he grows out of it and needs a new one. I explain my reasoning as I did to Abby. She is sweet and thankful and agrees to the plan. I will call my brother later to tell him the same thing.

Today Google Maps is telling me to follow Highway 114 East for forty kilometres. That's it. Then I'm there. One straight, paved road. I'm thrilled about this. It is exactly the type of day I need after yesterday. I begin singing "Country roads, take me home..." by John Denver as I ride along. But instead of saying "West Virginia" I say "Nova Scotia." I could completely make the cheesiest Canadian camp song album after this trip; all the songs I have written on my ukulele and the ones I sing as I ride.

I see a little, dead chipmunk on the side of the road. I make the sign of the cross. Poor little guy.

Roger, from the motorcycle club that I met outside of Fredericton, has been in rather frequent touch and it is lovely. He is sweet. I might be developing a small crush on him. He texted me this morning. Yesterday their crew did The Cabot Trail. He says there are long stretches of gravel where there is construction being done. Oh, man. It's one thing to deal with gravel and poor conditions when you're presented with them; it's quite another to know about it ahead of time and have the double duty of dreading them, too.

It happens again: a dog comes bounding out toward me from a house I pass when it hears me. Immediate and intense fear consumes me. I have my dog spray in hand within seconds. However, this time the scenario is less dramatic; this dog is on a long leash and stops before he can reach the road. I'm flooded with relief. Talk about an instant sweat.

I stop in a corner variety store in a little town called Crooked Creek. A car pulls up with a friendly-looking man behind the wheel and a woman wearing a colourful bandanna on her head. The woman sees my bicycle and begins asking me questions. I tell her my story. She tells me her name is Annie and that this is her husband, Jeff. Without pausing, she tells me they have a big barn and I am more than welcome to stay there for free rather than paying for a campground. And, she tells me, their place is only a few kilometres from the Hopewell Rocks, which is the exciting destination for my day. I take down her name and address and phone number and tell her I will let her know. I am amazed at the magnetism I keep exuding (or my bike keeps exuding) on these kind and generous souls.

I buy milk and a package of two cookies that the young lady behind the counter tells me are called macaroons. "Or, some people call them frogs. Other people call them haystacks," she says.

"My mom used to make these exact cookies and she called them "stovetop cookies," I tell her.

I don't have much of a sweet tooth, so it is for pure nostalgia that I can't resist buying them. My mom was the best cook. Every Valentine's Day she would bake Carolyn and I a huge, heart-shaped chocolate chip cookie, decorated with icing, scrawled with "I love you" and "Happy Valentine's Day" in thick, sugary icing. We loved this tradition. She would make the stovetop cookies now and again, and we loved them too. Even her spaghetti sauce, a plain tomato sauce, no meat, was delicious. I think this is a special accomplishment, to make such a tasty sauce from such a plain and simple medley of ingredients: tomatoes, onions and spices. I hold the good memories of my childhood near and dear to my heart. It wasn't always good, that is certain. But the good that there was, I remember. I cherish. This bike ride seems to be evoking not only joy from each day, but from the past, too.

I think about taking Annie up on her sweet offer but choose nature instead. I arrive in Ponderosa Pines Campground at quarter after one after a mere fifty-kilometre ride. My lot number is 409 and is just perfect. It has lots of trees creating shade and privacy and then a dense little clump of trees in the middle with two trees perfect to hang to hang my hammock tent from. I set it up and then go and take a shower.

Hallelujah. Sweet heaven. Glory be.

Showering is a particular joy today since yesterday, after the emotionally trying and particularly dirty, dusty day that I had, I was not able to shower. I feel like Queen of the Universe. I also do not one but two of the "White" cycles with my precious electric toothbrush. I am a new woman.

Shortly after three, I hop onto my super light, pannier-free bicycle. It is always a marvel and a joy when I ride my bicycle without its heavy load. I ride the mere one kilometre to the Hopewell Rocks. I need to go now while the tide is out and can walk the ocean floor between the rocks. I didn't even know about the Hopewell Rocks when I started this bike ride, which is shameful to admit. Bad Canadian. They are flower-pot shaped rocks that stand twelve to twenty-one meters high on the ocean floor when the tide is out. A natural wonder. I saw them on a magnet at that gift shop in Hartland, New Brunswick, beside the world's longest covered bridge. I decided then and there that I needed to see them.

I park my bike, pay my admission, and walk quickly and excitedly along the path through the dense, beautiful forest that leads to the rocks. I reach the ocean in about ten minutes. The tide is out. I am accosted by the wonder before me. Now I slow right down and just absorb. I descend the stairs, taking one million photos. My flip-flops are perfect for the muddy floor. We humans all look like tiny ants milling around these giant structures carved out by the Bay of Fundy's tide, the highest in the world, reaching over fifty feet. Today the tide will be out from half-past five until about seven in the evening.

I walk slowly, farther and farther along the coast, away from the entrance, though staying fairly close to the shore. I sink my feet into the slimy, silky, cool, refreshing mud, flip-flops and all. After that it is hard to walk. I am sliding all over. It's fun.

I climb up a set of stairs I find perhaps half a kilometre away from where I had descended then walk over to the Hopewell Café. I buy a lobster roll, a salad, and a carton of milk. The view is beautiful, overlooking the ocean, of course. Then I get a text from Roger from the motorcycle club. He tells me that he and the boys have been successful in putting in the necessary kilometres, about five hundred, to get to the Hopewell Cape in time for our paths to cross again. They are checking into the motel and then are coming down to meet me. I am flattered and elated. It is already after seven. I tell him that the park closes at eight. It seems like one second later when I get another text telling me they are here. I quickly finish up the remnants of my meal and run over to the front gate.

There they are. Just entering. All eight of them. I throw my arms around each and every one of them and tell them how happy I am to see them. One of the boys, the prospect (someone working toward becoming an official member of the club), gives me such a warm look. "I can see how happy you are, Christina. And I'm happy that you're happy," he says to me.

What a fantastic thing to say.

And so, little, chirpy me and eight tough-looking but soft-hearted bikers walk back down to the rocks. I am bouncing on cloud nine. I just love these guys. It's hard to explain but one thing I have learned on this trip is that you can love someone the instant that you meet them. Absolutely, yes, you can. I know this now because it keeps happening to me over and over on this trip. And to have that incredible feeling multiplied by eight in one shot is pretty overwhelming.

The boys are funny. They complain that the short walk is far and that this is the most exercise they have done in forever. We get to the rocks. They can't really walk on the ocean floor because of the mud. They are all wearing leather boots. Also because we are pretty pressed for time. The park is closing in ten minutes. Anyway none of them really care. They each take one or two photos of the rocks from the observation deck and then jokingly say, "Okay. Rocks. Done. Check."

I am laughing. We have someone take a photo of us together.

They buy tokens and we take the shuttle car back up to the parking lot. Roger invites me to dinner with them. Is that even a question? Of course, I say yes. I go and grab my bicycle and ride over to where all their beautiful Harleys are parked. Roger tells me that six of the guys will go to the restaurant to hold the table while Roger and another of the boys are going to escort me back to my campsite on their Harleys so I can drop my bike off. Is this sinking in? Little me, pedaling my little mechanical bicycle while two big, burly bikers on their beautiful Harleys ride slowly behind me with their flashers on, waving traffic on to pass us. I feel like supreme royalty. Now *this* is the true meaning of a glory moment. I am one hundred percent flying over the moon. I wonder and delight in what the people in the vehicles passing by think is going on here. It's funny. It is the most glorious kilometre of my ride.

I drop my bike at my lot then get on the back of Roger's bike. He has an extra helmet for when it is raining and this is what I use. He tells me that my bicycle helmet (which is actually a skateboarding helmet) is not regulation for motorcycles. Then we three ride the seven kilometres to the restaurant, which is attached to the motel where they are staying. It is called The Chocolate River Motel.

On the way I tell Roger what happened with Andrew yesterday. He is shocked. When we arrive, he tells the rest of the boys. They all have the same reaction: this guy must be some idiot, some *jerk*. I am relieved at their reaction. A part of me still believed that I was overreacting, being dramatic. I should have more faith in myself. I know I am not an alarmist. I am smart and reasonable and sensible. Andrew, on the other hand, acted stupidly and selfishly. And these eight men just confirmed that.

We order drinks and wait for our meals. Roger leaves to have a shower and is back quickly. The meals arrive. I have the seafood chowder. One of the boys and I take turns ordering half litres of red. Others start to partake as they wait forever for the beers that take an eternity to arrive. The service is slow but the waitress is quick-witted, funny, and handles the polite complaints with humour and facetiousness. While the general consensus is that the food is mediocre, my seafood chowder is savoury and delicious. The conversation is easy and excited and flows like the Chocolate River. The meal feels sacred. Eight apostles of the road, and one little apostle-ette.

The sun sets, the food is eaten, we pay our bills. We take our drinks around to the back of the motel. We sit around and chat, listen to music on one of the boys' laptop, and tell jokes.

One by one the boys start calling it a night. Soon it is just Roger and me left out there. He doesn't really drink. He has only had one whiskey and diet coke all night. It is late and time to take me home. We get on his motorcycle. In the pitch-blackness he drives me back to my campsite. He tells me he does not like riding at night because of the animals. Thankfully, none present themselves, we are safe and so are they.

We arrive at the park. I dismount from his Harley, but truthfully I don't want him to leave. I am attracted to this big, sweet man. I ask him to stay, to come see my hammock tent, and he agrees. There is a chain blocking the park entrance to motorists. I unlatch it and let him through. His bike sounds extra loud in the still of night. My site is not far, thankfully.

I proudly show him my little set-up; my hammock tent neatly nestled in the trees, my little outdoor living room, complete with fire pit and the small pile of firewood I purchased from the campground's office. A soft rain begins to fall. Roger helps me start a roaring fire. We sit side by side on the picnic table, faces glowing and warm from the blaze. And then we kiss. A soft, sweet, kiss, there in the light rain, under the open sky in the cool night air. It is innocent and lovely.

But the moment is cut short. There is sudden, angry yelling, coming from somewhere in the darkness. A golf cart bursts onto my lot out of nowhere, the man behind the wheel, menacing and livid. It is the owner of the grounds. He is more than upset about the noise that Roger's motorcycle made upon entering. Roger, who has such a way about him, a commanding presence, immediately takes hold of the situation. He carries himself with a quiet authority, with eloquence. His confidence is apparent but not at all overstated. He handles the situation with the utmost tact. He speaks calmly and respectfully to the irate owner. The owner's anger, however, is not at all assuaged. He informs us that the police are on their way.

By now it is raining harder. The police are coming, and, quite frankly, I still do not want Roger to leave. I ask if I can go back to the motel with him. He says yes. I get back on the back of his beautiful Harley and we set off for the motel once again.

As we are exiting the grounds, a cruiser from the RCMP shows up. The officer is completely laid-back and cool. He does his due diligence of taking Roger's information and then sends us on our way.

The eight boys have four rooms, two per room. I spend the night in Roger's shared room. I love curling up beside him, in his big, strong arms, snuggled in, safe and happy. It is late, after two. I fall fast asleep.

Roger and I both wake early. We go to the restaurant and have breakfast. Not only does he not drink alcohol, he also does not drink coffee. He is an alien. One by one, the boys start filtering in. I feel a bit awkward, wondering what they are thinking. But nobody says a word about me being there. They just greet me with the same warmth and smiles as always. I am relieved.

Their plan is to get on the road by nine. Roger informs me that all eight of them will be escorting me back to the campground, to make a statement, to make sure I am not hassled. I am absolutely delighted. I am being protected by a whole posse of bikers. It's thrilling.

At the campground entrance, I jump off the back of Roger's bike. I give each and every one of the boys a big hug, thank them again for the magical evening, and tell them to ride safely. And then I stand there, on the side of the road, and watch their small but mighty armada ride off down the road. Sigh.

Bye, Roger. Bye, guys.

"After climbing a great hill, one finds that there are many more hills to climb."
-Nelson Mandela

AUGUST 4TH – DAY 31

I pack up my camp and get on the road at around eleven. I pass Annie and Jeff's place and stop in to say hello. There are chickens and roosters roaming freely on their large front lawn in front of their big, charming, country house. Annie shows me her craft shop. She has a nurturing character and is deeply connected to nature. After about ten minutes, I tell them I will be on my way. They warmly wish me well and I set off again.

About fifteen kilometres into my ride, I approach a town called Hillsborough. It is appropriately named, my goodness—holy hills. There are many sweet little moments here. Just before entering the town, I am about to sail down a particularly long and steep hill. I notice a man standing outside of his car at the bottom of it, smoking a cigarette. I see him looking at me and my impending swift flight down. For his benefit and amusement, as I fly down the hill, I call out, "Woo hoo hoooooooooooooooooooooo!"

He starts laughing. I do, too.

Then, like seemingly always at the bottom of a big hill, I have to climb straight up another, this one unfathomably steep. It passes right through the middle of the town. I start up. It's tough. It's damn hot out. I am determined as hell. It's really steep. If I go any slower, I'll be going in reverse. I push and I push. I am determined to ride the whole way up without hopping off. When I finally near the top, I pass a man sitting in his truck. I guess he was watching me struggle all the way up.

As I pass, he says out the window, "You got to be in pretty good shape to do that."

"And a bit crazy," I reply.

We laugh as I trudge on. At the top of the hill I see a man on the opposite side of the street carrying the tiniest little baby.

"Wow! So new!" I call out.

The man breaks into the broadest smile. Proud daddy. I melt a little.

I pass a good-looking, young UPS guy making a delivery. He takes a look at me and my laden bicycle and then back at me, gives me a big smile. "How it's going?" he asks.

It seems he understands full well in this context that "it" is my long journey.

"Really well," I tell him.

He passes me in his truck a bit later and gives me a big wave.

I stop at a gas station and buy a carton of milk. There is a little boy there with the shyest eyes and the sweetest smile. I feel so connected to *everyone*. I carry on. And then, lucky me, a series of dramatically steep hills. Again, calling on every fibre of my quads, more than a little sweat, and a determination of steel, I make it up these hills too. When I saw this series of hills I thought for sure I'd have to end up walking at least part of them. But I didn't. I did it. I am now acutely aware of how very strong I have become. And then, guess who I run into at the top? The cute UPS guy again.

"Wow, you're really killing it!" he exclaims.

"You know what? After those hills there, I'm feeling pretty proud of myself right now," I reply.

"You should be. You're beating the UPS guy. You're making me look bad."

We laugh. He wishes me well on my journey.

All of these beautiful little moments lift me immensely. They put power in my pedal. They make my days happy and fulfilled. I am not alone.

The hills are numerous and steep along this stretch of the 114 North. Both working my way up them and profiting from the momentum gliding down them has prevented me from taking many photos today, which is a shame because today I have passed dozens of gorgeous vintage cars. Some for sale, too.

I arrive in Moncton at around quarter to three in the afternoon. I spot a Dollorama and get excited. This whole summer I have no need to buy anything and no room to store any purchases. So I buy nothing. It is liberating. This trip is certainly an effective way to curb spending habits. But at Dollorama I can buy a bunch of little things I do need and this has become my idea of fun. I buy: baby wipes, dolmades in a can, a Montréal Canadians lighter, and a package of four razors. However I am not successful in finding what I went in looking for; new sunglasses (I lost my Harley Davidson pair on the day of hell) and spray sunscreen for my poor face.

From Moncton I take the 134 North. This is when another modern-day miracle happens. For approximately twenty kilometres I ride a route that is one hundred percent flat or downhill. My mind is being blown as the flatness and descent go on and on. And on. Oh, sweet day. Kilometre after glorious kilometre. What a gift. A little voice in my head tells me that on another day I will pay, and pay dearly, for this gift. I will have to climb back up. But not today. Today I glide. Like an eagle, like the summer breeze.

When I left my friend Éric's house in Quebec City back on day sixteen, I had written on Facebook that his would be the last familiar face I would see on this trip. But as I continued to post my daily updates, this truth changed. Christina LaFlamme saw my route and said, "Come here." She was a virtual stranger but she opened her home to me and I gained a wonderful new cousin as a result. Now it's happening again.

I have an old friend whom I met when I was a mere sixteen years old, a boy named Dean, whose friend was dating my friend for a short while at that time. That was twenty-five years ago. Through mutual acquaintances and the mighty power of Facebook, he and I became online friends again and have been for years now. But. Still. I have not seen him since I was a teenager. He noticed my journey on Facebook, and made contact. "Come here. We have a house in Shediac Bridge. You will love my wife."

"Okay," I replied.

That is my destination today.

It is about quarter after five when, after sixty-nine kilometres, I turn onto Dean and Mireille's street. A little ways down the road, from the front porch of a lovely white house with green trim and green shutters, I see three hands waving at me. It is Dean, his wife Mireille, and their friend Ashley. They have seen me before I see them. What a moving sight it is for me. In theory, these people are strangers to me. Yet here they are, waiting on the veranda, for *me*, expectantly and excitedly, spotting me immediately and welcoming me with their waves. I am taken off guard, touched deeply. Dean gives me a hug and Mireille hands me a glass of wine she has already poured for me. This is the first sign of many that this pretty lady is a kindred spirit.

The conversation is immediate and overflowing and happy and full of laughter and without a breath. The wine continues to flow. I pull out the bottle I have brought, too. We drink it all. We never move from the porch. Mireille is like an instant old, dear friend. Ashley is looking at me in awe. He thought I would be exhausted but instead I am talking a mile a minute and need the wine to relax me. He leaves on his Harley at the arrival of a looming heavy storm cloud. He is getting married next week. I wish him good luck and congratulations.

Finally, I do start to unwind and slow down. We three talk and talk and talk. I learn about how Dean and Mireille met. They tell me about the trouble they had conceiving Romke, their ten-year-old son. I get a bit teary-eyed as I tell them about my miscarriage last summer. Mireille moves from the chair where she was sitting to beside me on the steps and gives me a wonderful hug. I tell them both how thankful I am to share this holy evening with them. Dean laughs and tells us that he knew that the two of us would hit it off.

Dean leaves to get more wine and cigarettes. Mireille prepares a lovely table of cheeses and pickles and breads and salami. I gave up pork and beef on July fifth purely as a defense against eating one million hotdogs while camping this summer. But, I maintained the caveat that if anyone were to welcome me into their home I would never tell them I don't eat this or that. I don't have an allergy, I am simply choosing to not eat meat. I maintained that I would eat whatever someone is kind enough to offer me. Here is just that situation. I am happy to enjoy the spicy salami along with the rest of the delicious charcuterie and cheeses. We eat, and then move back onto the porch for more wine and cigarettes and conversation.

Mireille plays a haunting tune on the stereo: "The Mistress" from Canadian folk singer and guitarist Amelia Curran. We all stop talking. We just listen. It is dark outside. We are all lightly buzzed. The good vibes are resonating in the warm air of this magical summer night. I am moved by the haunting beauty of this Miss Curran's song; her scratchy guitar, the melody, the wisdom of her lyrics, the timber of her voice. None of us says a word. The song mesmerizes us while the moonlight and still summer air suspend us there, too.

Almost abruptly, I know I need to go to bed. I had warned them that this might happen, that this is my nature: completely on or completely off. I wish them both a good night and thank them again for a wonderful evening. I don't even remember my head hitting the pillow.

I feel like a million ~~bucks~~ apples.

AUGUST 5ᵀᴴ – DAY 32

Miraculously, Dean and Mireille convince me to stay an extra day. They convince me to take a day off. To relax. I am in awe of their super powers.

Dean and I spend the early part of the day together while Mireille works. Our first stop is the touristy monument of a giant lobster and the town name, "Shediac" spelt out in giant Scrabble letter squares. I snap a few photos and we are off on Dean's motorcycle again. Next we lunch at The Sandbar in Pointe du Chêne, overlooking the Northumberland Strait. We both have double Caesars and bacon-wrapped scallops.

"What about your pork ban?" Dean asks.

"Oh, yeah. Oops," I reply.

I am still behaving in guest mode even though we are in a restaurant. Oh, well. Then we shop for seafood: oysters, salmon, and a 2.2 lb. lobster. Mireille has a dinner of fish cakes planned but Dean says, and I agree, that I should also try a lobster since Shediac is the lobster capital of the world. I think I have had a whole lobster maybe once or twice before in my life. Dean says the smaller the lobster the better and asks the lady behind the counter for the one with the darkest claws. He explains to me that dark claws mean the shell is older and there is more meat inside. Good to know. Then we go next door to the liquor store. I buy two bottles of red and two bottles of white. We now have everything we need and it is getting close to three when Mireille will be getting home and when Dean's parents and son will be arriving back from Nova Scotia.

Perfect timing. We arrive back at the house five minutes after his parents and son and five minutes before Mireille. Romke is such a handsome boy. He is interested in my hammock tent and contemplates sleeping in it that night. Dean and Mireille have a large backyard and a few acres of trees beyond it. In the end, he decides not to. I am kind of relieved. I know I can get scared out there in my hammock tent sometimes. I don't want him to have a bad experience.

Dean's parents, Sid and Sandy, are laid-back and friendly. At some point in the evening, Dean's dad says that I must be on some sort of special diet for this trek. Dean, Mireille and I all laugh.

"Yes. Red wine and cigarettes," I tell him.

We all sit to a fabulous dinner at around five or six. Mireille has made fish cakes and a remoulade from scratch and both are out of this world. She is an incredibly talented cook. The salad is made from different lettuce leaves and tomatoes she picked from their garden in the backyard. She serves all this with steamed string beans, also from the backyard.

Mireille explains to me how and where to crack the claw and the tail. I give one claw to Romke and the body to Mireille. She explains to me that the green, clumpy stuff inside the stomach is the lobster's undigested food and is called tomalley and is perfectly edible, a delicacy, in fact. She puts some on my plate. She should have told me what it was *after* I'd tried it. Sandy says that she has tried it and it is "okay." I stare at it, poke it, but I can't bring myself to eat it. What a wimp.

In the evening, Dean, Mireille, Romke, and I go to Cap de Cocagne beach to watch the sunset. It is spectacular; all kinds of vibrant colours and bursts of rays beaming through speckled holes in the clouds. There is no art like the ephemeral sky.

But as we drive back to the house, suddenly my reverie of being there with this amazing family, with my new best buddy Mireille, begins to break. The reality that I have taken a whole day off, that I still have a goal to accomplish, that the worst of the work is yet to come in Nova Scotia with its fabled hills and then the mountains of the Cabot Trail, sets in hard. Time is flying by fast and though I have already come so far, I still have no idea what lies ahead of me and how much time it will take me and if I am even capable of dragging my heavy bicycle up a mountain, up mountains. Shortly after we return to the house, I simply say to everyone, "I need to go to bed."

The paralysis of anxiety has taken hold. My day off is wonderful until it isn't.

I toss and turn all night. Sleep is completely unattainable. To make things worse, throughout the night, I start feeling nauseous. I make three trips to the washroom upstairs. I finally manage to fall asleep sometime after half-past three in the morning, but not for long, maybe two hours. I awake to make another trip to the washroom. I then manage another two hours of "sleep," which is more like being slightly unconsciousness as opposed to a legitimate, restful slumber. My short bouts of sleep are further sabotaged by nightmares of being cornered by strange men and of being blown off the Cabot Trail by wind. Sid mentioned last night that the winds were quite strong when they drove along it. He also said that there had been a huge accident, two cars flipped over. "Probably distracted driving," he said. Distracted drivers, wind, creepy people like Andrew, the mountains, the hills, too many fears…it is all swirling around in my subconscious. And even though I have come a long way already, in my mind I still believe that it has all just been a picnic compared to what must lie ahead. My fears and doubts are now haunting me in nightmares.

In the morning I am groggy, achy, queasy, still making frequent trips to the washroom. Mireille is making fish cakes with poached eggs for breakfast. I have no appetite, but I can't fathom passing up her home cooking. I tell her I am up for eating. But as she is cooking, she looks at me with scepticism. I cave in and agree. I just can't eat. What a crime. Passing up Mireille's cooking for breakfast is basically blasphemy and I am pretty upset about it.

Dean and Mireille feed me a shot of Pepto Bismol and give me two Gravol for the road. Dean brings out a scale to the front porch and weighs my bicycle with its panniers. Eighty-eight pounds. That's heavier than I had thought.

"And that's without wine," Mireille quickly and astutely points out. I marvel at how her brain works. I love this woman.

I set off shortly after nine. The whole family, Dean, Mireille, Romke, Sid, and Sandy, all give me hugs and come out onto the porch to see me off. Sandy has even added me on Facebook. As I pedal down the driveway, I call out, "I think I'm already starting to feel better."

"That's because you're moving again," Dean calls back.

There is wisdom in his words, no doubt. They wave, I call out a last goodbye, I ring my copper bicycle bell, and I look back and see them all there. What a sight. Again, I am moved. They are all standing out there for me, wishing me well, waving. Although I am physically ill, my heart has never been better.

Nova Scotia

"The greatest results in life are usually attained by simple means and the exercise of ordinary qualities. These for the most part may be summed in these two: common sense and perseverance."
-Owen Feltham

AUGUST 6ᵀᴴ – DAY 33

As I begin to ride, despite what I had said to Dean about feeling better, it turns out I am not feeling better at all. I feel weak, achy, nauseous, and poor-spirited as a result. My head and wrists are particularly sore. Even after the full day of rest, I am immediately tender on the hard seat. The only things that are just fine and pain-free, ironically, are my legs.

It is overcast and spitting and chilly and the wind is strong and relentless and all these things are trying on my already weakened psyche. Even on a downhill, I am blown to an almost full stop and am forced to pedal. On a bridge, the wind takes hold of my wheel and makes me fight to keep control and to not veer into traffic. It is a full-on fiercely forceful head wind. The mostly flat route with soft rollers that I am riding should be easy and fast, but instead it is slow with much-begrudged hard work. Although I feel weak I find enough energy to feel pissed about all this.

At around two in the afternoon I finally feel like I might be able to eat something. I stop on the side of the road and eat my last can of Alpha-Getti. I am able to get it down. I know that having some food in me will help me feel better. The sun comes out at this time, too. I slowly begin to gain a little strength.

I ride and I ride. There are some hills; mild whoppers, mild rollers. Then I come to a dead end in front of a construction site. I did see some detour signs earlier but I thought I was following them and that I am on the detour route. Apparently not. I ride past the "road closed / route barrée" sign and approach one of the on-site workers. With sugary sweetness, I politely ask him if I may please squeeze through here.

"Well, we're not supposed to. But I guess I can ask the foreman if it's okay," he replies.

They let me through. Bless them.

Then I see two signs that make my heart flutter and my pulse race in excitement. The first sign says: "Winery 6KMS." The second sign has an arrow and says: "To Nova Scotia." Nova Scotia. Holy shit. My delicate, fragile state begins metamorphosing into one of strength and exhilaration. It's the first sign I've seen bearing the province's name. I'm so close. This is exciting.

I stop at the winery, buy a bottle of Pinot Noir, and chat briefly with the girl behind the counter. She asks me how the wind has been for me.

"Yeah," I say, incredulously. "It's been hell."

I ask her how much longer it will be until I reach Nova Scotia. She says I have maybe one kilometre to go. One kilometre. Elation and anticipation levels are now at turbo levels.

And so, with sun and not rain, with returning strength and not illness, with happiness and not discouragement, and as quietly and unceremoniously as when I left my little apartment, just after sunrise, in Toronto, by myself, to begin this journey, I pass over into Nova Scotia. I keep looking for a sign: Welcome to Nova Scotia! But there is none. I look behind me. Along the opposite lane of traffic I see a sign giving directions to get to New Brunswick. I double check on my itinerary. Without a doubt, I am here. My smile is immense and wide and hurting my cheeks. *I'm in Nova Scotia.* Finally, in my damn little flip-flops, I've done it. I've reached this Maritime province where I have never been before.

I battle a few more whoppers and rollers before I arrive at Amherst Shore Provincial Park. Today I rode a hefty eighty-one kilometres. I snag the last available site: lot 17. And it is perfect. It is private and spacious. It is almost like an outdoor grand central living room with three little offshoots, bedrooms, into the tall woods. I even have extra "cushion" between myself and the next site because there is a little outhouse next door. Perfect. I set up my hammock tent then set off to shower.

Clean and refreshed, I lie down in my hammock tent. Like each and every time I climb into my little outdoor cradle, I cannot get over the perfection of the comfort. I lie there just revelling in the beautiful snugness for the longest while, just marvelling at how good it feels. I begin drifting off when it begins to rain.

I jump up and rush out to my picnic table. I pack up the loose items. I hang my panniers on some tree branches in my little forest bedroom. The rain dies down pretty quickly, however. Now that I am up and the rain has subsided, I sit at the picnic table and have a glass of wine and a cigarette. I feel pristinely clean, but the shower has not revitalized me. I feel sleepy. I know tonight I will sleep instantly and long and deeply which is exactly what my poor, ailing body needs. I'll be back in top form tomorrow for sure.

Minutes later, the rain returns. Then the thunder comes. I love it. I am glad for it. Now I don't need to feel guilty about not going down to the water or going to the eight o'clock park gathering where people share their stories and learn the park history. I was thrilled when I saw the notice in the outhouse advertising this little soirée. It is just the sort of thing that, earlier in this trip, I thought each campground should have. The closest and only thing I have seen that resembles my idea was at Camping Chutes et Gorge. There, they have a central room off of the laundry room with a picnic table and a large world map on the wall and above it the caption: "Where are you from?" There are tacks for you to mark where your home is. This gathering here at Amherst Shore Provincial Park is a great idea and I really want to go, but I am dead tired, and I know it just isn't going to happen. And it's okay, I console myself. *You can't do all the things.* I climb into my little cocoon at about seven-thirty. That's all she wrote, folks. I am out. Immediately.

Like a bear in December.

"You can't be suspicious of a tree, or accuse a bird or a squirrel of subversion or question the ideology of a violet."
-Hal Borland

AUGUST 7ᵀᴴ – DAY 34

While some sites are dominated by earwigs, others by mosquitoes, and many by both, this one seems to be overrun with spiders. I find one crawling down my leg as I begin to disassemble my hammock tent. Spiders have never bothered me. I flick it away. I find one crawling on the rope as I untie it from the tree. Sensing my presence, it hides around the knot. "I see you," I tell it. I blow on him to get him out of the way so I can untie the knot without accidentally squishing him.

The first tree I untie my hammock tent from has large, raised roots for me to step on to reach the rope. I tie it up pretty high now that I have my knot-tying skill down pat. So high, in fact, that I have to hop up to get in. I am proud of my acquired skill. I can jump into the hammock without fear of it coming loose.

As I am standing there on this beautiful tree's raised roots, untethering the straps from its strong trunk, I am struck by all that this beautiful tree has provided me with: shelter for the night, boundless beauty to be cradled in, protection from the rain, privacy, and now, even its roots are lifting me, giving me a stool to help me pack up camp. I think to myself, *My God, what more can this tree give me?*

"Thank you, Tree," I say out loud.

I run my hand over its smooth bark, and give it a little pat. I am suddenly deeply aware that it is a being rather than a thing. I have a little laugh at myself. I am now talking to trees, too. It feels good.

Then I untie the tent from the second tree. I say thank you to it, as well. I again, this time consciously, put my hand on it and give it a pat. It feels solid, smooth, and strong. I again think ahead to city-me and wonder how I will reconcile all my new habits; talking to animals, to the sun, and now to trees.

As I am packing up my panniers on the picnic table, a little chipmunk hops right up to me.

"C'mere, buddy. C'mere. I have something for you," I call out.

I take out one of my Nature Valley nut and seed crisps and break it up into a pile on the corner of the picnic table. He comes back, hops up, selects a chunk, and carries it away. He does this over and over. It is the cutest thing. He is brave, coming this close. I keep encouraging him and talking to him. I call him "Buddy." Eventually he carries away the last crumb.

I stop off at the washroom before leaving. I put on my mascara, and as I am doing so, a spider literally crawls out of my hair. I laugh hard. I change into my shorts. It is just before ten. Here I go again.

Some interesting and immediate changes to make note of about Nova Scotia: Number one, here even drivers of cars say hello. Many of them honk and wave. Previous to here, it was pretty much exclusively trucks and cyclists. Number two, here when drivers come up behind me they give a little toot of their horn to let me know they're coming. At first I didn't realize that the toot was a friendly warning. I thought they were honking *at* me. I gave a "What gives?" gesture with my arms and shoulders. Oops. Thirdly, the dirt here is red. Very cool. And fourthly, the signs are all English only, once again.

In Nova Scotia, the bike trail is called, "The Sunshine Trail." Fantastic name. And the route completely fits the positive vibe. The trail is mostly comprised of next-to-no-traffic roads that follow all along the coast. The scenery is stunning. I have the Atlantic Ocean on my left and beautiful countryside on my right and the sun on my face and the wind at my back and I am feeling pretty damn amazing.

I arrive at a really steep hill just before turning onto the 6 East. It's the kind of hill that is so steep that it doesn't visually flatten out when you arrive at it and start climbing it like most hills do. That visual flattening is a nifty little trick from Mother Nature specifically created to help us cyclists out, I'm sure. I am excited to tackle it. I'm ready for a challenge. Up, up, up I go, veering left, right, left, right in order to subtract some of the incline as I go. About halfway up I hear a car approaching from behind. Now I have to not only stick to my lane of traffic but I also have to move over to the shoulder and stay there, confronting the incline straight on and against its fullest force. There is no room now for any diagonal movement. The incline proves too severe to tackle straight up and I am forced to come to a stop. I am crushed.

I wait until the car passes and I have caught my breath. Then I roll my bike backward and adjust it to nearly perpendicular with the road. With all my might I step down on the pedal, trying to create enough momentum to bring my heavy bike to balance in order to take my other foot off the ground and continue pedaling. It is extremely challenging to begin pedaling on such a severe incline. But, I manage it. I successfully ride to the top.

I turn onto the 6 East. I pause to talk into my voice notes. As I am doing this, a car happens by. It just stops and waits. When I finally look in its direction, the man behind the wheel calls out, "Are you okay?"

I melt. "I am. Thank you."

Today I sing loudly as I ride. I sing "Flip-Flop Fantasy," a song I wrote on my ukulele along this trip. Then I sing "Good Tonight," another song I wrote on my ukulele. I sing "Amazing Grace" and "You Are My Sunshine." I love my ukulele. I love to sing. I love bicycle riding. Today I sing loud and proud as I ride along. My voice is clear and silky. Some days I sing better than others, and today I am in top singing form. I take full advantage and serenade all the trees as I glide along.

I stop in Port Howe where I write and mail off three postcards; one to my Aunt Gisèle, one to my cousin Danny, and one to my friend Kirsten.

Seconds after leaving the post office, I come to a fish and chip truck: Tess' Aus-some Fish & Chips. The owner, Tess, is from Australia. Before I order, I ask Tess if her ketchup is in a bottle or packets.

"A bottle," she replies.

Perfect. I am safe to order. I ask for the two-piece fish and chip meal; one-piece haddock and one-piece cod. I go to sit at a picnic table in the grass, but I am immediately and completely swarmed by a gang of mosquitoes. I look down at my leg and it is a perfect polka-dot pattern of the hungry blood-suckers. I freak out. I do a crazy, manic dance, flailing my arms and kicking up my legs. I dance my way back to the chip truck, out of the grass. I finally finish my performance by dousing myself in bug spray. My wonderfully tanned legs are now hidden behind a sea of mosquito bites, scratched to blood and scabbing or new and bulbous. My midriff is completely white. It hasn't seen a ray of sun all summer. And my arms are a light brown since some days I allow myself to not wear long sleeves. I am a walking bar of Neapolitan ice-cream with sprinkles. Sexy.

As I am once again riding along, out of nowhere, a new song comes to me. I swear these things write themselves and I simply scramble to remember and learn the right chords to match. I am calling this one "The Sunshine Trail," and it shares the trail's happy and sunshiny vibe. I sing it out as I ride. The joy is simply overflowing from me as I ride along the coast, the sunshine on my face, having accomplished so much and on the brink of realizing the ultimate goal of this trip: The Cabot Trail. I am singing out at the top of my lungs as I let myself fly down a hill. When I round the corner at the bottom, there are two, young, good-looking guys sitting on the porch of a house.

Before I have a chance to feel embarrassed, one of them calls out, "Absolutely beautiful!"

You see. I told you I was in good singing form today.

The next great thing that happens on this super fabulous day is I spot an NSLC sign. That's: Nova Scotia Liquor Corporation, my new happy place. I pick up a bottle of Marechal Foch dry red wine, made in Nova Scotia.

I am somewhat racing against the clock right now. I have 58% battery left, no extra charges and forty kilometres still to go.

With thirty-seven kilometres left to go, Google Maps tells me to turn onto the Trans-Canada Trail for three and a half kilometres. I decide to give it a go since I am now out of New Brunswick. Well, once again, the trail is an absolute nightmare; gravelly with pot holes and puddles. I may have lost my shit and said the "F" word angrily and loudly over a few moments. I feel horrible for this, for releasing such negativity out into nature. I feel embarrassed, too, for having a proper fit. I get to Thompson Road. Google Maps tells me to cross it and continue on the trail for thirty-two kilometres.

"Absolutely not." I state firmly out loud to absolutely no one.

Calm, blue oceans, I tell myself. *Calm, blue oceans*.

I turn left onto Thompson Road and pass a house. There is a man just out back.

"Excuse me!" I call out.

He is on his cell phone. He walks toward me as he is finishing up his call. I ask him if he would mind filling my water bottle.

"Sure, dear."

He lets the hose run awhile to get rid of the heated water that has been sitting in the tube in the hot sun. As he lets it run, I check with him that I am going in the right direction to reconnect with The Sunshine Trail. He confirms that I am. He fills my bottle and wishes me well. I thank him and climb up Thompson Road. I finally reconnect with The Sunshine Trail and happily remain there for the last thirty kilometres of the day's ride. It is hilly but paved. The sun is shining all day long. I am in a phenomenal mood.

I stop at Foodland in Tatamagouche, just five kilometres before my destination of Tatamagouche Provincial Park. I am craving some sort of salad or raw vegetables, which have been gravely lacking in my diet this whole journey. Inside the grocery store, there are three little boys wearing bicycle helmets, clearly having just rode their bikes there. I encounter the little crew in one of the aisles.

"I like your helmet!" one of the little boys says to me. I can't help but think of the little bike crew from Yogi Bear's Jellystone Park who also loved my hammock tent and told me it was cool. At forty-one years old, I seem to have really earned the respect and approval of the seven-to-ten-year-old crowd.

I arrive in Tatamagouche Provincial Park. Although I have only ridden sixty-one kilometres today, it is already half-past five in the late afternoon. The sign says: "No camping." Clearly I misread something in my planning or simply didn't bother to check if camping was available; most likely the latter. I have become pretty lax with details, preferring to plan less and just go and simply figure it out along the way. I could gorilla camp, of course, but there isn't much seclusion here to pull that off. I decide to go back into town since my phone is now dead. I did see a motel right across from Foodland. It looks pretty swanky compared to other ones I've stayed in; it might be pricey. But it offers free laundry and both my riding outfits are pretty damp and dirty and musty-smelling. I can recharge all my chargeables. Plus they offer a free breakfast in the morning. I am well under budget, I can afford a little splurge. Balmoral Hotel, here I come.

From my room, I have a lovely view of an open field. For my dinner I eat a sandwich I picked up earlier in the day from a gas station and the salad that I picked up at Foodland. For the salad, I use the last two dressings that Marc gave me way back in Montréal. Isn't that lovely, that his little act of kindness and generosity has stayed with me all this time? Each time I saw those dressing packets amid my collection of contraband condiments I would think of him. How long his kindness has lasted and the warmth over me has lingered. It's all about the little things, just like "they" say. I drink my wine, play my ukulele, smoke cigarettes on my front step, and then sleep peacefully like a tiny speck of a queen in a huge sea of a king-sized bed.

*"I may be ageing myself on the outside
but my soul is drinking from the fountain of youth."*

AUGUST 8TH – DAY 35

I sleep soundly until half-past three in the morning. Then I am up for two hours and when I finally get back to sleep, it's nothing but nightmares again. This time it is the kind of nightmare like when you try to scream but can't; that maddening helplessness. In my dream I keep getting lost or I can't get to my phone to take a picture and other minor dilemmas that seem to just go on and on.

I write out three more postcards to my mother, to my dad, and to my Aunt Denyse and Uncle Randy, while I eat the breakfast of scrambled eggs, bacon, whole-wheat toast, orange juice, and a coffee. There is no choice given; this is what is offered and that is that. It's fine by me. I am so full afterwards that I have to wait a bit in my motel room to let my stomach settle before setting off. While I'm waiting for my food to digest, I sit with my ukulele again. I haven't played it in a while but last night and today find me re-inspired and re-motivated to play it and learn it and write new songs. I sit long enough to figure out all the chords for my song "Good Tonight," including a mash-up part with a verse from "Patience" by Guns 'n' Roses. I finally leave at about ten- thirty.

The day begins with incredible and impeccable scenery, yet again. I love today's route. It starts with forty kilometres along the Six East. Incredibly, I write another new song in my head as I sail along. Like the others, it just comes to me out of the blue. I'm thrilled. It's called "When I Write To You." I can't wait to figure out the chords this evening.

In River John I stop at the NSLC and pick up a bottle of Nova Scotia red. Next door to the NSLC there is a post office. I mail the three postcards that I wrote out this morning.

Later on I stop at a general store. I buy a Nova Scotia sticker for my ukulele, some Nova Scotia postcards, a coffee, and a snack-sized bag of Old Dutch baked dill pickle chips. I sit at a picnic table out front and eat a chicken salad sandwich I purchased earlier at a gas station. Such beautiful weather. It is warm but not too hot—breezy. To add to the great weather, there are long stretches of flat spaces between the gruelling work of the hills. It's the perfect mix of satisfying hard work and well-merited breaks. I am absolutely loving today.

My lower back has begun spasming. It's nothing major but it's enough to alarm me. At the beginning of this journey I was quite nervous about freakishly tearing a calf muscle like I did as I skipped down my hall one Monday evening last January. However, upon further reflection, even with a torn calf muscle I think I could probably still pedal, putting pressure on only the ball of my foot. I don't think a torn calf muscle would stop me. But what if I threw my back out? I've only had a back issue once before and that was almost ten years ago while I was still in teachers' college. At that time, my lower back completely seized up on the right side. It was incredibly painful. It was so acute I couldn't stifle my screams of anguish and ended up at the emergency room, followed by a weeklong blur of greatly-needed Percocet relief. If something like that were to happen now, my ride would be over.

My original destination when I left this morning was Caribou Munro's Provincial Park. It was to be a ride of only fifty-eight kilometres. However, when I reach the turn-off from the Sunshine Trail to go to that park, it is only 1:30 p.m. There are only sixteen kilometres to go after the turn-off. I will finish incredibly early, yet I am full of gusto and ambition to keep going. With such perfect riding weather and still valuing my returned health, I want to take advantage of my energy and the lovely climate. I skip the park and carry on. I decide I will go as far as New Glasgow and then will re-evaluate a destination once there.

I pull over several times throughout my ride to stretch out my back. Just before New Glasgow, the spasms seem to be more frequent and a little more intense. I decide to resort to ibuprofen. I don't want to take a pain reliever because if it needs stretching I want to be able to feel the pain that is telling me I need to do so. But the spasms are frequent now. I need to treat and relax the tensing muscles. I take two extra-strength Advil and carry on.

I arrive at New Glasgow at half-past four. My back is still giving me trouble with frequent spasms, but it isn't getting any worse. It is still early and it's gorgeous out. I look on Google Maps and search for campgrounds. The next feasible destination is Cranberry Campground, another thirty-two kilometres away. Sundown is at 8:32 p.m. I have four full hours to get there. I don't need to think for long. I decide to go for it.

I pass through New Glasgow. I turn left onto Bridge Street. As I begin crossing over the namesake bridge, I hear a big thud. Simultaneously my back tire comes to a dead stop. It drags me to a halt. I wrestle with the weight of the bike to avoid falling over and succeed. I am standing there baffled.

At first I can't figure out what is going on. My tire isn't flat, and my panniers aren't caught onto a spoke. Upon further inspection I notice half a bolt on the ground. Then I notice my back bike rack. It attaches to the back wheel by a bolt on either side. The left side bolt is altogether missing. The other half of the bolt on the ground is still attached to the right side but now has no head and is flush with the frame and unreachable with any devices on my bike tool. The weight of both panniers has been riding on the single right bolt for who knows how long now? Bearing so much weight, it now has finally snapped.

So I'm suddenly halted and stuck. I am not panicking at all because I am in a relatively major city and not on some secluded path like Dark Hollow Road. As I stand there, trying to figure out how to handle the situation, a man comes walking by. He asks me if everything is okay. I tell him what has just transpired. He has a look at my bike, then turns and points to a tractor trailer truck maybe two hundred meters down the road. He says, "See that truck? That's McCullough's. It's a truck service station. They can fix this for you."

"Do you think they'll be able to get out that broken half-screw that's still stuck in the frame?" I ask.

"One hundred percent for sure, they can. One hundred percent," he says confidently.

"Thank you!" I gush.

What luck that this little mishap has happened in such an ideal location and also that this knowledgeable and helpful man just happens to be walking by and is able to inform me that help that is close by. Without his help, I would have ended up calling a taxi to take me to some bike shop or Canadian Tire who-knows-where with cab fare costing who-knows-how-much, getting my bike serviced who-knows-when.

I take my three back bike panniers and hide them in a bush beside the bridge. I use the two bungee cords, the ones that I always keep attached to my back bike rack for firewood lugging, to suspend the broken rack to the pole of my seat. Now my bicycle is rideable again, though this makeshift set-up could never support the weight of my heavy panniers. I ride over to McCullough's.

I enter the building and approach the counter, behind which there are several men in coveralls milling about. I explain what has happened and, as surely as the man on the bridge had promised, they tell me they can help me. They tell one of the younger guys to take my bike around back. I follow. I tell the young guy as we walk that it is ironic that this has happened, since just that morning I had noticed a loose screw on my water bottle holder and tightened it. I tell him, "I didn't think to check for other loose screws since I've never done anything like this before. This whole bike ride…I really don't know what the hell I'm doing at all."

He thinks this is funny and frankly so do I. We share a laugh as he removes the broken screw and puts on two new screws. My bike rack is like new. Upon my polite request, he also gives me two extra screws to keep just in case this should happen again.

I go around front to pay the man at the counter. He doesn't know what to charge me. He goes to ask another man, apparently the boss. The boss man looks busy and agitated and without looking up from what he is doing, replies grouchily to the first man, "I don't fucking know. Just tell her don't worry about it."

The man comes back with a bemused look on his face and says to me, "Well, I guess this is the freebie of your journey. No charge."

"Oh, wow, thank you so much!" I say excitedly.

Then he asks, "You doing this ride by yourself?"

"Yup," I reply.

"That sounds pretty boring," he says flatly.

I laugh and tell him, "I'm having a blast." Then I add with exaggerated enthusiasm, "And it's because of nice people like you!"

I add this last statement to purposely toy with his blasé attitude toward my little adventure. The young guy hears me and again cracks up. He gets my positivity and humour. I thank them all one more time, and then I take off once again.

I ride back to the bridge. My three back panniers are still safely hidden. I remove them and reattach them to my bike. I look at the time. I've basically lost forty-five minutes due to this little mechanical mishap. I now have around three hours to do thirty-two kilometres before sundown. That's cutting it pretty close and leaves no cushion for any other potential misadventures. Reluctantly, though with a respectable sixty-eight kilometres accomplished, I decide to just stay put in New Glasgow for the evening.

I arrive at the Tara Motel. The petite lady behind the counter tells me she indeed has a room for me. She says, "It's downstairs, around back, and beside the graveyard. Is that a problem?"

I laugh out loud. When I see she is absolutely serious about the details of the accommodation, I tell her I don't mind at all. Actually, I think it's hilarious.

She adds, "They're really quiet. You won't have any issues with the neighbours."

I'm sure she's told that exact joke one million times.

What a quirky, random day. I look out my window at the sea of graves. What a different view than the grassy field and distant trees I had yesterday. I love both views. I love the diversity of my days. This one definitely tops the list for its uniqueness. I continue to smile as I settle in my room.

By six in the evening, I am "moved in" and relaxing. I am lying on the bed, talking to my voice notes when someone comes up to my door, puts a key in the lock...and opens it. I thought that whoever it was would simply discover they had the wrong door when it failed to open, but no. In come two older women and an older gentleman. I call the front desk.

The lady says, "Oh, Christina, I gave you room 123!"

"No. You gave me the key for room 122 and you told me 'Room 122' and that's where I am."

"Oh, I'm so sorry about this," she says, after realizing that it couldn't possibly be my mistake but had to be hers.

"No problem," I say.

Yet another haphazard, comical detail to this unique and amusing day.

After a shower I sit down with wine and my ukulele. I figure out the chords to the song that came to me today and furthermore even write a bridge. I'm thankful that my sister Angela suggested I get a ukulele for this trip. It feels wonderful to write songs again. It's what I've done since I was a kid. I remember exactly how it all started. I was three years old there on Thomas Street in Oshawa when I first heard my parents play the *Grease* soundtrack on their huge stereo, the size of a large credenza and the commanding piece of furniture in our living room. The song "Hopelessly Devoted to You" was playing. I was mesmerized by the music. I listened and learned. I gathered my courage and ventured to sing along to the last two words of the song: "…to you." Somehow I got the notes right. And when I heard the music in harmony with my voice, I fell in love forever. I remember that moment. I was only three years old and I completely remember it. This magical journey has brought many marvels and amazements; it has even brought me back to singing and song-writing.

I speak with Roger briefly on FaceTime before he has to go back to work. He says he will call me back shortly. We have been speaking more and more, and I must admit that even though the song I wrote today isn't specifically for him, it is definitely his sweet texts and attention and our long conversations and budding emotional affair that has inspired me to write a love song at all. As promised, he calls back. I don't answer. I am already sound asleep.

"Fear is a wonderful feeling. Fear means that we are on the brink of learning new things and that our spirit will grow, whether through success or through failure."

AUGUST 9TH – DAY 36

I awake and have the continental breakfast included with my motel stay. I have two small bowls of Raisin Bran, a glass of orange juice, and two coffees. And a cigarette.

If I act like a car today I will have only a fifty-seven kilometre ride to my next destination. As a bike, it is seventy-five kilometres. I briefly ponder it but quickly choose the bike route that follows along the coast. It seems a bit contrary to what this trip is all about to just hop on an unscenic, boring highway. I'm glad I tried it; once was exciting, but also dangerous, and now that experience has been had. Check. The Sunrise Trail is calling my name. I leave shortly after nine.

A mere six hundred meters into my trek I turn onto Johnny Miles Memorial Trail. Since the horrors of the NB Trail in New Brunswick, anytime I hear the word "trail," except for the glorious Sunrise Trail, I am quite hesitant to follow it. However Google Maps says I am only to follow it for one kilometre and it looks decent so I am not too worried. Silly me. About four hundred meters in, the trail turns into that awful, uneven gravel that I had feared. Though a short distance to travel, I stop and debate continuing. I don't want a flat tire.

A lone man happens to be walking by and when he sees me stopped, he asks, "Well, where are you headed?"

"In that direction," I say as I point straight ahead.

"Well, where are you going?"

I look at the map and tell him I need to reach Walkerville Road. He points to another path and tells me it will take me to Walkerville Road, and though it adds a bit of distance it is smooth and rideable, unlike the one I am facing. Yet another random person popping up at just the right time to guide me the right way.

The day starts with fourteen kilometres of lovely, winding, hilly back roads. Then, I am taken along sixty-one kilometres straight of the glorious Sunrise Trail. I love these long stretches; there is no stress of being directed to a gravelly pass or a desolate road. I am quite happy. I am in love with the Sunrise Trail.

"How's the riding?" a woman asks me at the convenience store in Pictou.

"It's great!" I say.

"Well, it's kind of windy out there, isn't it?" she asks.

"Oh, nothing like a few days ago, that's for sure," I reply.

I see a roadside pizza oven and fish and chip truck called, "The Cabana." I pretty much stop at everything I pass. It breaks up the day. I am actually hungry, though. I order a two-piece haddock and chips. I eat one piece and take the second with me for later. The owner, who serves me, has a cool little plaque hanging at the condiment station. It reads: *Life is better in flip-flops.* Damn straight.

Before leaving this morning, my lower back gave one light spasm, a gentle reminder to stretch it and drug it, which I did. It has been good all day. Now, just after three in the afternoon, I start having a few spasms. I pull over and take two more Advil and have a good stretch. I put sunblock on my face, which effectively does nothing. I need to go back to the bandanna pirate styles. I have thirteen kilometres to go.

I ride through Antigonish. I have two more kilometres to go, or so I think. I pull over to make sure that I haven't missed it. I have pulled over right on the front lawn of Whidden Park Campground & Cottages. The campground is in a central location, not out in the country, not out in the middle of nowhere. It is inconspicuously tucked behind other houses and buildings off a main street. My seventy-five kilometre day is suddenly complete.

I pay to camp for the night. One of the staff members takes me by golf cart to check out the available lots to ensure that I find one with two trees where I am able to hang my hammock tent. Lot 157 is perfect. My hammock tent will hang directly beside a little babbling brook. I'm thrilled.

I set my tent up and then go for a shower. In the washroom there are all kinds of signs warning of theft. I have not encountered this at any other campground and know that it is not just standard operating procedure; there must be a reason for all the signs. That leaves me feeling more than a bit uneasy. I go back to my site and open my bottle of Wolf Blass Eaglehawk Shiraz. I look at my upcoming itinerary. I am dangerously close to the The Cabot Trail. I am flushed with equal parts excitement and fear.

I check The Cabot Trail website. It speaks of black bears, moose, and bald eagles. I Google "Cabot Trail accommodations." I see a couple of motels around the northern tip and nothing else. Will I be forced to gorilla camp in bear country? I become discouraged, drastically unconfident. I am in way over my head with this thing.

Then a man comes by throwing his ball into the babbling brook where his dog eagerly goes to fetch it. He asks me if I am biking far. I tell him that I started in Toronto and that I am going to The Cabot Trail.

"Whoa!" he replies.

I share my fears about finding accommodations along the trail. Well. This guy is from Cape Breton. He knows Cape Breton. He knows The Cabot Trail. He begins telling me stop-off points I should visit. He tells me there are lots of bed-and-breakfast spots along the way and that I will be fine. He also tells me that, yes, there is a lot of wildlife but there would not be any kind of direct interaction, and that I could do it and that I would be just fine. His name is Judson and he is camping there with his wife and two sons, who are doing some sort of hockey camp in the area. He tells me that they have made some sweet-and-sour pork in the crockpot with Greek salad and I am welcome to come have some. I tell him I have just eaten but thank him all the same.

He says, "Are you sure? It's really no trouble. We have so much."

I don't need any food, what I had needed was some insight about the trail and some reassurance that I would be okay, and he's given me exactly that. I let him know that he has come along at just the right moment when I was feeling overcome with fear and full of doubt, but that he has helped me immensely with his advice and his sharing his knowledge.

"Thank you," I tell him.

"I'll leave you to your evening. If you need anything, I'm just over there in the Zinger."

I look to my left. There is a big trailer with the word "Zinger!" on it.

"Thank you," I say again.

Then off Judson goes with his dog, Finn.

I sit and sip my wine. Right after Judson leaves, this little, tiny kid on this little, tiny bicycle with training wheels and a helmet that looks huge on his little, tiny body calls to me, "Do you want to see me do a pop-a-wheelie? I can do a pop-a-wheelie!"

I die on the spot from his cuteness and innocence. I call out, "Yes! Show me!"

He pedals really hard with his little legs, gets some momentum going, pulls back on the handle bars, and lifts his front tire off the ground, maybe a whole inch for maybe half a second. It's a start, it's something. It's a pop-a-wheelie, all right. He is beaming, darn proud. It is priceless.

I'm pretty overwhelmed by the amazing coincidences that have happened long this ride, the caring people who have come along at exactly the moment I needed some help. And this evening, as I am sitting here, scared, on the brink of the next and pinnacle leg of my journey, Judson, a complete stranger, stops by to chat and gives me all the information and assurance I need to carry on. Everyone keeps asking me: "Oh, you're doing this alone?" The funny thing is, I'm not; not by any stretch of the imagination.

I buy firewood and enjoy a roaring but short-lived fire. I am tired. I climb into my precious hammock tent. I listen to the soft murmur of the little rivulet I am hanging over. Its gentle gurgles and splashes coo me to sleep…

Cape Breton

"I am carefree and happy as a child. I could be in the Guinness Book of World Records for being the oldest girl in the world. It's how I act and how I feel."

AUGUST 10TH – DAY 37

In the morning, it is only thirteen degrees. If I stay nestled up in my furry socks, jeans, hoodie, and good-to-zero-degree sleeping bag, I am fine. If I wake in the small hours of the morning I need to pull closed the drawstring of my sleeping bag, so that I am completely entombed in it. My hot breath gets trapped inside the bag and it's sufficient to warm me. I know that is not a smart way to keep warm in the winter, but it isn't winter, so I do it. That is exactly what I am doing right now. I am basically trapped in this cocoon until it gets warmer outside. I am a wimp for the cold. Anyway, it is the perfect little pocket of time to do all my daily administration.

I am close to The Cabot Trail. Today, I should pass into Cape Breton, one milestone closer. In anticipation of the monstrous hills and mountains that I have been warned will be waiting for me there, both before starting this ride and by many people I have met during it, I am now planning for lower daily kilometres. Another reason I am now contemplating lower daily kilometres is that I don't want this experience, this magic, to end. Already my final destination is within sight. No need to rush. I want to relax and savour. But, truthfully, it is mostly that I am afraid that I am going to get clobbered by ridiculous hills and merciless mountains.

A woman in the lot across from me is watching me pack up my hammock tent. I notice her but pretend not to because it's amusing to watch her watch me. Finally she catches me noticing her. She just gives me a big grin and I give her one right back. I understand people's curiosity. My hammock tent truly looks like a mini hovering spaceship. I totally get it and love people's curious stares.

I eat a breakfast of a 500mL carton of milk and a granola bar. I think I have finally mastered the art of buying only just what I need. After this adequate meal, I am now out of food.

After packing up my camp I make a stop at the washroom where I change into my long-sleeved riding shirt. I am standing outside putting on my helmet and sun visor and sunglasses, replacements given to me by Dean, when a woman named Darlene happens by. She asks me about my trip.

When I tell her what I am up to you she says two words to me, "Smart girl."

What I am doing is not only not crazy or weird like my insecurities plagued and terrorized me in the weeks leading up to my departure, but it is smart. One of the smartest things I've ever done. Selling my car was another. Plus she called me a *girl*. Yep. I am the oldest girl in the world. My spirit never grew up and I reap the benefits of that every day, but especially now, on this ride of a lifetime.

Darlene wishes me well and goes on her way. I am just about to set off when Barb and her two sons come by. They are from Brampton, Ontario. They also stop to chat with me. My bicycle simply draws the curiosity and sense of adventure out of people. It's fantastic. I am blessed. Barb wishes me luck and I finally set out. I love these random chats with strangers. It is empowering to receive their warmth and encouragement. It puts wind in my sails.

Just before leaving, my back lightly spasms, just the same way it did yesterday directly before setting off. It's like a friendly but stern reminder to take some muscle relaxers (ibuprofen) before it completely seizes up. My legs feel quite solid and tight. I don't feel any pain in them, but I can absolutely feel their rock-solid response to all the hard work they did yesterday.

I stop at a drive-in style diner called Snow Queen along the Trans-Canada Highway. I stock up with a fish burger and a pulled-chicken burger. I pack both into my pannier, I'm not hungry quite yet, and continue on.

I'm finally hungry a short while later. I stop at Brosha's Short Stoppe, buy 500mL of milk, and then sit at the little table out front to eat. It's filthy, but that's one of the things baby wipes are for. I wipe it off, and eat the pulled chicken sandwich. It's crazy good. I have only travelled nine kilometres. From looking at the itinerary, I think it's going to be a long, boring day of unscenic highway.

At around nineteen kilometres into my ride, I see a sign that says "Cape Breton via Old Route 4." I check it out on Google Maps. It pretty much follows alongside the Trans-Canada Highway, which I am on now and dying from boredom on. It looks like taking this Route 4 will add some kilometres as it winds and twists a bit, but I decide to go for it.

I don't know why Google Maps isn't suggesting this route; I am acting as a bicycle today, after all. The journey along Route 4 lasts for a lovely ten kilometres. It is definitely more scenic than the Trans-Canada Highway, though it is a bit redundant; a tree-lined country road of ubiquitous natural beauty. It is peaceful with not much traffic. It is Anywhere, Canada.

When I return to the Trans-Canada Highway, it gets a bit treacherous. There is only half a metre of shoulder and some parts have overgrown bush jutting out and blocking my path. The vehicle lanes are narrow, as well. I am a bit nervous and am acutely aware of my surroundings and my steering.

I finally arrive at some scenery: water at last. I happily stop to snap up perfect photos. This section of highway is much calmer and the shoulder is much wider. I round a bend and there is a beautiful red ship docked in a harbour just beyond some train tracks. Just beside this beauty, there is a rugged stone cliff wall. Stunning. The scene is out of a seafarer's story book. I ride a few minutes, stop to take photos, ride another few minutes, and then stop to take yet more photos. The vivid colours; contrasting magenta-blue water with slate-grey rock walls, powder-blue sky, fire engine-red boat; the pretty, perfect placement of sky, mountain, train tracks, water, and boat, perfectly juxtaposing civilization and nature. I have somehow stepped onto the canvas of a vivid still life painting.

There is a green bridge just down the road a bit. I get a little closer. There is something written on the bridge. My heart begins to palpitate. I make sure what I am reading is what I am reading. Indeed, it is.

"Welcome to Cape Breton!"

My heart erupts like fireworks. It is the Canso Causeway Swing Bridge. I have arrived in Cape Breton! I am freaking out inside. My emotions are going ballistic. *Welcome to Cape Breton.* Holy shit. It is just before four in the afternoon.

Before even crossing the bridge and officially entering Cape Breton I snap a photo and send it to Roger, with whom I am pretty much having a full-blown emotional affair at this point. Then I post the photo to Facebook. I have stars in my eyes. I am giddy with my good news.

Just over the bridge there's a gift shop. I go in and buy a Cape Breton sticker for my ukulele. I also buy a fridge magnet for my mother and one for me too, and some postcards. I am fighting to hold back my tears of joy. I pay for my things and am getting back on my bicycle when I realize that in my preoccupation of sheer joy I have forgotten to ask something very important. I go back inside and ask, "Excuse me, do you know where a liquor store is?"

The Skye Motel, which is my destination for the day, is only about another kilometre away from the gift shop. However, the liquor store is another five kilometres beyond that. It is also uphill, the lady at the front desk of the motel tells me. So here is a, "You know you're an alcoholic when..." story and a "You know you're cheap when..." story: Instead of checking in, I decide I will carry on, get wine, then stop at the next motel I happen upon. Let me tell you: the hill leading up to Port Hawkesbury, where the liquor store is, is brutal. I get my precious wine. There is a motel directly across the street. It is $160 plus tax per night. I ride the five kilometres back to the Skye Motel.

When I am checking in, I ask if I can have a room at the back of the motel, which faces the water and that same beautiful red ship I passed coming in. She tells me that a room at the front of the motel costs $84.95 whereas a room at the back of the motel costs $89.95. I laugh. I decide to "splurge" for the room facing the beautiful water out back.

After sixty-eight kilometres spent in intense sunshine, now the sun's heat and radiance begin to soften. The deeper evening creeps closer. The view is serene, like a postcard. This is the perfect destination and place for me to stay on my first evening in Cape Breton. I shower and speak with Roger on FaceTime. Then I take out my ukulele and strum away as I sip wine. I am overcome with calm happiness; a bursting, joyful peace engulfs me. The sun goes down just beyond the mountains. The harbour looks beyond picture-pretty with the bright lights from the ship and the little lights that line the bridge reflected in the water, waltzing wistfully with the gentle waves. *I am in Cape Breton*, I think wondrously. *I am a whisper away from The Cabot Trail.*

At half-past nine I go outside for a cigarette. There is a light breeze coming from different directions. It tosses my damp, fresh hair to and fro and into my face. I love it. I feel holy in my rare pristine cleanliness. I can hear the leaves rustling in the wind. I can see the silent but sparkling harbour. I am lightly buzzed from the wine, the wine that I need to unwind from the days that often elate me, rather than fatigue me. I am ravished with this life. It is achievement wrapped in nature, how divine.

It has all unfolded so quickly, it seems. And now that I am here in Cape Breton, and nearing the Cabot Trail, I understand that it will all end and soon and that creates a panic and sadness inside me. I never want this to end. My memory is horrible and I look forward to re-reading and editing my notes when indeed this beautiful now becomes the elusive past.

I FaceTime with Roger again. I play him the song that I wrote a couple of days ago, inspired by him, called, "When I Write to You." He plays for me a bit on his guitar too. We say good night.

I fall sound asleep, like moss on a rock.

AUGUST 11ᵀᴴ – DAY 38

I awake early, just after five. I put a pot of coffee on and do my daily administration. I go outside and snap photos of the changing sky as the sun rises. And, of course, I chat with Roger. Yes, on top of all the other wonders of this trip, a beautiful new relationship is unfolding.

I eat a continental breakfast of two pieces of white bread toasted with four pats of butter and four slices of processed cheese. I also have a plastic cup full of apple juice and a mug of coffee with milk. Perpendicular to the motel is a little road called Lovers' Lane. I see the name on Google Maps. I go to the post office there upon setting out for the day, and I say to the clerk, "With a name like Lovers' Lane, it's a shame there isn't a street sign."

"Yeah, it tends to get stolen," she replies in a resigned tone.

Yes, of course. I laugh.

I am four kilometres into my ride and have just turned onto a ten-kilometre long stretch of a pretty isolated road called, ironically, Long Stretch Road, when I start getting terrible menstrual cramps. I am surprised I can even feel them since I have already taken two Advil in the morning for my back spasms. These must be pretty bad cramps. It couldn't hurt to take another two pills, I decide. I pull over and swallow them down with some water. As I begin pedaling again, I realize that I am going to have to find somewhere along the side of the road where I can conceal myself enough to insert a tampon. I spot a bush and into it I go. Wow. What a life. Here I am, on the side of the road, in a bush, with my finger up my vagina.

The glory moments.

After about another kilometre of riding, I'm passed by a blue car, which pulls over. As I approach, a woman in a pink sweater hops out and waits for me.

"Hi!" I call out.

Her name is Lorna and she tells me she just wanted to make sure that I wasn't lost. "I haven't seen anyone traveling down this road in forever and thought maybe you'd taken a wrong turn," she tells me. She is just coming back from the chiropractor. She warns me that there are a couple of kilometres of dirt road coming up. I review my directions from Google Maps with her and she says, "Oh yeah, oh yeah, okay, you're good."

Then Lorna invites me to her house, which is just within sight for a coffee. I admit to her that I have already had two double espressos in my motel room and then another one at the continental breakfast. She is speaking so fast and so excitedly that she is getting tongue-tied and laughing at herself. I put my hand on her arm and laugh and tell her that she completely reminds me of *me*. Lorna wishes me well and off we each go.

While I'm traveling the stretch of dirt road that Lorna had predicted, a car approaches, and slows down beside me. The man in the car rolls his window down and says to me, "Y're not lost, are ya'?" His voice is incredibly hoarse, like he has smoked more than one million cigarettes, but with a peppy twang. I assure him I am not and thank him. He drives off.

Here, in Nova Scotia, all of the dogs who have run out barking at me have only gone as far as their own front lawns. There have been no major scares like in Ontario and New Brunswick and Quebec…knock on wood.

All day I scan the trees looking for moose. I have never seen one of these magnificent creatures and I am determined to. Anyway, I have nothing better to do. I have no desire to listen to music. Except for at the statue of Dionne Le Semeur back in Quebec, I haven't. I am too tuned into the subtle sounds of nature, the silence, the hum of the insects, and the tickle of the wind on my ear. I have no need to escape or find a pacifier to occupy my mind. The entire ride is densely forested winding road and not a thing else. It is blissful monotony.

About thirty kilometres into my ride, my Google Maps itinerary instructs me to turn onto Ashfield Road and stay there for twelve kilometres. Ashfield Road looks alarmingly similar to Phil A. Munroe Road. There is no way I am riding even a single bike length of Ashfield Road. I change myself into a car on Google Maps. I then travel six kilometres on North Side River Denys Road to the Trans-Canada Highway and stay there until reaching Whycocomagh.

The yellow line in the middle of the Trans-Canada Highway now has divots in it, which makes it look like a super-long crinkle-cut French fry. I follow it and reach my destination of Glenview Campground at quarter after three. The two campsites they have left indeed have trees but they are entirely flush with the fence of a neighbouring house. Setting up my hammock tent on them, I would be lying directly against the fence. Not ideal. The woman then has her brother, with whom she runs the campground, take me in the golf cart down a new road they have just created, to a big piece of land they are still preparing and setting up to be future campsites. The plot of land is about two hundred meters long, beautiful, secluded, and full of tall trees. There is a little stream tucked into the far corner. I could have this entire space all to myself. I am torn.

In part, it is like an incredible gift and a dream. But, truth be told, I would feel a little isolated and fearful there away from all the other campers with not even a washroom close by or any lights. Even though I am open to gorilla camping, clearly I am still at level-one with regards to location comfortability. Furthermore, I can't get an Internet signal down here and, to top it all off, there is a fire ban. If I had no choice, I know I could face it and do it and even love it. But I do have the choice and I am choosing otherwise, though I am not sure what otherwise will be at this point. I tell the brother that I will think about it. Then I leave to go to the NSLC.

After buying a bottle of Lindeman's Shiraz, feeling grumpy, probably due to hormones, and seeing the impending rain, I decide maybe it is best to make it another motel evening. I don't want to spend the money and much prefer to camp, but I can feel my exhaustion increasing and I am simply feeling all around fed up and discouraged. At this moment, I've had my fill of all the riding and sweating and uphills and that damn helmet on my head all day long and the visor so tight around my head and the dull headache it gives me all day and the stupid mosquitos and the dirt. All of it. I start making my way to the Aberdeen Motel.

I get about two kilometres down the 105 East when I come upon Whycocomagh Provincial Park. Its sign displays that universal camping symbol I have come to know and love. I pull over and think about it. It's drizzling out. I would have to set up camp in the rain. But I'm right here, and I know I will be thankful once I'm nestled in my beloved hanging cocoon. Ugh. I might as well check it out, I decide, almost begrudgingly.

This park uses the "yellow phone system." Basically there is no person at the registration desk. Instead there is a yellow telephone. When you pick it up, it automatically connects you to a central calling center. You do speak to a live person, at least. As I am on the phone with the girl on the other end, I notice on the park map that there are three yurts at this park. I get a bit excited. I have never stayed in a yurt. I didn't even know what a yurt was until I started doing the weekend trial ride/camps in preparation for this expedition. I saw them for offer on some campgrounds I investigated online and had to Google them to figure out what they are. I ask the girl on the phone if one is available. She tells me two are definitely booked but "let me just check on the third one." When she puts me on hold I just know in my heart that she is going to come back and tell me it is available.

That is exactly what happens. My first yurt.

My yurt is on Lot 38 of the forty lots available. Lot one is at the bottom of a small mountain and the numbered lots ascend as you travel up a steep path up its side. I am able to grunt and stop to catch my breath but continue riding all the way up to lot 27 with my eighty-eight-pound-plus-wine loaded-up bicycle. Then I have to hop off. I am mad at myself that I am not able to get the whole way up riding. Now I am grumpy again, the thrill of the yurt quashed, like a gnat by a flyswatter. I'm definitely moody. I am frustrated and sick of riding my bike up these damn hills. Irritably, I push my heavy bike up to my lot at the top of the mountain.

Being as it is at the top of the path and above all the other campsites and on the side of a mountain, I have a gorgeous view of an opposing mountain and Whycocomagh Bay in between. The yurt is spacious and clean with two double bunk beds and a table with six chairs. I have my own personal outhouse just behind and a huge deck with bench and barbecue. (Though the barbecue is useless to me. Without knowing I'd have use of one beforehand, I have nothing to cook on it.) The view is the best part, for sure. It is magnificent and humbling, eerie and spooky with a light fog and a drifting mist. I am mesmerized.

I bring my four panniers inside and begin preparing my dinner of a salad with mozzarella cheese and a Greek dressing with feta and oregano. As I am preparing my meal, it begins raining hard. This makes me immensely happy, due to its perfect timing of arriving after I am settled into my home for the evening. It legitimizes the extra cost of my glorified tenting digs, too. I am happy and thankful for this new experience of staying in a yurt.

I enjoy a cigarette on the deck as I look on Google Maps and figure out that I rode fifty-two kilometres today. Then I go inside and eat as I listen to the calming pitter patter of the rain. It is such soothing drumming, the millions of tiny tappings, the incredible number of soft sounds creating an immense but gentle symphony on my vinyl roof. It reminds me once again of our family's thumbnail tapping as my Grandma and Grandpa entered the church that day in Oshawa, renewing their vows on their fiftieth wedding anniversary. Dull, perfect medicine for an agitated psyche and angry hormones. I drift into the lulls of a sweet nap in my cozy sleeping bag on a bottom bunk.

Finally, just before seven, the light rain stops and I am feeling refreshed enough to ride over to the communal tap and fill my water bottle. I spend the night in and around my little yurt; out on the deck having a cigarette or inside playing the ukulele and drinking wine, talking with friends on FaceTime, and running off to the outhouse. It's fun.

By half-past eleven I am deep asleep like a pebble in the bottom of a deep pond.

The Cabot Trail

"Achieving a goal is at least fifty-one percent mental."

AUGUST 12TH – DAY 39

Today is the day. Today I will enter the Cabot Trail. I feel immense, tall, and brave, like each of the twenty months leading up to this day are stand-up mirrors, all in a row, showing me my path here and the incredible scope of this journey. I see it all, I feel elation, I feel the hands of time pause. I already feel highly accomplished and amazed at getting even this far. I am wild with anticipation and wilder with fear here on this final leg of my journey.

I purposely did next-to-no research about my trip and about The Cabot Trail. I left it almost entirely up to discovery. Roger has asked me if I look ahead at each day's topography.

"No way," I told him. "If I have to ride up a mountain, why should I do it *and* dread it? I shall just deal with it as it comes."

I am overcome with excitement and curiosity, here at the brink of what is sure to be an experience of beauty and wonder, of self-test and challenge beyond anything I can imagine. I am at the cusp of achieving my ultimate goal. I am close, I can see it and taste it. This is the moment I have been looking toward, dreaming of, fantasizing, romanticizing, fearing. This is the moment where the unknown begins to morph into the known. I am wide-eyed and bursting with anticipation and readiness.

The miserable mess and discouragement I was feeling yesterday is gone. I am surprised, to be honest, that I haven't had more moments like that. I put on a fresh riding outfit and set off. It is half-past eight in the morning.

When a truck passes me going the same direction as me, and there is a pull, a sort of vacuum. It helps me, propels me forward. However, when a truck passes me going the opposite direction, it is like riding into a stone wall of wind. Today there are many trucks in both directions and I am being tossed about quite a bit. Most of the time, to the right of me, there is a guardrail bordering the road. But on my bicycle I am much taller than it. At other times there is no guard rail at all, just me beside a straight-down drop into tall trees, water, and a ground so far below I cannot see it.

I stop to eat a granola bar. I don't actually disengage from my bicycle, I just stand there with it between my legs, its weight leaning and balancing on my inner thighs.

Out of nowhere, over my shoulder, I hear, "Hello!"

I haven't heard him approach and pull up behind me. It is another solo long-distance cyclist. His name is Bertrand and he is from Montreal.

I am thrilled to see and speak with a fellow rider. "Hi!" I exclaim back.

We fall into an easy chat about our rides. He started in Montreal.

"I have you beat," I tease him.

He laughs. It turns out he also camped at Whycocomagh Provincial Park last night. Too bad we had not run into each other there.

We add each other on Facebook and then we begin to ride. We ride at fairly the same pace for a while, but eventually he drifts ahead of me. Even the slightest difference in natural pace can make a big difference after a short distance. I realize now how a trip like this, where there is demanding physical exercise all day long, every day, is probably best done solo. Each person will have a different threshold for pain, endurance, strength, resistance to the elements, level of camping, etcetera. I have had a hassle-free, argument-free, compromise-free journey, doing it on my own. It's smooth this way, but it doesn't teach you how to get along with other humans. As I have said, I'm going to be single forever.

After riding for twenty-six kilometres, I stop at the Red Barn Restaurant and Gift Shop. It overlooks the entrance to the Cabot Trail. Blood rushes to my cheeks. I could squeal like a pig. Utter and unequivocal jubilation. My dream is at hand, that sign, it is positively staring at me. It is, finally, the face of the voice that has tirelessly called to me these past twenty months.

I enter the restaurant and have my favourite and hearty meal of four sunnyside up eggs with hash browns and whole-wheat toast with butter and jam. I also have a small glass of grapefruit juice and a coffee with milk. I eat my breakfast slowly, or as slowly as I can manage. I am hungry, and I am raring to go. Still, I do my best to savour this exciting moment. The calm before the storm? I have made it all the way here, and now I will discover, wheel length by wheel length, just what the famous Cabot Trail has in store for me.

I finish eating and go into the gift shop to look for a Cabot Trail sticker for my ukulele, which is becoming as tatted up as I am. Billy, behind the counter, helps me find one. I tell him I rode here from Toronto and I am about to start the Cabot Trail, the final leg of my journey. He asks me if I am going to do it clockwise or counter clockwise. I tell him counter clockwise, to be ocean side for the ride. This was Roger's advice and how he and the boys had done it on their Harleys. Prior to that conversation with Roger, I had given it no thought. Taking one direction or the other had not at all occurred to me.

"I see. Well…" Billy begins. "Can I show you something?"

Billy turns out to be as knowledgeable as he is helpful. He brings me over to a map next to the gift shop entrance. He tells me the trail was the inception of Alexander Graham Bell (as was *National Geographic* magazine). Billy tells me the trail was actually designed to be done clockwise. He rattles off the names of several different mountains that are part of the trail. He tells me that if you do the trail clockwise, you roll down these with the view laid out in front of you. If you do it counter clockwise, you're doing a long climb of the mountain followed by a quick descent with the scenery behind you.

"Oh," I say, processing all this new information.

The entrance to go clockwise was this one, right behind the restaurant. To go counter clockwise, one must continue down the 105 East a bit still, to the other entrance. So really, the trail is like an elongated, upside-down horseshoe shape, both ends meeting the 105 East.

"Something for you to think about," he says.

I thank him, almost in a daze. I can't just flip my plans upside-down based on a random conversation with a stranger, can I? I think about it for maybe three minutes, then you know that that is exactly what I did.

Billy is from here and knows what he is talking about. I am going to go with his advice over Roger's. I look at the rough outline I have plotted for the Trail and simply start from the end. I get on my bicycle and head for Margaree Forks.

You see. If I had everything carefully planned out, I would have motels booked, shackles on me, unable to make a last-minute change like this. I fly by the seat of my pants, and I am free to listen and respond to the messages that the Universe sends to me.

I stop to take the token photo of my loaded-up bicycle; my good girl, my very good girl, my steed, in front of the sign to the clockwise entrance. Then, at half-past eleven in the morning, I begin my ride on The Cabot Trail. I am now too scared to be overly emotional. It's show time. Now is not the time for tears of fears. It's time to *giv'er*. I shall now finally encounter the fabled hills and mountains that I have been living in the shadow of my entire trip. Thoughts and feelings are for after the work is done. *It's time to do this.* I'm ready. I'm so ready.

And so it begins, and immediately. Hunter's Mountain is straight up like nothing I have ever encountered. Except, perhaps, for day twenty's psychotically hilly ride through L'Isle Verte, Saint-Paul-de-la-Croix, Saint Clement and Saint Cyprien. But as drastic and relentless as those hills were, they were hills. Now I am on a mountain. There is a noticeable difference. Granted, this first mountain is not too bad, even by my own petrified and ignorant standards. Albeit slowly, I am able to ride up the whole thing without stopping for a breath or walking.

And then you fly, fly, fly down the other side.

When a bug flies into your face as you're tearing down the side of a mountain it feels like someone has whipped a pebble at you. It hurts.

There is the odd raindrop here and there all day long but at twenty past one in the afternoon, it finally starts to rain down proper. I still have twenty kilometres to go. At twenty to two, my back starts to spasm. I want to take two Advil but I am out of water. The spasms become frequent and I have no choice but to gather as much spit up as I can in order to swallow down the pills. It doesn't work. I can feel them lodged in my throat and it is painful. I ride on in anguish. I am shocked at how much pain the two little wedged capsules are causing me. Thankfully, maybe one kilometre later, I happen upon the Lakes Restaurant and Cottages. Almost in a panic I buy some Gatorade G2 to flush the medicine down. They aren't easily dislodged and the pain is awful. Finally, the pills are freed and the pain is gone. It is two in the afternoon and I have fifteen kilometres to go.

I arrive at my intended destination at the Margaree Riverview Inn at twenty after three. It is full-on pouring raining and I am soaked and freezing when I arrive. The motel is full. No vacancy. I am a bit annoyed since I had tried to call earlier to reserve (or find out that they were full), but nobody had answered. The man at the front desk calls around and finds me another room - twelve kilometres away. He passes me the phone to make the arrangements. The lady on the other end is sweet and kind and especially attuned to the fact that I am on a bicycle. She tells me that there is a restaurant somewhat nearby but that she thinks it may be closed. I tell her I have food and she sounds relieved. I am impressed and touched that she is aware of the vulnerabilities of a self-supported cyclist, such as their potentially limited food supplies. I make the reservation and pass the phone back to the man behind the desk.

Then I just stand there. It's one thing to be mid-exercise with pulse racing and body heat flaring when rain arrives. It's another thing to be soaked and chilled to the bone and then have to head back out for more. But that is just what I have to do. I need a few minutes to gather up my courage. Then, finally, I am off again.

Thankfully, the route here is kind with regards to incline and the rain calms down quite soon too. After a seventy-five kilometre ride during my first day on The Cabot Trail, I arrive at the Duck Cove Inn at half-past four.

The lady at the front desk is kind and lovely. We chat about my bike ride. I tell her I am not really a long-distance cyclist at all but a marathon runner. She tells me that she also runs and that she did a try-tri (or "try a triathlon" with shorter than regular distances for all three challenges) with her sister recently. She admits that she had gained fifty pounds over the years without really realizing it, therefore training for the try-tri was difficult. I love that she is sharing all this with me. We banter back-and-forth about fitness and running and cycling. I am all registered and paid. The six postcards I had put on the counter she tells me are on the house. Another precious human exchange to sustain me.

My room is lovely and looks and smells like the house my Grandma and Grandpa Laflamme owned. I feel like I have stepped back in time and I am pausing and revelling in it. My view is spectacular. I feel a bit catatonic.

Although after that first, immediate incline up Hunter's Mountain it was pretty smooth sailing, still, with the rain pelting and the adrenaline now passing, I am beat. There is nothing I need to do. I don't need to set up camp or start a fire. I need to do nothing. I am feeling so lackadaisical that I even turn on the television. I haven't done that since Quebec. Then out my window I see a lady walking across the parking lot with a stack of folded laundry. I can do laundry here? So much for doing nothing.

I dig out my old, dirty riding outfit and throw it together with my fresher but soaked one and rush to the office. Sure enough, laundry is available. The older gentleman who is now there now gives me the six quarters and laundry soap necessary to do it. I promise to pay him back.

When I come back later to put my clothes in the dryer, I pay him back with a toonie. He won't take it, but I insist. He also insists. We are in a kindness stand-off. In the end, I win. Sort of.

He accepts the toonie but says, "Well can I at least pour you a glass of wine?"

Ding. Ding. Ding. Ding.

I am pleasantly surprised at his lovely offer. I accept with delight. People, hey? His name is Gordon and he is a retired teacher. He has the kindest eyes. We chat a bit, and then I carry the unfinished glass to my room. I finish it there, then open my bottle and finish that, too. I don't make it back to pick up my laundry. I fall asleep with the television blathering and the lights still on.

"Life is a constant battle, a tug of war between the head and the heart. An everlasting negotiation between the two. If the heart wins more often, I think it's a good life."

AUGUST 13TH – DAY 40

I awake at about half-past five to an infomercial blaring and the slightest glimmer of light coming from behind my curtains. I look at the time and realize the sun will be rising soon. I bolt out of bed as if it were on fire, much like back at Lac Témiscouata. I laugh at myself. I make a "real coffee" with the pot and coffee pouches provided. Then I go out into the cuttingly crisp, twelve-degree morning air. This motel is perfectly situated, facing the east. I sit on a bench facing the Margaree River and wait. It's freezing. I am now glad I am not camping, not that it was an option. I sip my coffee and have a cigarette.

Over the Margaree Harbour, an eerie band of mist floats over the still waters and beneath the masterpiece sky of a cottony web of clouds illuminated by the growing, smoldering orange caldron rising from behind the distant mountains. The mist is drifting hauntingly from the south and tracing the shoreline in a perfect and almost paranormal parallel. A smoky, silent, slithering snake, sneaking by…Yet again, like with pretty much all of these incredibly stunning and soul-awakening views, I am the only one out here witnessing it.

A truck pulls into the long, gradual uphill driveway to the motel. I notice it is pausing at the bottom. I finally look to see why. He is looking at me with my iPhone poised at the incredible sunrise. He is waiting for me to finish taking the photo. It's Gordon. I laugh and put my phone down and wave him on with a big smile. He drives through and waves.

After forty-five minutes of the splendour and glory unfolding over Margaree Harbour, I finally decide I can withstand the chill no more. I go back in my room and let the scene pour in from my east-facing window. I lie back down until it is time to go for breakfast.

At just after eight I walk over to the motel restaurant. First I go down to the laundry room. Gordon has already put my clothes into the dryer for me, "ten minutes ago," he tells me. Again, he won't take my two quarters that it costs to run the dryer. Oh, man. What a sweetheart. Is it silly that even this little gesture makes me feel happy and loved? I think not.

My breakfast is great. I even decide to break my little rule of no pork or beef and I order and enjoy sausage with my meal; three, in fact. I am almost at the end of my journey, after all. No fear of eating one million hotdogs anymore. What I should have banned was red wine. (No way, man.) I happily eat the sausages with two sunnyside up eggs, whole-wheat toast with butter, a glass of orange juice, and a coffee with milk. Yum. I am completely stuffed when I am finally done cleaning my plate.

I go to the front desk to pay for my meal. Gordon is there. He asks if I am checking out.

"Not quite yet, I just want to pay for my breakfast," I tell him.

He tells me I can pay later when I check out. "Are you checking out today?" he asks.

"Yes," I reply.

"No," Gordon cheekily replies right back.

He's funny. He tells me I should take a day of relaxation. I could just ride my bike around here, and then spend another night. His warmth and welcoming are palpable, and his eyes are so warm I am actually tempted to do as he suggests. However, even though I am thus far well ahead of schedule, the ants in my pants are telling me that relaxation is not in the cards for today. Also, hello, I am out of wine, although something tells me that Gordon would have been able to help me with this dilemma. We chat for a bit, and then I return to my room to digest my food and write a few more postcards.

I pick up my laundry, put on a fresh riding outfit, and almost sorrowfully, check out of the Duck Cove Inn.

I am on The Cabot Trail. I survived the first day and the first mountain. I set off full of energy and fear, much like yesterday. It's the best feeling: fear. It's exciting, it means new learning, and it means I am living, really living. What will today bring?

Upon my entering Cape Breton Highlands National Park, a woman in her SUV rolls her window down and offers to take my panniers to Pleasant Bay for me. Pleasant Bay is the next major stop, and is, as she correctly surmised, my destination for the day. She tells me I can pick them up at the hostel there and this way I can have a more enjoyable and easy ride through the park. I think about it for a moment but almost immediately decide that the bags stay with me. The bike, the panniers, all eighty-eight pounds of it; we're in this together. I can't even fathom separating from my stuff. It has been my everything, my salvation along this incredible journey. Furthermore, I didn't embark on this journey for "an easy ride." I want the challenge, the exercise. I want to do all the work and feel all the accomplishment. I realize at this moment I feel emotionally bonded to my bicycle and my panniers, fiercely protective, a dramatic "not without my panniers" type of attachment. While I recognize how kind and thoughtful this lady is to make such an offer, and to a stranger at that, I have to decline.

When the movie *Cast Away*, with Tom Hanks came out, I remember watching the part about his soccer ball "Wilson" and how he cried when he lost the ball to the sea, and thinking, "Oh, please." I thought the scene was just ridiculous.

Now I get it.

So here I am in Cape Breton Highlands National Park. The beauty basically slaps you across the face and immediately, knocking you out of reality and into an awe-struck state of humility and surrealism. Except it's all real. Oh, Canada! The first hill inside the park comes just after the Grande Falaise. It is killer. I have to stop twice to catch my breath, but I manage to get back on my bicycle and am able to ride up the whole thing. Initiating the upward propel of eighty-eight pounds of bicycle and baggage on such a steep incline is no easy feat. But I do it. I can feel how strong I have become. At the top of this first hill, and yes, frighteningly, this was just a hill and not a mountain, is the first observation point. I pull over and snap-snap-snap all the magnificent photos with my iPhone. The enormousness of the ocean in front of me, the majestic mountains around me, the trees, the coast, the waves, the high rock walls. The enormity of the moment and what I am doing, heightened by the salty smells, transports me to an elevated state.

The next hill, which leads to the second observation deck, is also killer but a bit more stretched out; longer, with a bit less of a dramatic incline. This time I am able to do the whole thing non-stop. Next, I inch my way up Cap Rouge. The incline is merciless. I do it, but I'm being clobbered. What have I gotten myself into?

And then I reach MacKenzie Mountain.

MacKenzie Mountain is three hundred fifty-five meters of unforgiving ascent. It isn't possible to go any slower than I am going, though I am using all my force to do so, yet only squeezing out a snail's pace. After each bike length travelled I am sure I am going to stop, give up. But I don't. *Not yet, one more pedal.* I feel delirious, gone. I have mentally retreated deep within, scouring my soul for the will to keep doing this. It's hard. Head hanging, glazed eyes drilling holes into the pavement beneath me, grunting, pushing, one more pedal, one more pedal. I can't fathom any farther ahead than the length of my bicycle. I dare not look. I just keep negotiating with myself, one more pedal, one more push.

I reach the top of MacKenzie Mountain, all riding, no walking.

No rest for the wicked, next comes French Mountain, four hundred fifty-five meters back up, up, half a kilometre into the sky. My head is empty, void of thought, thoughts would be dangerous; I just need to do this. I can't wrap my head around the climb, how badly it is beating me up. Me and my big mouth, my big ideas. My legs ache and grind and quiver. Up, up and more up. I give every ounce of my might to just propel my bicycle fast enough to keep balancing and moving and not stopping and falling. My mind is numb. *Just a few more strides, than maybe a rest. Keep going, keep going.* I am near growling like a rabid dog. *Don't look up, just keep going.* I am a machine, an almost broken one.

It is not only excruciating physically, but also mentally. It is exhausting, constantly coaching myself as I continuously feel on the edge of giving up. All day long. It just keeps going on this way. I can't help but wonder if I have bitten off more than I can chew—if I will be able to pull this off.

Thankfully, amid the gruelling work and heat and pain and slow, slow progress, my pride haunts fiercely. I carve up my heart and also my soul to find the will to just keep pedaling. Two female riders are gliding down the mountain pass. One calls out, "You can do it!" I can't even acknowledge her—I am in a fog. Head down, digging deep, drowning in the dirt of the depths I am digging.

Then I feel something, some ease to the ascent? I dare to look up.

I see a sign in the near distance: "French Mountain, 455m."

Well, holy frickin' shit. I am here, at the top. *I did it.*

I am at the top of French Mountain, all riding, no walking. I could just cry, but mentally and emotionally I am somewhere else completely and tears don't come. I am an empty vessel.

The views are spectacular and breath-taking and after following along the now more flat and manageable route, I slowly return from whatever subconscious, altered state I had retracted to. I take a million photos at each observation point. As well, since I am on bicycle and not confined to a car, I am able to stop whenever and wherever along the roads to take photos. I pride myself that I will have photos that most others will not have. My phone is full quite early. I am forced to keep deleting apps and music to make room for all the pictures. I can't imagine zipping through the entire three- hundred kilometre trail in a mere eight hours, as suggested by the Cape Breton website I visited. I am on day two and already it is whizzing by too quickly.

After seven gruelling hours, and gruelling is a massive understatement, I begin my descent back down to sea level at Pleasant Bay.

Woo. Freakin'. Hoooooooooooooooooooooo!

I am forced to brake because the speeds I am achieving as I drop down this mountain are crazy-fast, scary, exhilarating, dangerously fun, but too fast to negotiate the turns. I also remember the advice from the kind and helpful man at Sandbanks Provincial Park. He told me he'd blown out both his tires as he tore down the side of a mountain on The Cabot Trail, the heat making the air in his tubes expand and blow. I brake as lightly as I can while still trying to savour this incredibly well-deserved glide.

I make it to Pleasant Bay, sixty-four kilometres, all riding, no walking. I feel like a soldier after war. At The Rusty Anchor, a seafood restaurant at the foot of the descent and the entrance to Pleasant Bay, I have a bowl of seafood chowder, a half-dozen oysters, and a double, spicy Caesar. Highly-merited, to say the least, and if I do say so myself. I get back on my bicycle and ride one and a half kilometres further to my motel: The Midtrail Motel.

I am a shell of myself. I take a shower. This has been the most challenging, most beautiful, most intimidating, most wonderful, most daunting, most incredible, most exhausting day to date. Was that just a taste of what is to come? I truly need to offload the day's events, to tell them to someone, share them, cry about how difficult it was, divest myself of the enormity of it all. But it is not to be. There is no Internet connection. I also cannot receive or send texts or calls. The monstrousness of my day is erupting from me like a volcano with nowhere to spill. I am alone after a mammoth feat. I need connection. I need to unburden myself from the gravity of the events of my day. I desperately need encouragement and support; an ear. I am absolutely crushed. I flop onto the bed and unabashedly bawl my eyes out.

It is freezing. Sixteen degrees. My room had the air conditioning cranked when I arrived. I crawl under the covers for warmth. It is about half-past eight. The day hits me like a Mack truck. I am dead asleep like a pupa in a cocoon under a leaf in a deep, dark forest. Though not for long.

I awake at about eleven-thirty to the sounds of raucous laughter and talking from two doors down. I pour myself a glass of wine and go out onto my little back porch for a cigarette, shivering. I come back in almost immediately. Five texts from Roger have managed to come through during my sleep. I stand in different places in my room, trying to respond, almost desperately. After four tries, one somehow goes through. "I can't get a damn message through to you, Roger. Today was so hard. I feel like I'm in over my head."

Somehow a reply comes back. "You will be perfectly fine...you knew it would be challenging...you are amazing and will do this with your eyes closed...you're more than halfway already."

"I am?" I wrote back, incredulous.

But no response arrives. I don't think my message even went through. I let out a deep sigh.

Then I break down again. I quietly sob, alone. He's right. I knew it would be challenging, but I didn't know how much so and ignorance is bliss. Today, yes, I did this. But fear of the unknown is one thing. Now there is fear of the known and I am spiralling, petrified and dead tired. I gave my all and more today. What will I have left to give tomorrow for more and harder of the same? My legs are torn to shreds and so is my will. Today I did sixty-four kilometres and it damn near defeated me. Tomorrow I have seventy-one kilometres planned. Will one night be enough to recover physically and mentally? My muscles and my mind are either equal allies or foes. Today both stayed on my side. Will they tomorrow?

How will I ever convey to people what I've done? How I feel? I feel devastation at this thought. I feel an aching need to share this. I need to release this, find empathy. I feel lost. I finish the bottle, finally calm myself, have another cigarette, and then return to bed. There is nothing else to do. The best thing I can do is just get some sleep.

"Climb the mountains and get their good tidings."
-John Muir

AUGUST 14TH — DAY 41

In the morning, there is no glorious sunrise. The skies are heavy with a thick, grey cloud cover. It is only thirteen degrees. The forecast is calling for rain all day and a high of only sixteen. Even if I wear my warmest clothes, which consist of a pair of YOGAJeans and a hoodie, I'll be soaked and freezing. I want out of this isolated hellhole, but I have the feeling I should just stay put. However, tomorrow's forecast is almost the same; a high of nineteen and rain. Is it really feasible to think I can sit in one place for three days; financially and mentally? Especially this place, cut off from the rest of the world? And out of wine? I technically have the money to do it, but I begrudge spending that money here.

I have a coffee and a cigarette and go back to bed. The restaurant will open in two hours and I can connect to the Internet there. I will do my daily administration, have my eggs, investigate shorter routes, and decide what to do.

Two hours later I am seated in the small, busy restaurant. I eat a breakfast of four sunnyside up eggs, hash browns, whole-wheat toast with butter and Cheese Whiz and a coffee with milk. It has become a guilty treat, finding those little Cheese Whiz packets on the table. I pocket the ones I don't use.

With proper Internet connection at the restaurant I begin to look realistically at my day. I had planned to ride seventy-one kilometres to Ingonish Beach. In light of my experience yesterday with MacKenzie Mountain and French Mountain, plus the cold, rainy weather today, I think it is wise to revise my plans a bit. The option of staying here for another day is quickly tossed out the window. I need contact with the outside world and I need to put in at least a few kilometres toward my goal or I will be anxiety-ridden, it's certain. Cape North is just thirty kilometres and only one mountain away. I try calling to reserve a motel but even in the restaurant I still can't make calls on my phone. The waitress tells me there is a free phone for local calls beside the washroom. I use it but the call still isn't going through. The waitress asks where I am trying to call. I tell her. She tells me that Cape North is a long-distance call. I'm incredulous. It is a mere fifteen-minute drive away. It has already begun to rain. I tell her that I am on a bicycle and I am not leaving here without knowing I have somewhere to go in weather like this. She finally allows me to use their main phone but tells me to keep it short. I reserve a room at MacDonald's Motel Cabins and go back to my room.

Until today, I have never had to begin my ride in the rain and certainly never in temperatures anywhere as low as this. Do you know how deep you have to dig to choose to step out in a cold, heavy rain and drag eighty-eight pounds of baggage and bicycle and ride straight up a mountain? Deeper than North Mountain, today's taunting beast, is tall. And so, in my YOGAJeans and my hoodie over my long-sleeved Lululemon t-shirt, and my flip-flops, of course, I set out.

As I am leaving, texts begin to come through. Roger is sending texts that are light in spirit and are ending in "LOLs." I am far from any type of "LOL" mood and his jovial texts are irritating me and making me angry. I write, "Do you know how deep I am digging right now to go out in the freezing cold and rain to ride up a mountain?"

He responds with another LOL text.

"You're not getting that I could really use some encouragement right now." I angrily write.

"Lol...I know you are going to over-exceed your goal like crazy...I've realized you are super woman so you will be fine...lol."

"Why does everyone in this world think I don't need worrying after!? I'm not super woman. I'm a scared girl who needs support just like anyone else."

"You have your biggest supporter right here. And, yes, I have been worried about you since the second I met you. But I also believe in you huge."

The rain calms a bit. I bolt.

North Mountain is the same height as yesterday's French Mountain, four hundred fifty-five meters, but the route up it is much steeper. Even though I had said that it would be completely permissible to walk my bicycle at points along the Cabot Trail if need be, now that I am here, it seems my pride has something else to say about that. It would be way easier to walk my bike today up this insane incline. Instead, I am riding, slowly, terribly slowly, breaking the intensely steep climb up into twenty-two left/right standing pedal strides. One, one, two, two… I stop, catch my breath, and then do it again. Up, straight up, over and over. It is extremely cold, I am miserable. I am adding who knows how much distance as I meander across the road, right into the opposing lane, to reduce some of the incline.

Rock wall to my left, sea of treetops in front of me and beside me, mist and rain in my squinting eyes. Standing strides, left, right, I am bearing down with all my weight and might with each stride, desperate to keep this bike going. I try to add extra strides into the mix, twenty-four at a time, sneaking in extra distance, anything to get this shit over with. I remain lucid and present, though, unlike yesterday. The rain is remaining pretty calm. It even altogether stops for short stints. I zone out, turn off all thoughts.

I arrive on the top of North Mountain, all riding, no walking.

Due to the wet road conditions today, I have to be much more cautious and brake frequently as I make the steep glide down the other side of North Mountain. The breeze from the quick descent is not appreciated in my sorry, soaked state. I am chilled to the bone.

As I ride the last nine kilometres, I stop dead in my tracks when I see what I think is a black bear on the road ahead of me. It is moving slowly, in my direction. False alarm. Oddly, it is a man. A pedestrian. This is a much-unexpected anomaly. He is wearing a black sweatshirt. What a strange sight, to see someone on foot.

His name is John. He has walked and hitchhiked from Vancouver to Newfoundland and is now on his way back. Wow. We chat for a bit. He is not on Facebook.

"Oh, I have a couple of friends like you," I joke.

He doesn't have a camera or a cell phone. He hasn't documented his journey whatsoever. "I'm just doing it to do it," he states humbly.

I tell him how isolated I felt yesterday in my motel room with no calling ability or Internet connection. I admire his disconnect from the gadgets and distractions. He asks me if I am going to Meat Cove. He tells me how incredibly beautiful it is there. Gordon from Duck Cove Inn had also made a point of showing it to me on the map and telling me how gorgeous it is. It looks like I will be adding this to the itinerary.

The rain continues to be light and intermittent. It is early and I am already almost at my destination. I am just beginning to think that perhaps I wimped out prematurely by booking this motel room in Cape North, making for a mere thirty kilometre day, instead of continuing into Ingonish Beach, when about two hundred meters before arriving to the motel, it begins down-pouring. I feel redeemed and justified in my decision. I arrive at exactly two o'clock. The rain continues all afternoon.

In my motel room I wait and wait for the rain to die down. I am wineless, you see. Finally around four thirty, it does. I hop onto my super light, pannier-free bicycle and ride half a kilometre down the road to the Cabot Trail Food Market. I buy: two pizza slices that come with two free pops (President's Choice diet lemonades), two cans of Alpha-Getti, Krazy Glue to fix my ripped pannier pockets, a Sharpie Magnum marker, and a cheap bottle of Argentinian Malbec. There is a couple behind me in line and another young guy behind them. Someone asks me a question about my ride. I tell them my little spiel; that I rode here from Toronto. They ask more questions and I am happy to have some conversation to participate in.

When I come outside, the younger guy is standing there with his phone in his hands. "Do you mind if I take your picture?" he asks with a big smile.

I laugh and say sure. His name is Drew and his girlfriend in the car is Clarissa. The rain has started up again. I bike back up the road to the motel.

The woman who had checked into the motel just ahead of me is outside smoking. "I got my wine," I call out to her.

She and I had spoken briefly at check-in. When she overheard me ask the lady at the front desk where I could buy wine, she had chirped up, "I already have mine in the car, ready to go."

Good girl. As we stand now and chat, she tells me she thought afterward that she should have offered to take me to go get wine in her car. It's so close, I tell her it was nothing for me to have gone. Her name is Lisa and she is from

Newmarket, Ontario. I tell her I am from Toronto. She and her friend had just been to Meat Cove yesterday. She tells me some pros and cons and shows me some photos. We are so busy blabbing that I forget that I had unhooked the bungee cords that secured my reused-shopping-bag parcel of pizza and wine. Suddenly it crashes to the sidewalk. The bottle of wine shatters.

"Well, can I take you up on that offer to drive me to get wine?" I ask, laughing.

Lisa from Newmarket drives me to go get another bottle of wine. Bless her.

Back in my room, I don't turn on the television. I talk with my best friend, Darren. I speak with my brother, Jean-Guy. I tell him about the whole "bicycles for life" gift I want to give to Maya, his daughter, my niece, and he accepts and says thank-you. I have a good, long chat with my dearest buddy Donna. I write a postcard to Rosie. I wait for Roger to get home from Montréal. When he does, we talk on FaceTime for over two hours. I didn't realize how long we had been speaking and when he points it out, I am astonished. It is wonderful to have the emotional support of this good man.

Finally, after midnight, sleep beckons. Roger and I say our goodnights. Having spent many nights now in motel rooms instead of camping, I seem to have re-assimilated back into the whole normal bed thing. Or perhaps it is simply that I am so deeply exhausted, nothing could keep me awake.

"There's a flame
There's a fire
It lives within me
It is fuelled
And inspired
Between pedals and feet."

AUGUST 15TH – DAY 42

Even though Roger and I spent over two hours on FaceTime last night we have another forty-minute call this morning. I just can't get enough of him. I wonder how our emotional affair might play out in "real life." It may not, I realize. He is older. He has grown children and wants no more. I don't think I could enter a relationship where there are already closed doors. Then again, I am getting older. I am forty-one. Perhaps children are not in the cards for me. Perhaps the precious short visit from my little olive will be the sole gift I shall be blessed with and treasure in this life. I just don't know. That pregnancy was a surprise, unplanned. Darren has offered to be a donor for me. "You are a mother," he told me, resolutely, as he patiently let me bawl and bawl those days after finding out I had miscarried. But it is a lot scarier to choose to have a child then to simply find out you are having one. Darren's beautiful offer sways in the background. And Roger's warmth and companionship is wonderful now, no matter what happens later.

I have a shower and am packing up my bike to go when Lisa comes calling at my open door. She wants a picture with the two of us.

"I'd love that," I say happily.

"Can I give you my number just in case you need anything or if you run into any trouble? We're here until Friday."

We exchange numbers and add each other on Facebook. I have been so obsessed with the Cabot Trail these past couple of days that I forgot how much this journey has mostly been a human one and how well the Universe is taking care of me as I ride across the East Coast alone, yet not alone whatsoever.

This morning the forecast has changed from rain to simply cloudy. Three cheers for small mercies. I decide I will venture off the Cabot Trail and check out Meat Cove. I call the Meat Cove Lodge. They are full up. I try calling the only other place where you can camp or get a chalet but nobody answers. I ponder this. Lisa also told me that the roadway there is gravelly and she found it difficult to drive on in her car. I think about that, too. Finally, I decide that Meat Cove will have to go into the unfinished business file. At just after eleven, I set off for Ingonish Beach.

Wet roads, misty air, and a sixteen-degree temperature are perfect conditions for riding up hills and perfectly freezing for coasting down them. As Murphy's Law would dictate, today I am gliding downhill most of the day. I have to laugh at my luck. I take advantage of the easy ride and spend my energy scanning the dense trees for a black bear or a moose. I desperately want to see one or both before this trip is over.

Today's ride is all inland. From atop the mountain, it is nothing but a sea of leafy, needly treetops, too numerous to count, too tall to fathom ground. No coast, no water, no rocks, not an inch of clearing. It is a gentle wonder, almost hidden among the ubiquitous and never-ending green. I stop riding, slowly looking all the way around, trying to really appreciate how many trees I am standing among. The dead quiet. The misty skies, everything powdered grey. Not a sound, none at all, it's deafening, trippy. Imagine you had never even heard of Niagara Falls before, then found yourself in a boat at its feet, opened your eyes, and looked up. That's how I feel; a speck of dust in perfect nature.

The misty air soon turns into sheets of millions of tiny rain pellets that feel like wet sand being blasted into my face and onto my eyeballs. I squint through barely open eyes. My left pant leg is sopping wet. I am actually fine being soaked when I am stopped, but combined with the wind from riding, I am a human Popsicle and can't keep my teeth from chattering. I arrive in Neil's Harbour and decide to make a detour there, hopefully a short one, in search of some sort of temporary shelter where I can dry off and wait out the rain a little bit. Success. There is one road that leads, at its end on the coast, to the only restaurant: The Chowder House.

I arrive at a busy dining room. I am sopping wet and frozen to the core. Many people give me a warm and sympathetic smile when I enter and they see my sorry state. I sit at the corner picnic table. A waitress, an older lady, comes right over to me and says, "Do you have any dry clothes to change into, dear?"

"Yes," I reply, thinking of my warm, thick hoodie.

"Why don't you go get them and change in the washroom?" the sweet woman suggests.

I laugh to myself that I am in such a dreary, zombie-like state that I did not come up with this idea on my own. I go back out into the pouring rain where my bike is, open my pannier as quickly as possible so I don't drench the inside, and pull out my hoodie, which is safely wrapped in a Ziploc bag to protect it in just these situations. Pulling on my hoodie in the washroom proves difficult as it is close-fitting and my skin is still wet. After much tugging and pulling, I finally get it on and return to my seat.

Aside from my dry, comfy hoodie, do you know what else really helps to warm you up? A glass of wine. And do you know what's even better? Two. I also eat a bowl of the seafood chowder and a plate of mussels in a white wine sauce. I finish it all easily.

My corner table has a gorgeous view of the sombre skies and brooding ocean. It's enchanting. At the table in front of me, a woman in perhaps her mid-fifties, wearing a smart peach pant suit arrives and sits, facing me. She starts chatting away to me, friendly and happy as can be. She is also on her own, she tells me. She is on a spontaneous car trip from her home in Maine. I tell her she is the first woman I have met on my journey who is also on a solo trip, and I tell her I think she is fantastic for taking off and venturing out on her own. She likes this compliment and perks up. She proceeds to tell me that last year she embarked on a solo car trip to California. I tell her that is amazing and incredible. Then she tells me she had backpacked Europe for two months by herself in her early twenties. I tell her she is awesome and a superstar. Then she adds, "When I told people I was going alone, they said to me, 'Well what will you do if you break your leg? What will you do if you get a flat tire?' I told them, I'll do the same thing I'd do if I were with someone. You figure it out and people will help you."

She sounds exasperated that this wasn't already clear to these people.

Amen.

I love this woman. Her name is Lina, and Lina is a smart, independent, confident, vivacious, awesome cookie. Her wise words resonate. *You figure it out and people will help you.* Just before I set out on this journey, I had joined the "floating flowers" tattooed on my left arm with the first line of my favourite Emily Dickinson poem, "My wheel is in the dark." I still have the floating flowers on my right arm that I badly want to finish and join, but I have been waiting for the right words to join them with. I had hoped that those words would come to me along my ride. I think they just did.

Lina leaves. Another couple takes the seat where she was. I also chat with them a bit. They are both teachers, too. Then the rain finally pauses. I duck out of The Chowder House at about two-thirty. Neil's Harbour is beautiful. I take all the photos. Then I set off, yet again.

The scenery today along the eastern side of the trail is spectacular. I walk out to the tippy-tip of the rock outcropping of Green Cove. I take off my flip-flops and dip my feet in the little pools of warm ocean water collected in its crevices. I gaze out into the deep, enormous, commanding ocean sitting majestically beneath the iron, smoky sky. I breathe it all in. I do the same at Lakies Head. Today is a grandiose masterpiece of the Canadian coast.

The air, thick with moisture, morphs into light rain off and on throughout the entire day. It is nearly six in the evening. I have no accommodations booked for the night. I start my search. I see a sign for a restaurant serving all-day breakfast. Score. Accommodations can wait. I'm starved.

When I arrive there, I see that it is attached to a motel. Double score. When I inquire at the office if there is a room, she tells me they have just one left.

"I'll take it!" I exclaim. I ask the lady registering me, "Is there a liquor store around here?"

"Yes, ten minutes down the road."

Ten minutes in a car, she means.

"I'm on a bicycle," I tell her.

"Oh," she simply says with an apologetic and hopeless look on her face.

"We'll take you," the man behind me in line says.

I turn around, thrilled, surprised, and relieved. But my elation is quickly followed by zapped elation. I have just taken the last room.

"Will you still take me if you don't get a room here? I've just taken the last one."

The lady behind the desk chirps up. "Well, there are smaller rooms that the staff usually live in. You can have one of those," she tells him.

I interject: "I'll take the smaller room. It's just me and my bicycle. You can have the larger room."

I assume his "we" is him and his wife and possibly kids. He is hesitant to accept the larger room. I assure him, "I really don't care or mind. A small room is more than I need."

He accepts. Yay. Things have worked out for both of us.

In the end, the young man, Adam, and his girlfriend, Jaclynn, also take one of the "smaller rooms." They are forty dollars cheaper and they feel the same way as I do; all you really need is a bed to crash on for the night. Anyway, these rooms are not so small and are cute and perfect. Adam and Jaclynn end up being in the room right beside mine.

We all get into the car and Adam says to Jaclynn, "She rode her bike here from Toronto. We're driving her to the liquor store."

He says this succinctly, in a deadpan manner, like no other explanation whatsoever is necessary. We three chat as we make the short drive to the liquor store. They are friendly and relaxed, like old friends. They are originally from here but live in Alberta now. They are home for a visit. Adam asks me if there is anything else I need or anywhere else I need to go. I thank him and tell him I am good.

Back at the motel, I head over to the restaurant and have my all-day breakfast of three sunnyside up eggs, beans, oatmeal toast with butter, and four little potato cakes that are each just bigger than the size of a loonie. A perfect feast.

I go back to my room and shower. Just as I finish, there is a knock at the door. It's Jaclynn. She is inviting me out to watch some live Celtic music with her and Adam. I am thrilled. I absolutely want to accept, but I am extremely hesitant of being stuck out somewhere when my exhaustion from the day finally hits. I have no dimmer switch, as I have said.

As I am mulling it over, Jaclynn adds, "And why don't you come to Adam's parents' house tomorrow? They live just over in Big Bras d'Or. You can have a nice bath in his mom's claw-foot bathtub. You can camp in the backyard or sleep in a big, soft bed. We have a boat—we can go boating. We will have a delicious meal with everyone. His parents would love to hear about your biking story. We would love to have you."

All of that, all at once, just like that. I am blown away. It all sounds like heaven. I accept immediately.

I tell Jaclynn that in light of knowing I will have the amazing opportunity to hang out with them tomorrow, I am going to decline joining them tonight. I am already getting tired. I have no clothes (and certainly no shoes) for going out (not that it really matters, of course). I just need to unwind and get to sleep early. Jaclynn and I add each other on Facebook. She immediately messages me the address of Adam's parents' house. I wish them a good night and off they go.

I FaceTime with Roger, I drink my wine, and I stand out front of my motel room and smoke a cigarette. The night is charged with magic tonight. I can hear the thunderous roar of the waves rolling in and crashing on a shore I cannot see and it is bewitching. I listen for a long time. It is like a slow, haunting chant and I am in a sweet trance. Finally, I go back inside.

Today's ride was short, only thirty-eight kilometres, and relatively easy. There were some killer hills, but there was also a lot of flat sections and decline too. Still, I spent seven hours cycling, battling the elements, feeling the rush of adrenaline, and actively absorbing all the sights and sounds of the splendour and beauty that surrounded me. I am simply exhausted. I fall asleep, early and happy.

And tomorrow they are calling for sunshine.

"I am so glad I follow my heart, despite my head sometimes."

AUGUST 16TH – DAY 43

I had a terrible nightmare last night. In it, I am at a staff meeting. It is the day before school starts. It is in some strange building, not my actual school. All my colleagues are asking me how my bike ride went and if I had finished the Cabot Trail. I tell them no, not yet, I still have two or three more days to go and I will go back "soon" to finish. People look disappointed and embarrassed for me and begin to awkwardly look away, carry on with their business, and pretend I am not still standing there. Then the meeting begins. Excusing myself, I leave. But after I leave I get distracted and forget about the meeting. An hour later I remember about the meeting and panic. I rush back but it is already over. My principal just looks at me with disappointment and a clear loss of respect. The whole thing is just awful.

When I wake, I am spurred by the terrible dream. I think I know exactly what it means. I had suffered anxiety when I took a day's rest at Dean and Mireille's back in Shediac Bridge. Then, I chopped the route from Pleasant Bay to Ingonish Beach in half, too, adding another day. And now, here I am, so close to completing a goal that has been beckoning to me, haunting me for the past twenty months, and particularly for the past forty-three days, and I am going to go off-course to hang out in Big Bras d'Or? Do I even know myself? Clearly I will not be able to really relax and exhale until I have done this thing. Clearly I need to finish this task and achieve this goal, and apparently, I need to do it TODAY.

And I shan't beat myself up about it. I am a high-functioning, high-energy, type-A person. It is because of this that I am able to do the crazy things that I do, like run fifty-two marathons, sometimes eight ultra-marathons in one year, and jump on a bicycle and ride alone halfway across the country. If the flipside of this is that, sometimes, I am not able to relax, to unwind, then so be it. *I shan't beat myself up about it.* I accept all of me. It's a package deal, these human beings; the good with the "bad." I shan't beat myself up about being me, anymore.

I look on Google Maps. If I want, if I need, to finish the Cabot Trail today, I would have to complete an eighty-seven-kilometre ride. My longest ride so far has been eighty-three kilometres. I have no idea if there are more mountains…if this type of mileage is possible here, amid Cape Breton Highlands National Park.

There's only one way to find out.

I am on the road for maybe five minutes when a car pulls up alongside of me, driving bang-on in the opposite lane of traffic. The pretty, older woman in the passenger seat calls out to me, "How far are you going today?"

"Englishtown," I reply. "And I started in Toronto," I add proudly.

Her eyes go wide and she leans back and stares at me and says nothing. I smile and laugh. After a long moment, she says, "Be careful. The roads aren't great here."

She must be a local. I appreciate the tip.

"Okay. Thank you," I say.

"Have a great trip," she adds warmly.

At the top of a steep hill I find myself following behind a garbage truck. When it pulls up to its stop at the next house, a little boy jumps out. Clearly the nice garbage men had let this little boy come for a fun, short ride from his house to the next. As the little boy is walking back to his house, he looks like he's on top of the world, beaming. He notices me as I pass. Even this young child understands what I am up to. He stops, turns his body to face me, stretches out both his arms and calls out to me, "Welcome to Ingonish!"

I melt on the spot. That kid's parents are *so* getting a postcard. I take note of their house number.

Right after the Knotty Pines Cottages I come to a particularly long and steep hill. I brace myself and begin trudging ever so slowly up it. A man driving in the opposite lane of traffic shouts out, "Keep riding! You can do it!"

It is the kind of hill that when you get to the top and the road is flat again, you just can't bear to change out of first gear. You're that wiped from the climb.

As I round a sharp bend around a mountain, some motorcyclists appear from the opposite direction. The woman on the back of one sees me and points dead straight at me. The group of three motorcycles, two single riders and one couple, pull over immediately. I stop, too.

Remember Ashley from Dean and Mireille's front porch? It's him and his new wife, Nadine, and their friend Blair and his girlfriend, Denise. Dean and Mireille had told them I was currently on the Cabot Trail. Their crew of four was on a sort of "honeymoon ride" there too. Dean and Mireille had told them to watch out for me. And they did. I am over the moon to cross paths with them, that they cared enough to keep an eye out for me. And I love that it is Denise, someone I have never met before, who spots me.

"How did you know it was me? My flip-flops?" I ask Denise.

"No, your tan. Dean and Mireille said you are really tanned."

Ha. Okay.

We five exchange warm and excited hellos. I am thrilled to see Ashley again and honoured to meet Nadine, Blair and Denise. Blair tells me that what I am doing is amazing and they all tell me that they are impressed with and excited for me. I feel privileged to be the person that is doing something that thrills and excites others. I keep thinking about how scared and strange I felt before setting out on this soul-exploding adventure. Just look at the love and the beauty, human and landscape alike, that I have experienced and can now give testament to. We always hear about the bad stuff. There is way more good stuff. I am absolutely floating on it. We get a photo of us by a kind and obliging person nearby; luckily we are at an observation point. Then, we say our goodbyes and carry on our separate ways.

I am drifting blissfully, in an altered state. A man driving by in the opposite direction of traffic gives me a thumbs-up out his window. He's awesome, I feel his support, and as always, it invigorates me. There is no such thing as "alone" on this trip. No such thing at all.

The sun is shining beautifully. Today's ride is one of much downhill and long, sprawling views of the trail before me and the coast beside me. As I am on the brink of a downhill, I encounter two cyclists coming up the hill on the opposite side of the road. We three strike up a conversation. Their names are Nick and Don. These guys are experienced and have done many bike trips like the Cabot Trail. I tell them my little story, quite different from theirs. They are from Guelph, Ontario. We add each other on Facebook, and then they continue up, I continue down. I don't envy them at this moment.

I stop at Cape Smokey and have a lunch of a can of Alpha-Getti and left-over beans and toast from breakfast. I walk around, I take photos. Beauty, beauty, and more beauty.

A cyclist passing in the other direction calls to me, "Here we go!"

He gives his all and up he goes. I am nearing the end of my feat, but he is just at the beginning of his and I feel envy, admiration, and overflowing support.

"Enjoy!" I call out.

I come to the Wreck Cove General Store. I stop and have a snow crab roll and a carton of milk. I feel like I'm stalling now. I can feel that the end is near. I even ask a lady to take my photo with my bicycle in front of the "Welcome Bikers" sign, a sign clearly meant for counter-clockwise visitors. A rare photo of me, this mug of mine. It is my bicycle, my hammock tent, and my flip-flopped feet that have been the stars of all my photos.

Just after leaving the Wreck Cove General Store, an armada of about two dozen bikers on Harleys approach from the opposite direction. It is quite a sight to behold. I am in awe, and I stop as they get closer. I just watch them, I wave, and you know what? Every single one of them waves back at me and they give big smiles, to boot. One of them, a man with a long whitish-grey goatee, calls out to me, "Giv'er!"

I break out into a huge grin. I feel like they are part of a parade, the best floats saved for last, as I am on the brink of finishing my journey.

I arrive at the 312 junction. This is where I should turn to continue to Adam's parents' place. It is my last chance to change my mind, to go and enjoy their company and hospitality, and postpone finishing the Cabot Trail by a day or two. I pause for only a moment. I know I can't wait any longer. I need to get this done. Yes, it is about the journey. But it is also about achieving a goal.

I have loved my journey. Now, being this close, the end is calling me. I need to do what I came to do. I do not divert toward Englishtown and Big Bras d'Or. I take a right and continue along the Cabot Trail.

Only moments later, a motorcyclist passes me from behind. He shakes a "thumbs up" sign to me as he passes and calls out, "Way to go!"

He knows what I am doing, and he knows I am almost done. I can hardly believe it. I can taste it but I cannot wrap my head around the fact that I am this close, that I have almost completed the big, scary thing that made me lose sleep and question my sanity. That thing that has turned out to be the most self-validating, self-empowering thing I have ever done in my life.

A tractor-trailer approaches from the other direction, and the driver stops to ask if I am okay. I am stopped on the side of the road, talking into my voice notes. I assure him I am, and then ask him how many kilometres until the TransCanada Highway.

"About twenty-four."

Ouch. And here I am counting my chickens before they've hatched. I thought it was less; much less. I want to finish this today. It's already five o'clock. I still have about three hours of riding ahead of me.

My mind begins to wonder as I ride. Yesterday I watched a bit of the Olympics; the men's 100m hurdles. In a segue piece called "The Equalizer," CBC looked at legend Jesse Owens' 100m hurdle time of 10.2 seconds and compared it to Canada's Andre De Grasse's time of 9.91 seconds; a difference of less than 0.3 seconds. They posed the argument: Are athletes really going faster or are we just seeing the logical results of the advantages of advancements in technology? As an experiment, they had Andre run one hundred meters on the same dirt and cinder track that Jesse Owens ran on, in lieu of the bouncy, polyurethane track of today. They also manufactured the old, leather shoe that Jesse Owens wore in the 1936 Olympics; they made one for Andre, in his size. Andre ran in the plain, old, more natural conditions of Jesse Owens' day. Guess what time he ran the hundred meters in under these conditions?

ELEVEN SECONDS.

You see. It proves my flip-flop theory. I kept it simple for my ride. A three hundred dollar bike, only seven speeds, just two riding outfits, no fancy gear or nutrition. And I have been just fine. More than fine. Perfectly fine. When I worked briefly as a personal trainer, I saw people with the best of intentions and excited energy about achieving their fitness goals. And what is the first thing they do to "work" toward that goal? They spend a bunch of money on a bunch of gear they just don't need.

We need so little. I feel so free in my flip-flopped feet.

Over the past forty-three days, I have refrained from buying things; I have no use nor any room for anything I am not already carrying. But, now, I want a few token items to remember this momentous journey, and as gifts for others. I stop at Sew Inclined. I stop at Wildfire Pottery. I stop at Groovy Goat Farm and Soap Company. I stuff carefully-selected souvenirs into my bursting panniers. I ride and I ride. The sun is fading.

Minutes before seven in the evening, after eleven hours and seventy-seven kilometres of riding under cool skies with no one around, humbly and quietly, I officially achieve my goal. I finish the Cabot Trail.

There is a Quebecois saying that is, ironically, in English: "That's it, that's all." Today I have come to the end of my journey. I am emotional but calm. I have no energy for tears. I am soaring with a quiet sense of pride and accomplishment. I am thankful I will have my book to work on after this. I have never written a book, and I have no idea how to go about getting a publisher. I know nothing about any part of the process. But that was also true about this bicycle ride, and this has worked out pretty well, I think.

There are a couple of motorcyclists taking photos of themselves in front of the landmark sign. I offer to them, "Would you like me to take your photo for you?"

"Thank you. Yes."

I pride myself on being a pretty good photographer. We three start talking. They are from Vancouver and rode here from there. But now the woman has been called to start a new job and they have to get back, pronto. I tell them my story. They ask me if I would like my photo taken in front of the sign. I tell them no, it's okay, but thank you. But the woman does not accept my answer. "You need to take one photo with you and the bicycle and the sign, after what you did. Go stand there, I will take it."

Something inside me tells me she is right. This moment is special. I walk my bike over to the sign and stand in front of both my precious bicycle and the sign. And I smile. It's a smile that shines from deep in my gut, a place that no longer doubts myself. A place that is strong and believes in me, all of me, and is confident.

The St. Ann's Motel is directly behind the famous Cabot Trail sign, and incredibly, the vacancy sign is flashing. I ride to the office and ask for a room.

"Sorry, no vacancy," the woman behind the counter says flatly.

"But it says there is vacancy on the sign outside," I counter, a bit desperately.

"Someone just called. I have to change the sign."

Dejected, I turn around and get back on my bicycle. Sunset is in two hours. The next closest town that might have accommodations is Baddeck, twenty kilometres away. Ashley and crew were just there yesterday and they warned me that there are no vacancies anywhere. I have no other option than to try my luck. It isn't raining. It's fairly warm. Off I go.

If there is no motel or room to be found there and I finally have to pitch my hammock tent somewhere and at last do some gorilla camping, then so be it. In fact, it would be almost holy to have this new experience on this the last day of my great adventure.

I pedal like mad down the Trans-Canada Highway 105 westbound. I arrive in Baddeck relatively quickly; it is still light out. The first, second, third, fourth, and fifth motels I pass all have "No Vacancy" signs out front. Next I stop at The Telegraph Motel. There is a power outage here in Baddeck, and across most of the island, I learn. The gentleman at the front desk is serving the lady in front of me by candlelight and manually imprinting her card on a carbon triplicate form.

Finally she leaves and I approach. "I think I know the answer to this question, but do you happen to have a room available?" I meekly ask.

"Sorry, we don't," he says sympathetically.

"It's okay," I say.

Time to go looking for some properly-spaced and safely-concealed trees for the night. I am about to turn around and leave when he says, "Oh. Wait a minute. We did have a cancellation at our other place down the road. It's $140."

"I'LL TAKE IT!" I pretty much shout in his face.

How ironic. I am spending the most money for a place to stay on what is, by far, my latest arrival and to a room that is cloaked in pitch-black darkness. It is the pretty and quaint Dunlop Inn. I finally arrive there just before nine. It sits right on the water and the back porch faces out into a harbour with pretty boats, a picturesque little dock, and a view of a lighthouse. I take my bottle of wine and my package of cigarettes and go out to the back porch directly. I am hoping the lights will come back and I won't have to shower in the dark. I sit in blissful exhaustion and relief. Michelle and Jan, a couple also staying at the inn, come out onto the terrace, too. We three chat. After a long while, they leave and another couple comes out. We also chat a good long while. At just after ten, the power comes back on.

Poor Roger. When we finally have our FaceTime call I break down into quiet sobs and I can't stop. Again, I just need to release and offload this immense emotion I am feeling. *Today I finished The Cabot Trail.* I am also exhausted, of course, both physically, from my longest ride of the journey, ninety-seven kilometres in total, and mentally, due to scrambling at the end of a long, arduous day to find accommodations. Like always, everything worked out in the end. And so, since it is all finally done and taken care of, I can now allow myself to feel and express and to expunge, all the stress as well as all the success.

I don't make it to the shower. I flop myself onto the huge, luxurious, poufy, princess bed and, for a shatteringly still and quiet moment, I stare into the darkness. It finally registers. It's over. I did it. I rode my bike from Toronto to the east coast. I conquered the mountains of the Cabot Trail. I did it. I freakin' bloody well did it.

"I once was lost, but now I'm found
Was blind but now I see."
-Hymn

AUGUST 17ᵀᴴ – DAY 44

The next day it is pouring rain with a high of eighteen degrees. And the wind. It's a wonder to watch from indoors but miserable to be out in. There is a one hundred percent chance of rain all day. I don't think I have ever seen a forecast of one hundred percent chance of rain all day before. The bus to Halifax needs to be booked twenty-four hours in advance from Baddeck. It looks like I am staying put for the day. In the end, it is perfect. I need the time to find affordable accommodations in Halifax for the ten days that remain until my train back to Toronto. Airbnb has been fruitless in matching my schedule and budget.

Jerri-Anne, the lady running The Dunlop Inn, tells me that they have no availability for that night. Staying there is not an option. She calls over to The Telegraph Motel. They have one room left. I take it. Jerri-Anne takes my number and tells me she will call me as soon as the room is ready. Due to my situation, they are okay with an early check-in. In heavy, relentless rain, I ride over to the High Wheeler Café, panniers and all, to wait out the possible three-hour lapse between check-out from the Dunlop Inn and check-in at The Telegraph. Jerri-Anne texts a mere fifteen minutes later. My room is ready.

In my new room, which laughably has two queen-sized beds and a single bed, I book my bus ticket for the next morning. Then I send out ten Couchsurfing requests. I also put an all-call out on Facebook. I feel a little embarrassed doing the all-call, but these multiple motel stays this past week have killed my budget and I need to find somewhere inexpensive to pass my ten-day stay in Halifax.

On Couchsurfing, I write, "Hello! I have just finished a 43-day bicycle ride from Toronto to Cape Breton, including The Cabot Trail. Experience of a lifetime! I'm writing a book about it, too! As it turns out, I am actually finished almost two weeks ahead of schedule. My train from Halifax to Montréal is booked for the 28th. I have tried to find Airbnb places but with no luck re: dates. I certainly wouldn't expect you to host me all ten nights but any portion of that would be incredibly helpful. I am tidy and will be respectful of your home and rules. Let me know your thoughts. My fingers are crossed!"

On Facebook, I post: "Calling all cars, calling all cars!. I'm searching for affordable accommodations in Halifax but am having a bit of trouble. Anyone have a friend there that would like to rent their spare bedroom or couch out for a few days? I'm happy to pay. Please PM me. Thanks!"

As stunning as the scenery has been, it is the people who have been the most beautiful part of this journey. Seconds after my Facebook post, Mona, a friend I met in Cuba last winter, messages me immediately, telling me to contact her brother who lives in Halifax. Mireille reposts my post, asking for help. Lisa, a friend of Mireille's who became interested in my ride and added me on Facebook but whom I've never met, reposts my post, asking for help. Katherine, my long-time friend that I haven't seen in too many years, starts contacting her family and her family's family who live in Halifax. Sandra, my childhood buddy, contacts me to tell me that a mutual acquaintance is in the area and maybe could help. My old workmate from ages ago at The Black Bull, Jeff, who now lives in Newfoundland with his wife and kids, reposts my post, asking for help for me. With each new repost and reach-out, my heart is bowled over, flattened like the smooth, easy riding on the Sunrise Trail. This type of surrender, of defeat, is beautiful. This time I will accept help. Now, I need it.

Three people from Couchsurfing reply immediately. All three say they can host me the whole ten days. The first to reply is a gentleman named Ali. He responds telling me that he is also a cyclist and tells me that my bike trip sounds like it was amazing and he respects what I have done and would love to hear the story. He warns me, though, that he also has another friend living there temporarily; the friend has just moved here to Canada from Iran. I like the dynamic of three as opposed to just two or something larger. He also warns me that his place is not big. I tell him, "Hello, Ali! I don't mind cozy quarters with kind souls who would open their home to a stranger in need."

In the continuing rain and wind, I go out and do a bit of shopping and eat a pizza slice at Tom's Pizza, across the road from the motel. I'm actually glad that things have worked out this way, that I have this day of pause, of in between, of digestion, to sit with my story as it quietly winks at me and gives me a humble wave goodbye, before I begin the process of assimilating back to regular life. I'm toppled over with how quickly my problem of accommodations is solved, how strangers have gone out of their way to help me. Yet again.

My goodness, yet again.

I return to my ironically huge motel room and write out postcards. I write to Melody and Janet from Ontario, the two cyclist women I met early on in my ride. I write to sweet Denise from the Tracy Motel in Quebec. I write to my friend Éric in Quebec City. I write to my new cousin Christina in Fredericton. I write to Lonny, the pretty chocolate bark lady, from New Brunswick. I write to Elaine from Coy Lake, the sweet lady who drove me to the store to get cigarettes and made me a coffee in the morning and took out her maps to shorten my route.

I write to Myron, Darren, Kirsten, John, Donna, and Fotoula, some of my very best friends. I write to Robyn, Kelly, Stella, and Marni, my sweet colleagues who followed and supported me every day of this sacred journey like nobody's business and made me feel special and loved. I write to the staff at Cyclepath in Toronto, who sold me my bicycle and my panniers and heard me talk about this trip for nearly two years. I write to Marc in Montréal. I write to Lina.

I write to Gordon from the Duck Cove Inn. I write to Robert, the owner of the boat in Cobourg where I stayed at the beginning of this fantastic voyage. I write to Mary, whose backyard I had stayed in Bath. I write to the other Mary from Bath, the waitress who I chatted with there and who joined me in spirit, through Facebook, all along my ride. I write to Marc and Sherri, whom I met at Presqu'Ile Provincial Park. I write to my three sisters and my brother. I write to my mother. I write to the guy from St. Lawrence Park in Brockville who gave me the campsite on the hill "where the incident happened." I write to

Pat at Camping Chutes et Gorge in Grand Sault. I write to the three mechanics from Sandbanks Provincial Park who fixed my flat. I write to Sandra, my childhood best buddy. I write to my Dad and Helen. I write to Roger.

I write to Dean and Mireille. I write to the nice lady on the porch of the Bed and Breakfast in Alma, New Brunswick.

I say thank you, thank you, THANK YOU.

I try to gather the gumption to go out in the cold, windy rain and up the street to the liquor store. I decide instead to simply go back across the street to Tom's Pizza. It is about five or six in the evening. I order a small vegetarian pizza and a glass of Jost red. I pay ahead for the second glass that I know I will want, and soon. I go into the dine-in area. I immediately notice a microphone stand and guitar case. How wonderful; live music. I settle in as the rain continues to pour outside.

His name is Jon MacLean and his voice is a perfect, soothing blend of purr and rattle. The whole room is under his spell. He plays "If You Could Read My Mind" from Gordon Lightfoot. He plays "Blackbird" from The Beatles. He plays "Fire and Rain" from James Taylor. He asks if there are any requests.

"Can you please sing 'Farewell to Nova Scotia?'" I pipe up.

"Never heard of it," he shoots back.

We all laugh.

He begins to quietly strum as he tells the history of the song. He tells how Helen Creighton found the lyrics and music written out on sheets of paper, authorless, in an abandoned cottage in Nova Scotia. And then he begins to sing. I let my emotion rise as close to the surface as possible without letting it overflow and making me blubber and sob. That would be a bit awkward as I sit alone here in public.

Next, Rob sings "Jet Plane" from John Denver. He encourages the crowd to sing along. When I do, he immediately stops playing and singing, mid-song, and turns to me. "You've been holding out on me," he says.

I smile. He plays "Sweet Caroline" from Neil Diamond followed by the Cape Breton National Anthem, called "The Island." I request "Country Roads" from John Denver. He plays "Try" from Blue Rodeo, "I've Got a Name" from Jim Croce, and then "Ready for the Storm" from Dougie MacLean. Then it's "Free Falling" from Tom Petty. You can see the air because the clock has stopped ticking, time is nothing, there is just this magical, melodic now.

"Where are you off to next?" Rob asks me between songs.

I tell him about my plan to take the bus to Halifax and then the train home from there.

"This is the perfect ending to my journey. I can't thank you enough."

In total, I sit there for nearly four hours, from before Rob started his magic, through my pizza, through four or five glasses of wine, until he says simply, "Okay, I'm tired. Three hours, no break. I think that's enough."

Mercilessly, I ask for one more. He plays and I sing, "Amazing Grace."

I buy his CD. We add each other on Facebook. He mentions something about using me for back-up vocals on a recording. He is only conjecturing, of course. But, just in case, I want him to be able to find me.

I walk across the street to my big, charming motel room. I leave the two double beds untouched and crawl into the single bed, as happy as can be. I'm out like the power yesterday across my beloved Cape Breton Island.

"Imagine I'd given into fear and not done this."

AUGUST 18ᵀᴴ – DAY 45

The next morning I have what will probably be my last, tap water morning coffee. The rain has finally stopped. There is a light trickle from the eaves trough that sounds peaceful and soothing, like a little river. I sit in calm bliss on the porch. I am fully entrenched in this moment. The air is still. The cloudy sky is a warm blanket.

I ride to the Irving only two kilometres away. I unhook my panniers, and I disassemble my very good girl, my steed. A man comes over and places a clean piece of torn shirt on my pile of bike. I look up. He rubs his hands together and smiles. "Thank you." I laugh at my dirty, blackened, grease-covered hands. I finally get it all apart and not twenty seconds later, the bus arrives.

I sit second seat from the front (there is already a man in the front seat). Then, so quickly, or so it seems, we rattle down the 105, the same way I had come, pedaling, slowly, wide-eyed, open, a hungry vessel. We pass the Red Barn Restaurant and Gift Shop. We pass Whycocomagh Provincial Park. Finally, I say to the man in front of me, "Do you mind if I sit up there with you?"

"Sure, dear."

And this is how I meet Keith, a large, jolly old fellow. We chat non-stop the whole drive.

We pass Brosha's in Antigonish. Finally, we head on a route more southwest from the one I had taken to arrive at the Cabot Trail. The trip down Memory Lane is over for now. I'll enjoy it again once I am on the train home.

Keith gets off in Truro.

"Oh. Well, who will I talk to now? The bus is probably happy that I'll finally shut the hell up," I tell him as he leaves.

We share a last laugh.

The bus arrives in Halifax at around five in the evening. I reassemble my bike. I also tighten the back brake and oil the rusty chain. I time myself. I do the whole job in sixteen minutes. Before today, I had never disassembled nor reassembled a bicycle before and I'm proud of my time. I ride to Ali's.

I spend a wonderful ten days with him and his friend, Hamed. I spend every day, all day, at the beautiful Halifax Central Library, working on my next adventure, *this book*. Ali spends his days at work or working on his thesis, and Hamed spends his days studying, preparing for school in September. Then, every night, we three meet back at home and break bread together. They are great cooks, Ali and Hamed. They prepare traditional Iranian dishes every night. They are delicious. My new favourite dish is Shirazi salad.

At the library, I begin sorting through my daily emails from my ride, the beginnings of assembling this book. As I do this, I start to think of the obvious: about going the other direction, by bicycle; Toronto to Vancouver. Now that I have the confidence and experience and accomplishment of my east coast ride, I begin to wonder: Could I ride, in one summer, all the way from Toronto to Vancouver, a ride that is at least double in length?

Within an hour I have a rough itinerary plotted out over fifty days. I imagine long, flat stretches of nothing. I envision having to be better prepared for longer periods of solitary riding. I foresee less wine. I predict there may be a lot of necessary gorilla camping. The wheels are turning.

Roger ends our emotional affair the day before I catch my train home. I didn't see it coming and am shocked. I am also shocked at how quickly I realize it is for the best. I remind myself of my own doubts and scepticism of our relationship's sustainability. I am thankful for the time we shared; the amazing memory of him and the boys meeting up with me at the Hopewell Rocks, his friendship and support during our brief, mostly virtual, relationship. He is a good guy. He has made the right decision. I am happy that our story is confined to my time out here and has not messily spilled over into "real life" or with physical attachments. In this way, it is beautiful.

"Do you feel like a different person?" my best friend Darren asks me when I arrive back in Toronto.

I stay with him for the first three days while I wait for my Airbnb guest to finish his stay at my place. His question startles me. I had been upset that he wasn't following my daily posts, liking my pictures, posting comments of support like many of my other friends were, on Facebook. When I had raised this issue with him, earlier during my ride, he had responded, "I call you."

Well. That was true. I couldn't argue. Still I couldn't help but wonder if maybe he wasn't interested in what I was doing, or if maybe he didn't comprehend what an enormous personal feat this was. But his simple and pointed question makes me understand that he most certainly does.

Facebook can be great but it isn't everything.

Any imagined neglect or hurt I felt is immediately assuaged. A wave of warmth and love washes over me.

"No. Not at all. I feel like exactly the same person as before. But I finally, finally feel comfortable with who I am," I tell him.

No more weirdo.

My journey was both big and small. Like me. This ride was not transformative, it was affirmative. Of me, exactly as I am. And of fellow humans. I figured it out as I went along, and people helped me. I did it. All by myself, but not at all alone.

I wonder what beautiful adventure is next.

The Summer Day
Who made the world?
Who made the swan, and the black bear?
Who made the grasshopper?
This grasshopper, I mean-
the one who has flung herself out of the grass,
the one who is eating sugar out of my hand,
who is moving her jaws back and forth instead of up and down-
who is gazing around with her enormous and complicated eyes.
Now she lifts her pale forearms and thoroughly washes her face.
Now she snaps her wings open, and floats away.
I don't know exactly what a prayer is.
I do know how to pay attention, how to fall down
into the grass, how to kneel down in the grass,
how to be idle and blessed, how to stroll through the fields,
which is what I have been doing all day.
Tell me, what else should I have done?
Doesn't everything die at last, and too soon?
Tell me, what is it you plan to do
with your one wild and precious life?

—Mary Oliver

"He who would travel happily must travel light."
-Antoine de Saint-Exupéry

WHAT I CARRIED

PANNIER 1 — AXIOM 45L SADDLE BAG
BACK RIGHT (MORE ACCESSIBLE THAN LEFT)

1A Main pocket
(Each outfit is individually wrapped and sealed in a large Ziploc bag. The panniers are "waterproof" but NOTHING is waterproof.)

1 Old Camping Hoodie
1 pair YOGAJeans
2 bikinis (one would suffice)
1 Joe Fresh camping dress (cheap cotton dress)
1 Joe Fresh camping dress (cheap cotton dress)
1 pair MEC riding shorts and 1 white long-sleeved Lululemon top
1 pair MEC riding shorts and 1 white long-sleeved Lululemon top
1 pair Capri pants and tank top
1 pair Capri pants and tank top
7 pair's underwear
Extra Ziploc bags
Baby wipes on top (for easy access)

1B Front outer pocket

Plastic camping mug

Stainless steel stemless wine glass

Hot mitt

Grill

500mL pot

775mL pot

Corkscrew

Can opener

Plastic camping fork

Plastic camping knife

Plastic camping spoon

1C Side outer pocket

Sunblock

Bug spray

PANNIER 2 — AXIOM 45L SADDLEBAG BACK LEFT

2A Main pocket

Hammock tent (There is a pocket that hangs inside the hammock tent. I kept a phone clip/stand and headphones permanently there.)

Sleeping bag good-to-zero degree from MEC in a stuff sack

Bike repair bag

+ Two spare tire tubes
+ Two tube tools
+ 5 bungee cords
+ Rope
+ Patch kit
+ Chain lube
+ Bike tool
+ Bike pump
+ Phone cords

- ◆ Two rechargeable bike lights
- ◆ Matches and lighters

Bottle of wine

2B Front outer pocket
Single-charge battery for phone
Ten-charge battery for phone
Pens
Postcards
Stamps

2C Side outer pocket
7" retractable saw
Tent pegs

PANNIER 3 – 20L MEC

All toiletries, including my electric toothbrush.

PANNIER 4 – 9L AXIOM HANDLEBAR PANNIER

Bike lock key
Dog spray
Change purse with money, debit card, and credit card
Sunglasses
Food

*Bear spray should be suspended from front handlebars.

"Make a plan and then don't stick to it."

FINAL ITINERARY

DAY 1

Tuesday July 5
74kms from Toronto to
Darlington Provincial Park
1600 Darlington Park Road
Bowmanville, ON L1C 3K3
$41.50 (electric)
Free showers
Branches for food hanging
No raccoons

DAY 2

Wednesday July 6
60kms to
Old Flat Top @ Cobourg Marina
103 Third Street
Cobourg, ON K9A 5W9
$49

DAY 3

Thursday July 7
52kms to
Presqu'Ile Provincial Park
328 Presqu'Ile Pkwy
Brighton, ON K0K 1H0
$36.50 (no services)
Free showers
No branches for hanging food
Diligent raccoons.

DAY 4

Friday July 8
62kms to
Sandbanks Provincial Park
3004 County Rd 12
Picton, ON K0K 2T0
$39.75 (no services)
Free showers
Branches
No raccoons

DAY 5

Saturday July 9
54kms to
Mary's backyard tent
Bath, ON

DAY 6

Sunday July 10
57kms to
Angela's summer digs
Gananoque, ON

DAY 7

Monday July 11
56kms to
St. Lawrence Park
Brockville, ON K6V 5R9
$11.87 for cyclists (no services)
Free showers
Branches
No raccoons

DAY 8

Tuesday July 12
69kms + + +
Upper Canada Migratory
Bird Sanctuary
5591 Morrisons Rd
Ingleside, ON K0C 1M0
$? got a freebie. (no services)
Free showers

Branches
No raccoons

DAY 9

Wednesday July 13
60kms to
Glengarry Campground
20800 S Service Rd
Lancaster, ON K0C 1N0
$43.44 regular rate (electric)
Free showers
Branches
No raccoons

DAY 10

Thursday July 14
62kms to
Parc National d'Oka
2020 Chemin d'Oka
Oka, QC J0N 1E0
$7.48 for cyclists (no services)
$1 for 4-minute shower
No branches
Huge families of super dili-
gent raccoons

DAY 11

Friday July 15
51kms to
Marc's place
Verdun, QC
51KMS

DAY 12

Saturday July 16
28kms to
Parc National
des Îles-de-Boucherville
55 Île Sainte Marguerite
Boucherville, QC J4B 5J6
$12.50 pour cyclistes (no services)
$1 for 4-minute shower
No trees so no branches
No raccoons

DAY 13

Sunday July 17
62kms to
Motel Tracy
3330 route Marie-Victor,
Sorel-Tracy, QC J3R 1N9
$49 (if booked through Airbnb)

DAY 14

Monday July 18
74kms to
Motel Bellefeuille
2070 rue Bellefeuille,
Trois-Rivières, QC G9A 2T6
$78

DAY 15

Tuesday July 19
72kms to
Camping Panoramique de Portneuf

464 Rte François Gignac
Portneuf, QC G0A 2Y0
$28.74 for cyclists (electric, water)
$0.75 for 5-minute shower, no pause
Branches
No raccoons

DAY 16

Wednesday July 20
79kms to
Éric's place
Quebec, QC

DAY 17

Thursday July 21
61kms to
Camping Coop des Érables
de Montmagny
860 Boulevard Taché O
Montmagny, QC G5V 3S9
$18.87 for cyclists
Free showers
Only $3 for firewood.
Branches
Few raccoons, some skunks

DAY 18

Friday July 22
83kms to
Camping Rivière-Ouelle
176 Chemin de la Pointe
Rivière-Ouelle, QC G0L 2C0

$20.70 for cyclists
$6 for firewood
$1 for a 4-minute shower, no pause
Branches
No raccoons

DAY 19

Saturday July 23
68kms to
Camping municipal de la Pointe
2 Côte des Bains
Rivière-du-Loup, QC
$26 (not a participant in Bienvenue
Cyclistes, this is the regular rate)
Campfires not allowed, though there
is a communal area where a campfire
is permitted
Free showers
Branches

DAY 20

Sunday July 24
77kms to
Éco-Site de la Tête du
Lac Témiscouata
140, route 232
Saint-Cyprien, QC G0L 2P0
$16
Free showers
Branches
No raccoons

DAY 21

Monday July 25
60kms to
Ritz Motel
810, chemin Mont-Farlagne Road
St-Jacques, NB E7B 1V3
$55

DAY 22

Tuesday July 26
73kms to
Camping Chutes et Gorge
120 Manse St.
Grand Falls, NB E3Z 2R2
$28
Free showers
Branches
No raccoons
Pat is great.

DAY 23

Wednesday July 27
80kms to
River Country Campground
69 Lahue Rd
Clearview, NB E7L 1X6
Campsites $30, Cabin $50
Free firewood.
Free showers.
Branches
Kenneth is the sweetest.

DAY 24

Thursday July 28
63kms to
Yogi Bear's Jellystone Park
174 Hemlock St
Lower Woodstock, NB E7M 4E5
$45
Free showers
Some branches
No raccoons

DAY 25

Friday July 29
42kms to
Sunset View Campground
and Cottages
45 Hawkshaw Rd
Hawkshaw, NB E6G 1N8
$29
$1 for 6min shower, no pause
Branches
No raccoons

DAY 26

Saturday July 30
66kms to
Christina LaFlamme & Family
Fredericton, NB

DAY 27

Sunday July 31
57kms to

Coy Lake Camping and RV Park
1805 NB-102
Upper Gagetown, NB E5M 1N3
$29
$0.25 for 4-1/2 min shower.
Branches
No raccoons
Elaine is darling and helpful.

DAY 28

Monday August 1
78kms to
Town & Country Campground
133 Aiton Rd
Sussex, NB E0E 1P0
$40.71
Free showers.
No branches.
No animals
Lot 26

DAY 29

Tuesday, August 2
56kms + + to
Cleveland Place (cherry tree
in backyard)
8580 Main St
Alma, NB E4H 1N4
The lady on the porch who was the
owner would not take my money so
I don't know the cost.

DAY 30

Wednesday August 3
50kms to
Ponderosa Pines Campground
4325 Route 114
Lower Cape, NB E4H 3P1
$31.65
Free showers.
Branches
No raccoons
Lot 409

DAYS 31 – 32

Thursday August 4 & Friday
August 5
69kms to
Dean, Mireille & Family
Shediac Bridge, NB

DAY 33

Saturday August 6
81kms to
Amherst Shore Provincial Park
6596 NS-366
Northport, NS B0L 1E0
$26.70
Free showers.
Many branches.
No raccoons.

DAY 34

Sunday August 7

61kms to
Balmoral Motel
131 Main St.
Tatamagouche, NS B0K 1V0
$113.85
Includes breakfast
Free laundry.

DAY 35

Monday August 8
68kms to
Tara Motel
917 E River Rd
New Glasgow, NS B3H 3S5
$126.50
Includes breakfast

DAY 36

Tuesday August 9
75kms to
Whidden Park Campground
& Cottages
11 Hawthorne St
Antigonish, NS B2G 1A2
$26.50

DAY 37

Wednesday August 10
54kms to
Skye Lodge
160 NS-4
Port Hastings, NS B9A 1M5
$102.35

DAY 38

Thursday August 11
52kms to
Whycocomagh Provincial Park
89 Provincial Park Rd
Whycocomagh, NS B0E 3M0
$59.95 for a yurt (there are three)

DAY 39 CABOT TRAIL

Friday August 12
75kms to
Duck Cove Inn
10289 Cabot Trail
Margaree Harbour, NS B0E 2B0
$90
$1 wash, $0.50 dry
Gordon and wife are amazing.

DAY 40 CABOT TRAIL

Saturday August 13
64kms to
Midtrail Motel
23475 Cabot Trail
Pleasant Bay, NS B0E 2P0
$123.16
No calling ability. Limited
Wi-Fi access.

DAY 41 CABOT TRAIL

Sunday August 14
30kms to
McDonald's Motel

37 MACLEODS LANE
Victoria, Subd. A, NS B0C 1C0
$75 plus tax ($87.98)

DAY 42 CABOT TRAIL

Monday August 15
38kms to
Glenghorm Beach Resort
36743 Cabot Trail
Ingonish, NS B0C 1K0
$98 for a room, or $78 for smaller
quarters, plus tax

DAY 43 CABOT TRAIL

Tuesday August 16
97kms
The Dunlop Inn
552 Chebucto St
Baddeck, NS B0E 1B0
$140 plus tax

DAY 44

Wednesday August 17
400m
The Telegraph Motel
479 Chebucto St
Baddeck, NS B0E 1B0
$135 plus tax

DAY 45

Thursday August 18
3kms to
Irving/Circle K
Bus to Halifax

DAYS 45 TO 54

Hamed & Ali's place, my lovely
Couchsurfing hosts who put me
up for ten days, free of charge.
Thank you!

DAY 54

Train home.

TO CONTACT THE AUTHOR

for questions or speaking engagements, please email:
flipflopfantasy@outlook.com

Printed in Canada